UNAUTHORIZED
FREUD

UNAUTHORIZED
FREUD

Doubters Confront a Legend

Edited by

Frederick C. Crews

Viking

VIKING
Published by the Penguin Group
Penguin Putnam Inc., 375 Hudson Street,
New York, New York 10014, U.S.A.
Penguin Books Ltd, 27 Wrights Lane, London W8 5TZ, England
Penguin Books Australia Ltd, Ringwood, Victoria, Australia
Penguin Books Canada Ltd, 10 Alcorn Avenue,
Toronto, Ontario, Canada M4V 3B2
Penguin Books (N.Z.) Ltd, 182–190 Wairau Road,
Auckland 10, New Zealand
Penguin India, 210 Chiranjiv Tower, 43 Nehru Place,
New Delhi 11009, India

Penguin Books Ltd, Registered Offices:
Harmondsworth, Middlesex, England

First published in 1998 by Viking Penguin,
a member of Penguin Putnam Inc.

1   3   5   7   9   10   8   6   4   2

LIBRARY OF CONGRESS CATALOGING-IN-PUBLICATION DATA
Unauthorized Freud : doubters confront a legend /
edited by Frederick Crews.
p.   cm.
Includes bibliographical references and index.
ISBN 0-670-87221-0
1. Psychoanalysis—History.   2. Freud, Sigmund,
1856–1939.   I. Crews, Frederick C.
BF173.U49   1998
150.19'52—DC21   98-11418

This book is printed on acid-free paper. ∞

Printed in the United States of America
Set in Berkeley Book
Designed by Betty Lew

For Alejandro César Márquez and
Rebeca Josefina Márquez

"At this point Freud's big chow was heard scratching on the door, and Freud rose, as he often had before, to let the dog in. She settled on the carpet and began licking her private parts. Freud did not approve of this behavior, and tried to make her stop. 'It's just like psychoanalysis,' he said."

—Joseph Wortis

PREFACE

Unauthorized Freud is the work of eighteen authors, but I am the only one of them who should be held accountable for its intent: to restore the mythified "discoverer of the unconscious" to human size and, in the process, to expose his system of psychological propositions to the same kind of scrutiny one would apply to any other aspiring science. There is no team of "Freud bashers" at work here. True, the book shows psychoanalysis to have been a mistake that grew into an imposture. But some of the contributing scholars hold milder views, and I ask the reader to note that their raising of objections to specific points of theory and method doesn't necessarily imply a sweeping attack on Freud's tradition. Nor should the irreverent chapter titles, only two of which (Chapters 3 and 17) match the originals, be taken to represent anyone's chosen emphasis but my own.

I am, of course, hardly the first student of Freud to have concluded that psychoanalysis was built out of straw. That judgment can be found in a number of other recent books (see, for example, Jurjevich, 1974; Szasz, 1978; Eysenck, 1985; Torrey, 1992; Scharnberg, 1993; Esterson, 1993; Wilcocks, 1994; Dawes, 1994; Webster, 1995; Gellner, 1996; Macmillan, 1997; Cioffi, 1998). We will see that no milder verdict is warranted by all that has been learned since the tradition of revisionist Freud scholarship was seriously launched by Paul Roazen (1969), Henri F. Ellenberger (1970), and Frank Cioffi (1970) almost three decades ago, and especially since the uncensored, startlingly credulous letters of Freud to his friend Wilhelm Fliess were rescued from sequestration by Jeffrey Moussaieff Masson and published in 1985 (*The Complete Letters of Sigmund Freud to Wilhelm Fliess, 1887–1904*). By synthesizing expert judgments about Freud's career and the various kinds of knowledge claims he put forward, *Unauthorized Freud* shows, in a uniquely accessible form, the damning consistency of the record.

Obviously, a psychoanalytic partisan could assemble a more soothing book by calling on further scholars, such as Lisa Appignananesi, Ronald Clark, John Forrester, Sander Gilman, Ilse Grubrich-Simitis, Patrick Mahony, William J. McGrath, and Carl Schorske, who have enriched our understanding of Freud without mounting a challenge to psychoanalysis itself. It is possible to be objective about many details of Freud's life and milieu, and even about some of his unlikely culture-bound notions, while skirting the self-validating character of his method. But why should that all-important fact—the black hole of circularity that renders the very term "psychoanalytic knowledge" an oxymoron—be omitted from consideration? The chapters and editorial comments below not only take the full measure of Freud's well-documented conceptual errors, relentless apriorism, disregard for counterexamples, bullying investigative manner, shortcuts of reasoning, rhetorical dodges, and all-around chronic untruthfulness; they also show that contemporary analysts possess no reliable means, internal to "clinical evidence," of locating and correcting their own misconceptions.

Whatever is said here, people who have publicly committed themselves to the psychoanalytic worldview are unlikely to acknowledge that the game is finally up. This book is not addressed to them. But readers who entertain mixed or uncertain feelings may find themselves engaged by *Unauthorized Freud*. If they can put in abeyance the much-rehearsed Freud legend, they may discover something amazing, liberating, and finally, I think, rather comical: that our great detective of the unconscious was incompetent from the outset—no more astute, really, than Peter Sellers's bumbling Inspector Clouseau—and that he made matters steadily worse as he tried to repair one theoretical absurdity with another.

Unfortunately, however, there is nothing comical about the uses to which Freudian ideas are being put in our own time. During the 1990s, the most fervent trend within the English-speaking analytic world has been a sinister revival not just of Freud's pretensions to veridical memory retrieval but also of his rash efforts a full century ago, just before "psychoanalysis proper" was born, to ferret out repressed sexual abuse in the histories of his patients. Bizarre as it may seem, quite a few analysts have now cast their lot with the so-called recovered memory movement, which has been causing incalculable personal, familial, and social havoc since the mid-1980s (see, for accounts of that movement, Loftus and Ketcham, 1994; Ofshe and Watters, 1996; Pendergrast, 1996; Van Til, 1997). Mainstream analysts have largely refused to admit that any of their mostly younger, mostly feminist colleagues are engaged in this backward time travel (see, for example, the bald denials in Gabbard et al., 1995; Lear, 1995, 1996; Michels, 1996, 1997). Yet the analytic community's own recent books and journals abound in naive tales about memories of violation retrieved through the modified exercise of classical Freudian technique. (See, for example, Hedges, 1994; Prozan, 1993, 1997; Gartner, 1997; and for critical commentary from a psychoanalytic perspective, Brenneis, 1997; Galatzer-Levy, 1997.)

The emergence of latter-day psychoanalytic incest inquisitors constitutes the most dramatic sign that the work of this present book is neither antiquarian nor superfluous but urgently practical. As I have shown elsewhere, every feature of recovered memory therapy, even the crudest, was pioneered by Freud, and nearly all of those features were retained in his practice of "psychoanalysis proper" (*Memory Wars*, pages 71–73, 206–223, 274 note). Moreover, the recovered memory movement would have been inconceivable without our society's more diffuse allegiance to the Freudian psychodynamic paradigm. Since the very ineffability of psychoanalytic theory allows a user to reassemble its parts so as to rationalize any number of new or revived enthusiasms, only a thoroughgoing critique can discourage further reckless attempts to disclose the purported contents of "the repressed."

Nevertheless, I grant that a book of this kind incurs the risk of overkill. Multiple paths of inquiry must be broached, but they all lead inexorably to the wizard's empty palace. I have made for variety, however, by excising inessential material and redundancies of discussion wherever possible, by giving close attention to some of Freud's inherently fascinating case histories, and by concluding with a segment of chapters about the human consequences of his therapeutic regimen and personal influence. By the end of Part I, readers will already have reason to doubt that Freud possessed either the fruitful theoretical premises, the evidential base, or the methodological prudence needed for the breakthrough in knowledge to which he would lay claim at the turn of the century; yet the logical and empirical case against his brainchild will still lie ahead in Parts II and III.

Unauthorized Freud has been conceived with the general reader uppermost in mind. Although the book is meant to be self-sufficient as a demonstration, it barely samples the vast field of critical discourse on its subject. Major contributors to that field such as Henri F. Ellenberger, Edward Erwin, Hans J. Eysenck, Phyllis Grosskurth, Han Israëls, Ernest Nagel, Paul Roazen, and Max Scharnberg remain unrepresented, not because of any deficiencies in their work but simply because this book has its own work to do: displaying the emptiness of Freud's claims and the whimsical nature of his interpretations. To that end, writings that synopsize and build upon earlier scholarship have occasionally been preferred to the original statements.

For ease of reading and economy of space, the selections themselves have been stripped of their footnotes and citations and subjected to some minor reconciling in the handling of conventions. (However, British authors' national conventions of spelling have been preserved.) Except for the most trivial omissions ("As we saw in Chapter Four," for example), all splicing within the texts is indicated by ellipses. Where ellipses occur in the originals, they have been placed within brackets: "[. . .]." I encourage readers not only to consult the source articles and books in all their amplitude but also to look into other works that are cited in my editorial comments and fully identified in a list at the back of the volume.

Within the editorial material, a few frequently cited works are designated by shortened names or titles:

CLFF   *The Complete Letters of Sigmund Freud to Wilhelm Fliess, 1887–1904*, translated and edited by Jeffrey Moussaieff Masson (Cambridge: Harvard University Press, 1985).

Jones   *The Life and Work of Sigmund Freud*, 3 volumes, by Ernest Jones (New York: Basic Books, 1953–57).

Memory Wars   *The Memory Wars: Freud's Legacy in Dispute*, by Frederick Crews et al. (New York: New York Review, 1995).

SE   *The Standard Edition of the Complete Psychological Works of Sigmund Freud*, 24 volumes, translated by James Strachey (London: Hogarth Press, 1953–1974).

A suggestion by Marion Maneker set this project in motion. I am grateful to my coauthors not only for allowing their work to be reproduced here but also, in many instances, for sage advice. Mikkel Borch-Jacobsen and Allen Esterson have been especially generous and informative. I thank Robert Wilcocks for an early and extremely useful critique of my proposal. As always, Elizabeth Crews has been the shrewdest and most watchful reader of my drafts. And Kristine Puopolo of Viking Penguin has helped me immensely with her critical support, her high standards, and her sense of the proper relation between editorial commentary and the main texts.

Frederick C. Crews

CONTENTS

III PSYCHIC INSPECTOR CLOUSEAU

IV WE FEW

INTRODUCTION

On July 31, 1995, conferees at the annual gathering of the International Psychoanalytical Association in San Francisco found themselves treated to an agreeable piece of news. At the outset of his remarks officially opening the conference, Dr. Harold Blum, executive director of New York's Sigmund Freud Archives, announced with pride that, "at a time when psychoanalysis is so challenged, and when we have so much Freud denigration and throughout the world the devaluation of psychoanalysis," a major Freud exhibition was to be mounted by the Library of Congress in the fall of 1996, "under the virtual sponsorship of the United States government" (Blum, 1995). The coming show would educate the public not only about the origins and history of Freud's thought but also about "the importance of psychoanalytic ideas," or what Blum has elsewhere called "the enduring discoveries of [Freud's] revolutionary genius" (*Memory Wars*, page 105).

This didactic effort, Blum continued, would reach perhaps 250,000 visitors to the exhibition hall and be further prosecuted through "a catalog, a scholarly conference, a public lecture series, a festival of films . . . , educational materials and workshops for teachers, and . . . electronic outreach through the internet," plus television coverage of the main event itself. Meanwhile, a portrait of the master psychologist would "hang in the great rotunda of the Library of Congress where so many of our presidents' portraits have also been placed." After closing in Washington, moreover, the show would be reassembled in Vienna to adorn that country's celebration of its millennial year. Thus—though Blum didn't make this point—

there would be a handsome ideological return to the show's main financial backers: his own Freud Archives, the Freud Museum (London), the Sigmund Freud Gesellschaft (Vienna), the Mary Sigourney Charitable Trust (a psychoanalytic foundation), and the touchily image-conscious, post-Waldheim government of Austria, which had already placed the visage of its newly discovered favorite son on every fifty-schilling note.

When plans for "Sigmund Freud: Conflict and Culture" were announced to the American taxpayers who would be footing the rest of the bill, a less cheerleading tone was understandably adopted. The exhibition, said the official announcement of the Library of Congress, would not only expound Freud's "fundamental contributions toward understanding the origins of drives and conflicts within the individual psyche and in society" but also address the "close critical reexamination" of his ideas since the 1970s (Library of Congress, 1995)—the ground shared by this present book.

Knowledgeable observers, however, scrutinizing Blum's privately recruited lineup of advisers and catalog contributors, perceived with alarm that nobody remotely qualified to deal with "critical reexamination" had been appointed. As a journalist subsequently noted,

> the exhibit's advisory committee was hand-picked from scholars hewing closely to the Freudian line. . . . Some of the "exhibition consultants" aren't scholars at all but practicing analysts. Most troubling, no prominent (or obscure) revisionists of Freudian orthodoxy were invited to contribute to the exhibit catalogue—though major essays were assigned to partisans like the Vienna Freud Museum's Harald Leupold-Löwenthal and the London Freud Museum's Michael Molnar (Zalewski, 1995, page 75).

It seemed to many students of the psychoanalytic movement, and above all to the independent historian Peter J. Swales, that Blum and other members of the Freud establishment were well advanced toward staging a federally sanctioned coup against history. And that suspicion was reinforced when Swales, whom guest curator Michael S. Roth had been consulting by phone and mail about Freud's life and how best to represent it, learned that the organizers disapproved of such collaboration with someone regarded by analysts as a blasphemer against Freud's gospel. It was then that Swales decided to circulate a petition, framed in measured and courteous language, asking the head of the library's Manuscript Division to ensure that the exhibition "suitably portray the present state of knowledge and adequately reflect the full spectrum of informed opinion about the status of Freud's contribution to modern intellectual history." The petition also requested that the advisory committee be expanded to include a member from the library's own staff who could keep the scholarly community informed about the hitherto confidential planning process (Swales et al., 1995).

Swales's petition eventually garnered fifty signatures from a broad range of Freud scholars and others, including not only outspoken critics like me but also historians who harbored some sympathy for psychoanalytic method, a number of practicing psychoanalysts, the president-elect of the psychoanalytic division of the American Psychological Association, and even Freud's own granddaughter Sophie Freud. Here, patently, was a heterogeneous assemblage of voices whose continuing disapproval could jeopardize the intellectual legitimacy of the show.

That point was not lost on guest curator Roth, whose primary ties lay with the academy, not with the lucrative business of psychodynamic therapy for which a larger-than-life Freud still serves as logo. Roth was clearly uncomfortable with the propagandistic emphasis that director Blum had sketched with such relish in San Francisco. At once, Roth set about to discover what might appease the petitioners. They, in turn, though wary of co-optation, were willing to offer their advice and even, in some instances, their open enlistment in the project.

Thus two of Freud's most penetrating critics, Adolf Grünbaum and Frank Cioffi, accepted offers to join the list of catalog writers, and another eminent critic, Malcolm Macmillan, was engaged to evaluate a draft document outlining the exhibition's rationale. Although the library at first ignored and finally rejected the petitioners' request that an observer be appointed, and although the old-line Freudians remained well positioned to exercise ultimate spin control, the petition had done its intended work of nudging the organizers toward a less tendentious presentation. As Roth graciously wrote to each signer on October 5, 1995, "Your petition alerted me to the dangers that the exhibit might unwittingly contain a partisan defense of Freud, or that we might not have paid sufficient attention to the recent historical and philosophical critiques of psychoanalysis" (Roth, 1995).

There the story would end on a conciliatory note were it not for a development that threw all parties into confusion. On December 4, 1995, the library announced to an incredulous nation that because of a $352,000 shortfall in funds, the exhibition would have to be indefinitely postponed. Sensitized by earlier, politically motivated cancellations, many citizens concluded at once that the library must have caved in to extremists who had petulantly resolved that if they couldn't dictate the tenor of a Freud exhibition, there would be no exhibition at all. This theme was soon embroidered by Michael Roth himself, who, although he knew that no Freud critic had asked the library to cancel the show, now saw fit to maintain the opposite in published articles, decrying as censors some of the very scholars whose judgment he had hitherto been soliciting (Roth, 1996a, 1996b). Meanwhile, much sympathy was expressed for the gate-keepers of the Freud Archives, who, though they had done their best for four decades to prevent open access to key research materials, were now transformed into beleaguered champions of free inquiry. And Freudian pundits like Peter Gay, quoted with approval in the *New York Times* and elsewhere, were quick to opine that infantile oedipal rebellion, not a concern for truth, underlay the critics' attempt to usurp Father Freud: "Society wants people to behave, but the kid in us wants everything" (quoted by Smith, 1995, page 14; Phillips, 1996, page 11).

Before long, the imaginary "campaign to sideline the Freud exhibit" (Phillips, 1996, page 1) was being treated as an incontrovertible fact by psychoanalysts, other Freudians, and deceived commentators who had been distressed by political interference with other shows (for example, Gifford, 1996; Gitlin, 1996; Kurzweil, 1996; Zaretsky, 1996). In France, meanwhile, Jacques Lacan's biographer Elisabeth Roudinesco began recruiting international signatures on a rival petition to the library denouncing the "unheard-of violence" of the critics and characterizing them as "puritans" and "inquisitors" whose nefarious scheme must not be allowed to prevail (Roudinesco et al., 1996).

It seems doubtful that any of the 180 Roudinesco signers had actually seen Swales's text pointing out his group's possession of "no common doctrinal commitment" and asking only that a decent eclecticism be observed. One American psychoanalyst likened that plea for fairness to "the Ayatollah's *fatwa* against Salman Rushdie" (Gifford, 1996, page 16), while Roudinesco herself hinted that the original petitioners could be understood not just as allies of the Christian far right but as latter-day

Nazis hunting down "Freudian Jews" (Roudinesco, 1996; see also Gifford, 1996, page 16)—a considerable surprise to the many Jewish signers of Swales's petition, including at least one refugee from Hitler's terror.

All this furor abated when, in February 1996, the Library of Congress reported that the necessary funds could be raised after all in time for an opening date of fall 1998 (Library of Congress, 1996). In announcing the news, the library pointedly reaffirmed its trust in the analytic insiders who had first proposed and would still oversee the show. For gratified Freudians, the only remaining question was which group of their lobbyists deserved major credit for what the president of the International Psychoanalytical Association called "the large mobilization which led to the exhibition being reprogrammed for 1998, without altering its previous organization" (Etchegoyen, 1996; see also Basseches, 1996; Kaley, 1997). The strongest claim apparently belonged to the American Psychoanalytic Association's at first secretive but later self-congratulatory "Task Force to Monitor Freud Exhibit" (see Benson, 1996b), which had solicited analysts to urge sympathetic academics, whose university stationery would give no hint of Freudian bias, to flood the library's directorship with letters about the dire threat to intellectual freedom (Benson, 1996a).

A reader who fully digests the import of *Unauthorized Freud*, attending especially to the sectarian mentality explored in Part IV, cannot be surprised by this combination of deviousness and probably heartfelt alarmism. Most analysts even to this day recoil from exposure to scientific give-and-take, preferring Freud's own conception of a heroic band of the enlightened who are holding out against a vindictive established order—as if psychoanalysis weren't itself an ornament of that same order. Thus the enemy is never far to seek. Even the "normal" mind, in a Freudian view, is thought to consist of encrusted reaction formations against hideously aggressive impulses that remain capable of eruption; and what target of philistine malice could be more suitable than Freud and Freudians themselves, the bearers of the frightening news about those subterranean forces? To such a mindset, irreverence toward the official though mythical account of Freud's triumphs (pages 3–9 below) takes on the appearance not just of a private neurotic ailment (see *Memory Wars*, pages 285–289) but of a pogrom in the making.

More broadly, the farce surrounding the Library of Congress exhibition has been amplified at every turn by the general public's ignorance of Freud's actual career. Though it is easy in retrospect, for example, to condemn the library's directors for placing a national historical project in the hands of an interested guild, those directors couldn't have known what we will demonstrate below: that the "history" cherished by psychoanalysts consists largely of untruths meant to promote a deluxe mode of treatment by exaggerating the founder's originality, concealing his therapeutic botches, and granting him powers of discernment that he proclaimed but didn't come close to possessing. Likewise, nonanalysts who misconstrued the controversy as a matter of "professional historians [running] into flak from outside the profession," and who thus saw the dissenters as mere cranks who ought to be satisfied with "publish[ing] pamphlets denouncing the show" (Gitlin, 1996), failed to grasp that historical fidelity was precisely the bone of contention. All of which suggests the need for a book like this one, in which general readers can at last meet the Freud who walked the earth, not the one who walked on water.

Did Freud plumb the depths of the psyche, as many pilgrims to the Library of Congress exhibition will doubtless assume and still believe on their way home? Or did he just clog *our conception* of the psyche with a maze of misaligned plumbing, leaving the effluent of his own strange imagination to circulate through our medical and cultural lore? To entertain such an impious question is to consider whether the self-satisfied intelligentsia of our epoch may have been—may still be—no less deluded than were earlier believers in master keys to meaning. But what could be more likely than that? After all, psychoanalysis would not be the first belief system to have exacted loyalty from modern secular intellectuals without being either methodologically scrupulous, vindicated by facts, or free of harmful consequences.

Freudolatry in its most exalted mood verges on outright religious worship—as when, for example, an otherwise canny philosopher portrays his idol as a great sage and healer who did "as much for [humanity] as any other human being who has lived" (Wollheim, 1981, page 252). The majority view, however, is more mixed, combining doubt and respect in roughly equal measure. Yes, many fair-minded people tell themselves, Freud made some missteps that are traceable to his late-Victorian zeitgeist, but he was also a trailblazer who provided us with a new way "to explain our quirks, fantasies and neurotic miseries by reference to unconscious beliefs and desires" (Rorty, 1996). Wasn't he one of our "founders of discursivity," a titan of innovation who therefore shouldn't be "required to conform to the canons of science" (Goodheart, 1997, page 132)? And surely, it is presumed, he remains our only stay against reversion to a shallow positivism and associationism (see, for example, Robinson, 1993; Prager, 1996; Edmundson, 1997). As one advocate has put it, "Are we to see humans as having depth—as complex psychological organisms who generate layers of meaning which lie beneath the surface of their own understanding? Or are we to take ourselves as transparent to ourselves?" (Lear, 1995, page 24). A vote for complexity, it seems, is automatically a vote for Freud.

Though initially attractive, this line of reasoning is both unhistorical and illogical. As Lancelot Law Whyte (1960) and Henri F. Ellenberger (1970) showed long ago, Freud deserves no credit for having introduced us to "the unconscious," a Romantic commonplace with ancestry stretching to Plato. Nietzsche in particular anticipated most of what sounds deep in Freud, and he did so with spirited wit instead of with diagrams and with false and self-aggrandizing tales of healing (Anzieu, 1986; Lehrer, 1995; Gellner, 1996). Nor should we confuse Freud's *psychodynamic* unconscious—an unsubstantiated portion of the mind that allegedly schemes and subverts, lusts, atones, remembers, symbolizes, plays on words, encodes its thoughts in symptoms, and quarrels within itself while the subject remains oblivious—with *unconscious mental functioning,* whose existence is uncontroversial and can be readily demonstrated (Kihlstrom, 1987). (For egregious confusion of the two kinds of unconscious, see Erdelyi, 1985, 1996.)

Freud's originality, we will see, lies exactly where he is most vulnerable, in maintaining that allegedly psychogenic lameness, spasms, rashes, sores, phobias, compulsions, and obsessions can be both understood and cured by pouncing on telltale characteristics of the subject's "free associations" and pressing for regurgitation of the memories or fantasies lying behind them—a method said to yield up the secret thoughts determining dreams and slips as well. That diagnostic and therapeutic stab in the dark, in combination with the quaint etiologies, the several models of instinct management, and the wild explanations of history and prehistory that were extrapolated from it, makes up Freud's *specific and unique* contribution to the received wisdom of our age.

Just where in Freud's *Standard Edition of the Complete Psychological Works* can we find the needed evidence to begin authenticating his central claims? The surprising answer is: nowhere at all. True, Freud's texts offer many assurances that he indeed cured such-and-such a patient or satisfied himself that he had solved such-and-such a mystery; but any charlatan could say as much. Mention is also made of past and forthcoming proof resting on impeccable research, but that proof can't be located anywhere in the twenty-four-volume set.

The closest thing to tangible data in Freud's psychological writings would appear to be the ingenious and amusing strings of puns that he tells us he gathered in his consulting room—puns allegedly showing just how, in a given instance, the patient's mind followed a chain of association expressing a disguised sexual or aggressive motive. But the puns turn out to have been Freud's own, misascribed to his patients' unconscious so as to forge thematic connections that no one but a Freudian could detect. Accordingly, the daring biographical inferences that Freud based on such "evidence" are not compelling. The entire system of classical psychoanalytic thought rests on nothing more substantial than Freud's word that it is true. And that is why the late Nobelist in medicine Sir Peter Medawar famously condemned that system as a stupendous intellectual confidence trick (Medawar, 1982, page 140).

In recoil from such a disillusioning prospect, a number of philosophically inclined apologists have recently asserted that psychoanalytic tenets are merely a plausible extension of our usual way of drawing inferences about motives (Davidson, 1982; Wollheim, 1993; Cavell, 1993; T. Nagel, 1995; Rorty, 1996; Lear, 1996; Levy, 1996; Forrester, 1997). If these thinkers are right, to challenge Freud would be to cast needless doubt on common sense itself. But the truth is that classical psychoanalysis flouts common sense at every turn.

Ordinary experience does not teach us, for example, that benign-looking sentiments are always defenses against more primary hostile and/or libidinous ones; that the strength of a desire can be gauged by the severity of the social prohibition against it; that each peculiarity in someone's behavior must stem from a specific childhood ordeal; that a symptom must allude symbolically to the repressed trauma lying behind it; that a certain buried trauma must be relived in order for a neurosis to be vanquished; or that every custom, every civic ideal, every work of art must be purchased with sums of irreplaceable libido that leave "civilization" ever more erotically impoverished. These are all idiosyncratic and counterintuitive assumptions, yet they stand among the axioms enabling Freudians to put aside appearances and achieve what they take to be explanatory depth.

Some features of classical psychoanalysis, to be sure, do have a ring of initial truth about them. In particular, one cannot easily dismiss the proposal that "defense mechanisms" such as projection, identification, and denial affect mental productions. Even so trenchant a critic as Adolf Grünbaum has repeatedly granted the intuitive attractiveness of such concepts. And unquestionably, their invocation allows hermeneutic feats of quite dazzling ingenuity to be performed on utterances, texts, and works of art.

However, there is a crippling problem here that psychoanalytic advocates steadfastly refuse to address. Freud left us with no guidelines for perceiving whether a given expression should be taken literally or regarded as a compromise formation shaped by this or that unconscious defense against a wish or fantasy. Thus we cannot maintain that awareness of defense mechanisms puts us on a path to reliable knowledge about any given subject's mind. On the contrary, the notion of those mechanisms merely expands the scope of arbitrary license available to the interpreter, who will have no difficulty, as Freud certainly did not, in grinding the patient's conduct and history into the sausage of standard complexes, repressed primal scenes, and the like. Ironically, it is just this superabundance of opportunities to draw thematic connections that prevents Freudian method from ever doing justice to the intricacy of motivation that must actually be at work all around us, not least in the endlessly devious and self-dramatizing Freud himself.

Indeed, the almost infinite pliability of defense mechanisms can ultimately be seen not only as the Freudians' insurance against ever encountering uninterpretable material but also as the deepest source of their internecine strife and disarray. Every psychoanalytic interpreter can readily assemble an "unconscious logic" to account for a given attitude, credo, protestation, poem, or dream, but other psychoanalytic interpreters will inevitably disagree; and since all parties are merely following their hunches, playing a riff on a haphazardly chosen tune, no empirical basis for deciding among the versions can possibly be found. The very bounteousness of ingenious but contradictory readings, all appealing to exactly the same means of drawing inferences, thus constitutes a progressive crisis for the system, whose institutional development must continue to be drastically centrifugal, spinning off ever more numerous, mutually excommunicating schools and cliques.

By now the reader will understand that I cannot count myself among those—some of whom will be met in these very pages—who see enough plausibility in psychoanalysis to hope for a future clarification of ambiguities and a rapprochement with the values of responsible science. I consider the plight of Freud's system to be more desperate than that. As Frank Cioffi in particular has shown (pages 116–128 below), Freudian theory is not a set of adequately delimited, operationally meaningful, but largely untested propositions whose advocates just happen to have shielded those ideas from rigorous evaluation. Rather, the cloudy propositions themselves appeal to evidence from a calculatedly unexaminable realm, and a full correction of that flaw would simply make the body of doctrine disappear. In Ernest Gellner's biting but judicious words, "[t]he evasion is not brought in to save the theory: it is the theory" (Gellner, 1996, page 164).

Think again, for example, of Freud's way of construing the unconscious, or what Ludwig Wittgenstein sarcastically called "Mr. Nobody" (Wittgenstein, 1958, page 69). This was a personification of the not-known who initially spoke only to Freud and, later, only to Freudians. By invoking a preternaturally clever, absolutely unforgetful, multilingually punning second mind that absconds yet leaves its mark even on seeming accidents, Freud gave notice that he would improvise laws and interpretations without empirical check, plucking "evidence" from the most innocent happenstance and declaring it to be traceable, with gnostic certainty, to deformative events in his patients' earliest years. Thus the unconscious, "dynamically" conceived, is not so much a segment of the mind as it is a password for overturning appearances and arriving at prearranged conclusions.

Much the same must be said about Freud's rule of strict psychic determinism—the idea that every single action, even the choice of a number at seeming random, is traceable in principle to the workings of unconscious mental conflict. That notion has proved thrilling to academic humanists, who still marvel at what they mistakenly consider to be Freud's ascetic obeisance to the scientific ethos. No, strict determinism was just another name for Freud's hubris, his refusal to acknowledge that any thought, act, or physical state might lie beyond the reach of his hermeneutic steam-roller. Likewise, the so-called "overdetermination" of psychic causality, whereby one action or expression can carry a variety of secret meanings, was the permission Freud granted himself to spin out multiple interpretations without being troubled by their cross-purposes.

These were the tools not of a scientist but of an intellectual megaloma-niac. Accordingly, classical psychoanalytic theory is best regarded not as a set of sober if perhaps improvable inferences from "clinical experience" but rather as a perpetual motion machine, a friction-free engine for generating irrefutable discourse. As for those "fundamental contributions toward understanding the origins of drives and conflicts" that the Library of Congress press release charitably ascribed to Freud, we will find that they evaporate just as soon as one asks what they might be.

Freudians are finding themselves on the defensive, and the strategies of special pleading that they adopt are themselves symptomatic of intellectual bankruptcy. Rather than attempt to show that Freud did correctly infer childhood trauma from free associations, or that his mental laws really are clear and adequately linked to observation, they appeal to more relaxed standards of proof. The critics, they maintain, are ignorant of postmodern insights into the relativistic nature of science. Thus we are often treated to a tendentious synopsis of Thomas Kuhn's conception of scientific history, whereby a supposed incommensurability between competing paradigms is taken to mean (in defiance of Kuhn's disclaimers) that "evidence" is whatever the partisans of a given paradigm declare it to be. We needn't worry about Freud's enlistment of his own theory to justify that theory's claims, the argument goes, since we now realize that all theories take comparable liberties.

But as Barbara Von Eckardt shows in Chapter 9 below, this fashionable position is vacuous. However theory-laden our perceptions and ideas in general may be, it is both possible and necessary to be theory-neutral in the one way that matters: excluding circularity from a test or justification. Thus the fact that scientific claims are never devoid of presuppositions is no excuse for the blatant question begging of psychoanalysis. Moreover, as Sebastiano Timpanaro's Chapter 8 emphasizes, the indictment to which Freudianism is liable has nothing to do with rarefied debates in the philosophy or sociology of science. Instead, it is lodged at what Timpanaro calls "a much more modest and artisanal level," that of shifty moves that would be deemed unacceptable not just in science but in the conduct of everyday affairs. The real issue is simple: How indulgent do we wish to be when faced with the heads-I-win-tails-you-lose posture of an idolized thinker?

The answer, for many Freudians, is that we should be no less indulgent than Freud's contemporaries were. It would be anachronistic, we are admonished, to hold Freud to standards of proof that were conceived much later. But this is to do an injustice to the shrewdness of our scientific forebears. In the years before Freud rewrote psychoanalytic history as a fetching Promethean myth, he was received *more* skeptically than in the six decades since his death. His unconverted contemporaries saw the hollowness of his pretensions with admirable clarity.

Thus it was Freud's closest friend Fliess who pointed out in 1901 that Freud was ascribing his own thoughts to the minds of his patients (CLFF, page 450). It was C. G. Jung in 1906, long before he fell out with Freud, who remarked that psychoanalytic therapy "does not always offer in practice what one expects from it in theory" (Jung, 1953–1980, 3: 4). It was Gustav Aschaffenburg, again in 1906, who complained that Freud's presentation of case material was inadequate, that he guided his patients toward specious sexual revelations, and that he insisted on favored dream interpretations without considering equally plausible alternatives (see Kerr, 1993, page 117). And the very first number of *The Psychoanalytic Review* in 1913 contained an article asserting,

> There is absolutely nothing in the universe which may not readily be made into a sexual symbol. . . . We may explain, by Freudian principles, why trees have their roots in the ground; why we write with pens; why we put a quart of wine into a bottle instead of hanging it on a hook like a ham, and so on. . . . [C]ures resulting from Freudian treatment have no value as evidence in support of the Freudian dogmas (Dunlap, 1913–14, page 151).

It was no recent critic, moreover, but Freud's contemporary Pierre Janet who, in 1925, laid down these devastating strictures against both his theory and his therapy:

[N]o factor can have pathogenic importance which operates in equal measure among the sick and the well. . . . To me it seems that the psychoanalytical method is, before all, a method of symbolical and arbitrary construction; it shows how the facts "might be" explained if the sexual causation of the neuroses had been definitively accepted; but its application cannot be insisted upon so long as that theory is still unproved. . . . [T]he mere fact that a happening played a part long ago does not prove that it still plays an important part to-day. . . . A microbic infection in the past may have weakened the sufferer irreparably, and yet have quite ceased today. In the latter case, we shall not now do the patient any good by disinfective procedures (Janet, 1925, 1: 623, 627, 652).

In the light of such discerning early statements, the only parties harboring lax criteria of validation would appear to be the Freudians themselves—especially those who now maintain that science has no more claim on our propositional assent than literature does.

Another variant of the antiscience argument is voiced by those who tell us, following Paul Ricoeur (1970) and Jürgen Habermas (1971), that psychoanalysis is not a science but a hermeneutic (interpretive) activity, in which case it should be judged only on intuitive and empathic, not empirical, grounds. Freud himself, however, repeatedly and emphatically declared his brainchild to be a science (see Macmillan, 1997, pages 590–593). Unlike Ricoeur and Habermas, he grasped that even his "meaning" claims were tied to causal assumptions that couldn't be set aside without disemboweling the entire system. And he knew that assertions about etiology, diagnosis and prognosis, psychosexual development, mental structure, the formation of dreams and errors, and paths to cure are no more interpretive in nature than assertions about geological strata or germs. The fact that Freudian beliefs are underwritten by nothing but interpretations is doubtless awkward, but efforts to turn that deficiency to argumentative advantage are doomed to be unavailing. "What are we to do," asks one hermeneutically inclined analyst in mock alarm, "give up interpreting people?" (Lear, 1996, page 583). No, just recognize the glaring difference between interpretations and would-be mental laws. (See generally Grünbaum, 1984, pages 1–94.)

Still another strategy, by no means incompatible with the last, is to sacrifice Father Freud to the perpetuation of his horde. Freud had his limitations, this argument goes, but we psychoanalysts have long since corrected them and proceeded to new clinical discoveries and refinements of technique (see, for example, Gabbard et al., 1995). But just who has made the alleged progress? Would it be the classical Freudians, the scholastic Anna Freudians, the resurgent hands-on-the-patient Ferenczians, the Frommians, the Sullivanians, the Horneyans, the Eriksonians, the Kleinians, the Bowlbyans, the Winnicottians, the Rapaportians, the Schaferians, the Kohutians, the Mahlerians, the Kernbergians, the Lacanians, the Kristevans . . . ? Is it the id psychologists, the ego psychologists, the self psychologists, the feminists, the constructivists, the dissociationists, the explorers of the inner child . . . ? We know that the progress in question wouldn't be ascribed to circles standing still farther from the Freudian center, such as the Rankians, the Adlerians, the Jungians, the Reichians, the Laingians, the Gestaltists, or the Transactionalists. But on what generally accepted principle has *any* way of "moving beyond Freud" been proven superior to its myriad rivals? Those who boast of progress are hoping we won't glance past their own table of wares in the ever-expanding bazaar of certified and black market "psychoanalysis."

Furthermore, the conflicting innovations in the field all appeal to the same knowledge source—namely, the clinical interaction between therapist and patient, with particular stress on the two features that remain virtually universal, the analysis of free associations and the analysis of the transference. In Chapters 6 through 8, and again in Chapter 17, we will see in detail why neither process is trustworthy, but logic alone can show that if one supposedly reliable method produces an endless sequence of incompatible findings, and if no means of even beginning to resolve the differences can be specified, something has to be fundamentally amiss.

Having backed away from Freud yet still finding themselves under attack, some analysts are prepared to make one last adaptation—a more drastic and promising one than any we have yet considered. They tacitly or even explicitly admit the justice of revisionist critiques and, accordingly, bid farewell to the whole body of clinical and metapsychological doctrine about traumatic memories, repressed complexes, libidinal stages, and drives and inhibitions. Psychoanalytic theory, it is now said, ought to restrict itself to what can be observed about the operation of transference and countertransference in the clinical setting. Instead of trying to dredge up traumas, the doctor and patient should jointly fashion an ego-enhancing fable of identity by which the patient can henceforward be guided and uplifted.

This minimalism is in most respects a welcome development. It has the considerable virtue of doing away with Freud's creaky psychodynamic model and with his always disingenuous curative claims. Yet something is still being overlooked here. Where has it been shown that the most efficient means of addressing a patient's presenting complaint is a prolonged emotional entanglement with the therapist? Freud's rationale for that taxing regimen was faulty, but at least it *was* a rationale; he never imagined that transference ought to be pursued for its own sake. As psychoanalysis heads into its second century, however, this costliest and most time-consuming of therapies is attempting to survive while its intellectual structure topples all around it. "Freud's ideas, which dominated the history of psychiatry for the past half century," writes Edward Shorter, "are now vanishing like the last snows of winter" (Shorter, 1996, page vii). Can psychoanalysis as a treatment for neurosis be far behind?

Even then the enigmatic and fascinating figure of Freud remains. That he could have portrayed himself so winningly as a hero and a prophet, selling that image to present-day thinkers who pride themselves on tough-minded skepticism, indicates that he really was one of the most extraordinary personages of the modern age. Yet even his genius for rhetoric cannot be fully appreciated until we grasp that, from the beginning, the rhetoric had to cover a therapeutic and scientific fiasco. Only Freud, as stubborn, resourceful, and cynical as he was ambitious, could have turned failure into self-promotional success on such a grandiose scale.

I

WRONG
FROM THE START

*"I confess that he made on me personally
the impression of a man obsessed with fixed ideas."*
—Josef Breuer on Freud

OVERVIEW

Thanks to Freud's own efforts, endorsed and amplified by partisan biographers, psychoanalytic doctrine has reached most of us packaged within a heroic story about the discovery of the unconscious. Critics call that story *the Freud legend*. Its intended upshot is that Freud, having defied the opprobrium of his contemporaries and broken through the repression that had held our species in thrall for millennia, can be trusted as the authenticator of his own revelations. If the legend is gospel, the voicing of empirical doubts about psychoanalysis is blasphemy, and the skeptics must be "Freud bashers," or compulsive naysayers whose own repressions and resistances cry out for Freudian explanation and treatment. But if the legend bears only a distant relation to historical fact—and that is what we will find in these five chapters—psychoanalysis will have to justify its claims in the same mundane, evidence-based way as any other body of scientific thought.

The Freud legend consists of six elements that add up to a gripping account of the hero's apprenticeship, his struggle with error, and his eventual world-historical breakthrough:

1. *Charcot's lesson.* Sitting at the feet of the great French neuropathologist Jean-Martin Charcot in 1885–86, the twenty-nine-year-old Freud learned that unconscious ideas can produce symptoms and that hypnosis is a reliable means of triggering a display of those symptoms

without suggestive interference from the hypnotist's expectations. Thus when Freud later acquired hysterical patients of his own and began interrogating them under hypnosis, he could attend to Charcotian signs of split consciousness, or the operation of a subterranean second mind—the unconscious.

2. *Breuer's success—and his failure of nerve.* Freud next learned from his mentor Josef Breuer that hysterics, like Breuer's successfully treated "Anna O." (Bertha Pappenheim), suffer from repressed memories that can be brought to the surface in therapy, resulting in permanent relief from symptoms. This is the story told in Breuer and Freud's *Studies on Hysteria* (1895), a collaboration that could barely be maintained because Breuer, lacking Freud's moral courage, could not own up to the exclusively sexual etiology of psychoneuroses. Breuer had, in effect, founded psychoanalysis through inadvertence; Freud alone had the greatness of scientific character needed to face down the demons of the unconscious. Hence:

3. *Sexual candor and professional isolation.* Startled though he was by the sexual material that his patients kept presenting to him, the good bourgeois Freud steeled himself to acknowledge the role of taboo erotic themes in the formation of neuroses. Announcing his findings to his prudish and disbelieving colleagues, he underwent an ostracism that, however, failed to deter him from adhering to the hard and lonely scientific path.

4. *"Seduction" stories and their true basis.* In 1896–97 Freud was briefly deceived, by his women patients' insistence that they had been molested by their fathers in early childhood, into believing that those stories must be true. Hysteria, he held in that period, must result from the repression of such awful experiences. But when the implausibility of so many "seduction" tales was borne in upon him, he grasped the revolutionary truth: hysterics have repressed the memory of *their own* unacceptable incestuous wishes and early masturbatory practices.

5. *Self-analysis.* Between 1895 and 1899, and particularly after the collapse of the "seduction theory" in 1897, Freud, "following a path hitherto untrodden by any human being" (Jones, I: 287), smashed the barrier of repression to retrieve memories of his oedipal desires from the first two years of his life and then realized, in a transcendent flash, that his case could stand for that of everyone who had ever survived childhood and become "civilized."

6. *Farewell to Fliess.* At that momentous juncture, Freud was ready at last to abandon his neurotically tinged dependency on Wilhelm Fliess, a nose specialist from Berlin who, despite his vast intellectual inferiority to Freud, had been his best friend since 1887. Freud had overrated Fliess while he needed the latter's emotional support, and thus he had acquiesced in some of Fliess's dubious biogenetic notions about periodicity in both sexes. But once Freud began verifying his new, "properly psychoanalytic," psychology by producing spectacular cures, he could dispense both with Fliess personally and with Fliess's system of thought. Psychoanalytic doctrine thenceforth emerged directly from clinical experience, without any deductive Fliessian residue.

The chapters in Part I do not address these six points in order, but they do bear upon them in the course of telling the real, and very different, story of Freud's founding of psychoanalysis—a story of initial errors compounded by ignoble dodges and fibs. To begin with, Freud was ill advised to take his first bearings from Charcot. The very malady, hysteria, whose fixed traits Charcot had "demonstrated" to Freud's satisfaction now appears to have been a cultural artifact, a product of precisely the kind of suggestive collusion between doctors and patients that Freud, following Charcot, ruled out as either easily corrected or flatly impossible. This means that Freudian "cures" of hysteria, had there been any, would have occurred through the patient's decision to abandon symptoms that had stemmed from hypochondriacal contrivance, not from repressed memories. In short, the determining features of psychoanalytic "knowledge" were gleaned from attempts to treat a nondisease that was never admitted to be such.

Charcot's incautious view of hypnotism, without which Freud could never have imagined that his own hypnotized patients were giving him direct intimations of "the unconscious," was decisively refuted by his great rival Hippolyte Bernheim of Nancy. But though Freud himself translated Bernheim and practiced, for a while, Bernheim's therapeutic method of *open* hypnotic suggestion, he failed to learn Bernheim's more important lesson that hypnosis is essentially compliance with instructions, not the genuine eliciting of a prior state on the subject's part. Hence the tool of inquiry that Freud first employed to ferret out the sexual basis of psychoneuroses was ideally suited for getting the patient to act out the doctor's pet ideas. Still more damningly, we will find that when Freud gave up the practice of hypnosis, first in favor of his "pressure technique" (placing a hand on the patient's head and demanding that memories and confessions be produced) and then for "free association," those methods proved every bit as contaminating as hypnosis had been. Freud employed them so coercively that they were guaranteed to yield "confirmations" from those patients who elected to stay in treatment.

The remaining elements of the Freud legend fare no better. The Anna O. case, we will learn in Chapter 1, was anything but the model of a cure achieved through memory retrieval. In 1880–82 Breuer had been check-mated at every juncture by Bertha Pappenheim's morbid ingenuity, but at least he hadn't falsified his original report. Freud, however, cajoled him into allowing the tale of Bertha's cure, which they both knew to be ficti-tious, to serve as the foundation stone of psychoanalysis.

When word began leaking out that Pappenheim hadn't been cured or even helped by Breuer's treatment, Freud circulated an alternative version of the story. According to this variant, Breuer's discomfort with sexuality had made him panic when Bertha, impelled by "transference" longing toward him, expressed her love by experiencing a hysterical pregnancy. Had the courageous Freud been in Breuer's shoes in 1882, the story goes, he would not have fled from Bertha, and the therapeutic outcome would doubtless have been more satisfactory. But we will see in Chapter 1 that there is no factual basis for this ingenious effort at damage control, which nevertheless helped to solidify Freud's reputation as the unflappable sexual investigator par excellence.

Was Freud, as he sometimes claimed, the sole theoretician of his era to come to grips with sexual problems and perversions? No, he was one of many, including Albert Moll, Leopold Löwenfeld, Albert von Schrenck-Notzing, Richard von Krafft-Ebing, and Havelock Ellis. He often bor-rowed ideas from them, even while trying his best to consign them to historical oblivion. Among those sexologists of the 1880s and 1890s, however, he was by far the least enlightened in his view of nonstandard sexual practices and their consequences. Indeed, his adherence to, and active implementation of, Wilhelm Fliess's idea of corrective nasal surgery for "reflex neuroses" in the sexual sphere (see pages 54–55 below) aligned him, however uneasily, with the already discredited crackpots of the 1870s who had treated "hysterical" women through gynecological mutila-tion (Bonomi, 1997). (Butchery of the nose instead of the clitoris, uterus, or ovaries can hardly be counted as progress.) Thus Freud's stirring portrayal of himself as isolated and ostracized in the nineties because of his sexual candor was utterly at variance with reality. If he suffered disapproval, it was for his rashness in proposing wild etiologies that he himself eventually repudiated.

Freud did, however, set out to extract sexual confessions from his patients, and he was already doing so in the early nineties, *before* he had settled upon hysteria as his main topic of inquiry. "The sexual business," he wrote to Fliess in 1893, when he was interested in correlating other neuroses with such unhygienic practices as coitus interruptus, masturbation, and contraception, "attracts people who are all stunned and then go away won over after having exclaimed, 'No one has ever asked me about that before!' " (CLFF, page 57; see also Macmillan, 1997, pages 117–138). Hence he was being disingenuous as usual when he characterized himself as having stoically tolerated sexual material that spontaneously arose in his consultations with hysterics. If Freud had admitted the extent to which he was extorting revelations about sex, psychoanalysis would have impressed the world not as a medical breakthrough but as an exercise in question begging. And that, in fact, is just what his medical colleagues correctly understood to be the case.

We will devote two chapters (3 and 4) to Freud's still controversial seduction theory, which will prove once again to revolve around the issue of who told stories to whom. It took Freud until 1925, when "seduction" was itself a faded memory, to announce the face-saving claim that is still being endorsed by loyal Freudians—namely, that his female patients had besieged him with tales of molestation by their fathers. That claim was crucial for making the theory of oedipal fantasy look like a corrective to the seduction theory. But in the first place, those freely volunteered tales would have been incompatible with his dogma that only *repressed* sexual memories can bring about hysteria. And second, Freud's own papers published in 1896 make it clear that he was the one—just like a modern recovered memory therapist—who urged his patients to imagine scenes of childhood rape and then to regard those scenes as memories.

As for Freud's Promethean self-analysis, which we will be slighting below, it was nothing more than a sequence of contradictory dreams and hallucinations that he entertained and overinterpreted with cocaine-enhanced feverishness (see Crews, 1986, pages 61–62). The centerpiece of that effort was the "recovery" of memories from an age when, as we now know, long-term memory cannot be established at all. And Freud's instant generalization from those dubious retrievals, entailing everyone else's oedipal case in his own, merely illustrates his impetuousness as a self-styled intellectual "conquistador" (CLFF, page 398). When, after Freud's time, the idea of the universal Oedipus complex has been subjected to independent anthropological scrutiny, it has fared very badly (see, for example, Wallace, 1983; Daly and Wilson, 1990; Degler, 1991; Erickson, 1993).

And then there is the question of whether Freud truly abandoned Wilhelm Fliess's psychobiological speculations when he founded psychoanalysis as we know it. We will see in Chapter 5 that Freud's doctrine became more "Fliessian," not less so, as he was resigning himself to the collapse of the seduction theory. Lacking even one single patient who could supply good evidence for his views, Freud turned at once inward toward his own case and outward toward Fliess's parascientific systematizing. Though he would later grant himself full credit for "clinically" deducing such ideas as infantile sexuality, polymorphous perversity, innate bisexuality, latency, and the psychosexual developmental stages, each with its favored zone and mode and "fixation point," all of those notions owed much to Fliess, as did a host of other explanations for such diverse phenomena as thumb sucking, bed wetting, night fears, gastric pains, even hemorrhoids. Freud had become a virtually complete Fliessian, but with no intention of admitting that fact. And that is why Fliess, having come to regard Freud less as a friend than as an outright plagiarist, refused to have anything further to do with him (see Sulloway, 1992, pages 217–235).

Finally, we must remark on the important connection between Freud's defective ideas and his progressive ineptitude as a therapist. Equipped at first with an empathetic manner and a ready store of narcotics, the Freud of the late 1880s could at least impart some calm to a chronically agitated patient such as Anna von Lieben (Chapter 2). But that minimal degree of competence vanished as Freud became increasingly dogmatic about his etiological laws. By the mid-nineties, he had already changed his manner from that of a bedside comforter to that of an implacable sleuth, a seeker of mechanical links between childhood shocks—sexual abuse, a glimpse of parental intercourse, a surge of guilt over masturbation—and specific neurotic disorders in adulthood. And since he was by then convinced, on a priori grounds, of the shameful secrets that needed to be brought to light, the sleuth typically gave way to the third-degree prosecutor who would brook no denials or excuses. Such zeal was incompatible with the therapeutic attitude. We cannot be surprised, then, to learn that Freud's record includes not a single validated cure. It was precisely his growing certitude about the wiles of the unconscious that guided his evolution from an ineffective but harmless therapist to the actively dangerous one of the "seduction" period and beyond.

Anna O.: The First Tall Tale*

Mikkel Borch-Jacobsen

The saga of Freud's great therapeutic triumphs begins with a precursor case, that of his mentor Josef Breuer's "Anna O." (Bertha Pappenheim), who was treated for hysteria from 1880 to 1882. According to Breuer and Freud's *Studies on Hysteria* of 1895 (SE, 2: 3–305), Pappenheim's shrewd directions to her therapist led Breuer to the revolutionary insight that hysterical symptoms can be permanently removed by retrieving buried memories that underlie them. Freud further concluded that there must be a mental repository for storing those not-yet-accessible memories. Here in the Anna case, then, "the unconscious" had left its spoor for the big-game hunter Freud to stalk more assiduously in later years.

As Borch-Jacobsen narrates, the positive outcome of Pappenheim's "cathartic" treatment has been exposed as a falsehood jointly perpetrated by Breuer and Freud (see Jones; Ellenberger, 1970, 1972; Hirschmüller, 1989; Jensen, 1984; Swales, 1986, 1988a; Schweighofer, 1987). But the initiative for the deception was all Freud's. As early as 1888, he was already publicizing Breuer's (nonexistent) "successful cures" with catharsis, while Breuer was making no such claim; and later, it was the importunate Freud who overruled Breuer's scruples and insisted on showcasing Anna O. as both the first beneficiary and the prime begetter of "the talking cure."

The fact that Pappenheim did eventually recover from "hysteria" and

* From *Remembering Anna O.: A Century of Mystification* (Routledge, 1996).

become a vigorous social activist emboldened Freud and subsequent Freudians to count that happy outcome as a vindication of cathartic therapy. Yet members of Freud's circle were well aware that Breuer's treatment had left Bertha more wretched than before, with her symptoms exacerbated by dependency on the morphine and chloral hydrate that Breuer and others had employed to treat a persistent facial neuralgia. Her recovery was to be postponed through another six or seven years of suffering and at least four hospitalizations, with no further contribution from the school of memory-retrieving therapy that she clearly regarded as worthless. Pappenheim's belated return to health does, however, tell us something important: she probably hadn't been suffering from the organic brain damage that some observers have hypothesized (see Thornton, 1986; Orr-Andrawes, 1987; Webster, 1995).

What was ailing her? Conceivably, a manic-depressive disorder or a grief crisis over her father's terminal illness and subsequent death had left her prone to the "conversion symptoms" that were considered in her day to be signs of hysteria (Merskey, 1992; Shorter, 1997). But whether or not she was depressed, Borch-Jacobsen's book *Remembering Anna O.* shows that, in all likelihood, she was hypnotically and autohypnotically manufacturing symptoms both to meet Breuer's expectations and to prolong a hypochondriacal condition that insulated her from more objective annoyances and frustrations. If so, the disappearance of certain symptoms was no more significant than their production in the first place.

This chapter offers a useful glimpse not just into the proximate antecedents of psychoanalysis but also into its more remote ancestry in suggestion-based "magnetic" treatment. Likewise, Borch-Jacobsen astutely sketches the legacy of Freud and Breuer behind the recovered memory movement that is still unfolding today. The whole tradition of teasing out the secrets of the unconscious, from Mesmer in the eighteenth century straight through to the latest purveyors of multiple personality disorder, is characterized by indifference to what are now called experimenter effects: artifacts of the treatment itself that are mistaken for independent phenomena.

Finally, the text below is of interest for the light it throws on Freud's habits of invidious mythmaking—in this instance, on his tale of Breuer's supposed flight from Pappenheim's sexual advances and her disconcerting hysterical pregnancy. The charm of that fable is so powerful that its documented refutation a quarter century ago (Ellenberger, 1972) has had no dissuasive effect on the Freudians who continue to pass it along (see, for example, Erdelyi, 1985; Safouan, 1988; Gay, 1989; Kurzweil, 1989; Forrester, 1990; Appignanesi and Forrester, 1992; Micale, 1995; Showalter, 1997).

Mikkel Borch-Jacobsen is Professor of Comparative Literature at the University of Washington. In addition to *Remembering Anna O.*, his writings include books on Lacan, Freud, and hypnosis.

Every society has its therapeutic myths, meant to explain why we fall ill and why we get well, and our society is no exception. To be sure, we no longer imagine that our ills are caused by spirits or evil omens, nor do we believe any longer in curative power derived from the laying on of hands or from magical formulas. But we are quick to believe that certain troubles, which we call *psychological* or *psychosomatic,* are due to traumatic events in our personal histories, and that by recounting these events to a doctor we will cure ourselves of their effects. It is necessary, we believe, to name the ill, narrate it, *make the evil speak,* in order to be rid of it. . . .

. . . Here, we recognize the story that Josef Breuer told about the spectacular cure of Fräulein Anna O., his patient: "It was in the summer during a period of extreme heat, and the patient was suffering very badly from thirst, for, without being able to account for it in any way, she suddenly found it impossible to drink. She would take up the glass of water she longed for, but as soon as it touched her lips she would push it away like someone suffering from hydrophobia. [. . .] This had lasted for some six weeks, when one day during hypnosis she grumbled about her English lady-companion whom she did not care for, and went on to describe, with every sign of disgust, how she had once gone into that lady's room and how her little dog—horrid creature!—had drunk out of a glass there. The patient had said nothing, as she wanted to be polite. After giving further energetic expression to the anger she had held back, she asked for something to drink, drank a large quantity of water without any difficulty and woke from her hypnosis with the glass at her lips; and thereupon the disturbance vanished, never to return."

This, to be sure, is still a far cry from the tales of childhood "seduction" that Freud would obtain from his patients between 1896 and 1897, and farther yet from the sensational accounts of incest and satanic ritual abuse that have become all the rage lately among American therapists. Right here, however, in this rather innocuous account of Anna O., is where the idea was born that "hysterics suffer mainly from reminiscences," as Breuer and Freud state in *Studies on Hysteria*, and that these traumatic memories can be "talked away" under hypnosis. Of course, this sturdy theory soon underwent a number of metamorphoses: Freud reconceptualized Breuer's indeterminate "trauma," first as an actual sexual assault suffered in early childhood, then as a fantasy having to do with perverse infantile sexuality, and finally as a fantasy of oedipal origin. As for cathartic hypnosis, it was abandoned in favor of the method of so-called free association, which itself gradually came to be recentered on the analysis of resistances and of the transference. But none of these reshufflings ever called the fundamental, seminal idea into question: that *to remember is to heal*. Heal from what? From the amnesia that "dissociates" the psyche, from the forgetting that breaks the continuity of my history and therefore keeps me from being my *self*. Ever since (and because of) Anna O.'s miraculous cure, forgetting has ceased to be a simple lapse of memory and has become, under various names—"dissociated consciousness," "the unconscious," "repression"—the supreme form of remembering, and the very key to our identity as subjects.

Freud himself said this quite overtly in 1917: "This discovery of Breuer's is still the foundation of psychoanalytic therapy. The thesis that symptoms disappear when we have made their unconscious predeterminants conscious has been confirmed by all subsequent research, although we meet with the strangest and most unexpected complications when we attempt to carry it through in practice." Are we much more advanced now that a hundred years have gone by since the publication of *Studies on Hysteria*? Apparently not, to judge by the spectacular comeback, in the United States, of the traumatic-dissociative etiology of neurosis, with its parade of "traumatic memories" abreacted under hypnosis. And even if the theorists of "recovered memory" do refer to Janet more than to Breuer or Freud, it is clear that their utter trust in remembering, with its "integrative" power, takes us more directly back to Anna O.'s "talking cure" than to the suggestive manipulation of memories practiced by the author of *Psychological Automatism. . . .*

Myths are notoriously thick-skinned, and here we have a fine example. It may be true that the cure of Anna O. consisted—*partly*—in her relating "memories" to Breuer, but it is just plain untrue that this treatment ever got rid of her symptoms. This fact became well known in 1953, when Ernest Jones revealed it publicly in the first volume of his biography of Freud, and it has since been amply corroborated by the painstaking research of Henri Ellenberger, Albrecht Hirschmüller, Ellen Jensen, and Peter Swales, among many others. No one today can remain unaware that the treatment of Anna O. (whose real name was Bertha Pappenheim) was very different from what Breuer and Freud have told us about it—so different, in fact, that we can legitimately wonder what remains of modern psychotherapy's origin-myth, now that the historians of psychoanalysis have so thoroughly debunked it. But that hasn't prevented this myth and its derivatives from perpetuating themselves and proliferating in psychotherapeutic discourse. . . .

Everything—the whole enterprise of modern psychotherapy—starts from this marvelous tale of Breuer's, almost too good to be true. And it isn't true. In the early 1970s, the historian Henri Ellenberger, curious about what eventually had become of Bertha Pappenheim, managed to determine that Breuer and the patient's family had placed her in the Bellevue Sanatorium at Kreuzlingen, Switzerland, where she was a patient from July 12, 1882—barely a month after the end of her treatment—until the following October 29. Her file contains a very interesting report from Breuer to the director, Robert Binswanger (father of Ludwig), as well as a second report, dated October 1882, from the sanatorium's Dr. Laupus. The report by Laupus wastes no words in establishing that Bertha Pappenheim has been suffering for six months from a serious "trigeminal neuralgia," which itself has brought about the patient's addiction to the high doses of morphine that Breuer has been administering to dull her pain (Breuer was also giving her chloral to help her sleep). This facial neuralgia, which Breuer mentions nowhere in the *Studies on Hysteria* (he likewise refrains from any mention of Bertha's embarrassing morphine addiction), appeared briefly in the spring of 1880 and played only "a quite subordinate role" in Bertha's illness until "the middle of March" 1882, when, quite possibly as a result of surgery performed in February on the patient's upper left jaw, the pain became "persistent and very excruciating." The patient's pain has persisted throughout her stay at Kreuzlingen, Laupus notes, and all attempts to break her addiction to morphine have been utter failures, despite some apparent success at the very beginning of treatment. Dr. Laupus also reports that the patient has continued to exhibit "genuine signs of hysteria," moving from depressive states (during the day) to playful ones (in the evening) to "dramatic" enactments in her "private theater" to intermittent loss of German (at night, as soon as her head hits the pillow).

Albrecht Hirschmüller, following up on Ellenberger's research, was able to dig up other documents from the Bellevue Sanatorium, among them a "report" written in English by Bertha Pappenheim herself, in which she complains of periods of "time-missing." There are also letters from Breuer to Robert Binswanger that show Breuer making preparations for his patient to go to Kreuzlingen. In one, dated November 4, 1881—immediately after the patient's return from the first sanatorium, at the point where the "talking cure," according to the *Studies*, had rendered her condition "bearable, both physically and mentally"—Breuer writes that the attempt to acclimate Bertha to her family "will probably fail," and that it will be best to prepare for her immediate hospitalization. In another letter to Binswanger, from mid-June 1882 (only a few days after Bertha's allegedly definitive "cure"), Breuer states that Bertha is "very agitated," adding, "Today, the patient is suffering from slight hysterical insanity, confessing at the moment to all kinds of deceptions, genuine or not, occasionally still seeing bits of nonsense such as people spying on her, and the like, and exhibiting perfectly odd behavior on visits." Other archival documents unearthed by Hirschmüller demonstrate beyond a doubt that Bertha Pappenheim's symptoms, both somatic (neuralgia, morphine addiction) and functional, persisted well after her discharge from the sanatorium at Kreuzlingen. Indeed, between 1883 and 1887, Bertha made at least three prolonged visits to the same sanatorium in Inzensdorf where she had first been confined in 1881, and the doctors reached the same diagnosis every time: "hysteria."

Breuer, who declined to resume treating Bertha Pappenheim after her stay at Kreuzlingen, could not have had any illusions about the results of Anna O.'s "talking cure," especially since he had kept in touch with the Pappenheim family and enjoyed ample opportunity to inquire after his patient. We can easily understand, then, why he refrained for thirteen years from talking publicly about this "cure," and why he "at first [. . .] objected vehemently" to the idea of doing so when Freud brought it up. If Freud was ultimately able to prevail, it was certainly less because of his powers of persuasion than because of the fact that Bertha Pappenheim, toward the end of the 1880s, had gradually recovered and, starting in the early 1890s, took up the literary and philanthropic activities that were to make her a pioneer of feminism and social work in Germany. Obviously, without this unexpected recovery—which owed nothing whatsoever to the "talking cure"—it would have been impossible to ring down the curtain on a happy ending for this case history (too many people in Vienna knew the true identity of Fräulein Anna O.).

As for Freud, he was completely aware of the whole situation. We know from Freud's unpublished letters to his fiancée, Martha Bernays (letters cited by Jones in his biography), that Breuer first spoke to Freud about Bertha Pappenheim on November 18, 1882, making no attempt to conceal the disastrous outcome of the treatment; and on August 5, 1883, Freud wrote to Martha: "Bertha is once again in the sanatorium in Gross-Enzensdorf [sic], I believe. Breuer is constantly talking about her, says he wishes she were dead so that the poor woman could be free of her suffering. He says she will never be well again, that she is completely shattered." Moreover, because Martha Bernays maintained quasi-familial ties with Bertha Pappenheim and saw her regularly, Freud could not have avoided hearing about the evolution of Bertha's illness. Martha (by then Martha Freud), in two letters to her mother from January and May of 1887, writes that her friend continues to suffer from hallucinations in the evenings. Not that any of this deterred Freud, later on, from pressing Breuer to publish Bertha's case history and thus to provide an a posteriori validation of Freud's own cases: nor did he scruple to make false claims for Breuer's "method," as early as 1888, by comparing it favorably to the treatment of hysteria by suggestion: "It is even more effective if we adopt a method first practised by Josef Breuer in Vienna and lead the patient under hypnosis back to the psychical prehistory of the ailment and compel him to acknowledge the psychical occasion on which the disorder in question originated. This method of treatment is new [to riot in understatement, since at this point it has been used on precisely one patient], but it produces successful cures [sic] which cannot otherwise be achieved." . . .

The Pappenheim affair, carefully concealed from the public, seems nevertheless to have been an open secret among psychoanalytic insiders. As early as 1916, in his book *The History and Practice of Psychoanalysis*, Poul Bjerre noted almost in passing, "I can add that the patient was to undergo a severe crisis in addition to what was given out in the description of the case. Since then, however, she has lived, and still lives, in the best of health and in widespread activity." And Carl Jung, in a private seminar of 1925, went even farther. Referring to confidential remarks made by Freud about the "untrustworthiness" of some of his early case histories, Jung stated: "Thus again, the famous first case that he [Freud] had with Breuer, which has been so much spoken about as an example of a brilliant therapeutic success, was in reality nothing of the kind." In fact, so little does the whole business appear to have been a secret within Freud's inner circle that Marie Bonaparte, upon returning from Vienna, where Freud had told her "the Breuer story," noted in her diary on December 16, 1927, "*The rest is well known:* Anna's relapse, her fantasy of pregnancy, Breuer's flight"[emphasis added].

It wasn't until 1953—some sixty years after Breuer's initial publication—that Ernest Jones, with the first volume of his biography of Freud, rattled the skeleton in the psychoanalytic closet. And, conveniently, this noise was drowned out by one that was even more sensational. According to Jones, Freud privately confided to him (as he had to Marie Bonaparte) that Breuer developed an intense countertransference to Bertha Pappenheim, which not only made his wife jealous but also, at the end of the treatment, resulted in an episode of pseudocyesis (hysterical childbirth), "the logical termination of a phantom pregnancy." Breuer, the story goes, frightened at having the sexual nature of Bertha's illness so abruptly exposed, and hoping to calm her down, hypnotized her and then fled in a "cold sweat." He left Vienna the next day for a second honeymoon in Venice, where he played his part in producing his wife's actual pregnancy with their youngest daughter. And meanwhile poor Bertha, abandoned by her phantom love, was forced to content herself with fulfilling her sterile fantasy of maternity by becoming the "'Mother' of an orphan institution." The subtext of this tale is that Bertha Pappenheim's botched treatment was due to a serious underestimation of the role that sexuality played in her case, as well as to insufficient analysis of the transference and the countertransference. Breuer had failed, for want of courage and determination, where Freud doubtless would have triumphed. The failure belonged to Breuer, not to psychoanalysis. *Q.E.D.*

A lovely story, and one that has thoroughly made the rounds—but here again, careful research by Ellenberger, Hirschmüller, and Swales shows that this ingenious explanation of Bertha Pappenheim's failed treatment doesn't hold up. Mathilde Breuer probably *was* offended by the intense "rapport" that developed between her husband and his patient, but it simply isn't true that Breuer forsook Bertha for a hasty flight to Venice with his wife. Quite the opposite: Breuer arranged, very professionally, for his patient's transfer to Binswanger's sanatorium and then continued to work normally until he left to spend the summer with his family at Gmunden. Nor is the rest of the story true: Dora Breuer was born on March 11, 1882, three months before her alleged conception in Venice: and Breuer's custom when a patient needed sedation was not to induce hypnosis but to administer injections of morphine or chloral.

As for the juiciest part of this story, the pseudocyesis, or hysterical childbirth, it is mentioned nowhere in Breuer's report to Binswanger, nor does it appear in Dr. Laupus's report or in letters sent to Binswanger by Bertha's mother and cousin: there is every reason to believe that it is sheer invention. Had the episode really taken place as Jones claims, Breuer's failure to mention this spectacular symptom to the colleague who was about to receive his patient would have been unthinkable. But here is what Breuer's report actually says: "The sexual element is *astonishingly underdeveloped:* I have never once found it represented even amongst her numerous hallucinations" [emphasis added]. It is hard to see why Breuer, noted for his diagnostic skills, would have exposed himself to the indignity of having his medical opinion immediately contradicted by his patient's maternal-erotic delirium, and harder still to see why he would have taken such pains to assure Binswanger that Bertha was neither a liar nor a malingerer: in those days, he certainly would have aroused his colleague's suspicions of an affair between patient and doctor. All the evidence indicates that the story peddled by Jones is a psychoanalytic myth based on rumor and professional gossip.

Who is the beneficiary of this myth? Because no one can still claim to be unaware that the official history of psychoanalysis is a vast anthology of tall tales, psychoanalysts customarily profess to be amused by Jones's "mistakes." But, here as elsewhere, Freud himself is to blame. There is no particular reason for believing that Jones unduly elaborated on the story Freud told him: after all, Freud was more than capable of embellishing the story himself. In fact, the pseudocyesis story has been handed down in a number of versions which vary considerably according to when Freud told the story and to whom: taken together, they give the clear impression of being a spiteful piece of slander that was built up over a period of several years. . . .

But didn't Bertha Pappenheim do better whenever she could talk about the origin of her symptoms? Yes—and no. When we examine the case history published in 1895, or especially the initial report of 1882, we see that the theme of memory emerged only gradually over the course of treatment. For the first four months, Bertha Pappenheim gained relief by telling fairy tales of her own invention. Over the next two months, the same effect was obtained through her recounting—or, more precisely, acting out ("tragedizing")—morbid hallucinations. Only after August 1881 was the "talking cure" directed toward her recounting the memories that supposedly were at the root of her symptoms. Therefore, we have no grounds for assuming that the temporary remission of Bertha Pappenheim's symptoms owed more to her remembering their origin than to her telling fairy tales or even, as Lacan would have it, to her "verbalizing" her hallucinations instead of acting them out, since each of these procedures finally had the same effect. Peter Swales puts it very well: "the cathartic treatment, involving a detailed biographical accounting for the symptoms, exerted an essentially *placebo* or *suggestive* effect."

Remembering and narration, obviously, were only two elements among others involved in what amounted to a negotiation of symptoms between Breuer and his patient: "You give me this, and I'll give you a symptom." Thus Breuer, in the sanatorium at Inzensdorf, literally had to beg Bertha and recite a ritual phrase in English ("And there was a boy") before she would agree to begin telling her purgative stories. She also insisted on feeling Breuer's hands, to make sure it was really he. As Henri Ellenberger has aptly pointed out, the treatment of Bertha Pappenheim bears an unmistakable resemblance to courses of magnetic treatment from the late eighteenth and early nineteenth centuries, whereby patients prescribed for themselves the therapeutic procedures that would heal them and accurately predicted the moment of their own healing. . . .

Breuer, in fact, in his original report of 1882, has nothing at all to say about "memories" or "reminiscences" (by contrast with what he would have to say in 1895): he speaks only about "*caprices*" (in French) and "fantasies." What is even more striking is that these two terms make their appearance just at that point in the report where Breuer mentions the episode in which Bertha's hydrophobia was cured, an episode described in the *Studies* as the true beginning of the "talking cure," centered as it was on memories of *actual* traumatic events. In the 1882 report, however, this episode is immediately preceded by what Breuer, in a charming phrase, calls Bertha's "stocking caprice": "When she was awoken and put to bed in the evening, the patient could not bear her stockings being removed; only on awakening at 2 or 3 o'clock would she occasionally do this, complaining at the same time of the impropriety of allowing her to sleep with her stockings on. One evening she told me a true story of long ago, how at night time she would creep in to eavesdrop on her father (at that time, night nurses could no longer put up with her), how she slept in her stockings for this reason, then on one occasion she was caught by her brother, and so on. As soon as she had finished she began to cry out softly, demanding why she was in bed with her stockings on. Then she took them off, and that was the last we saw of the stocking caprice."

Is it any wonder that Breuer, in the *Studies on Hysteria*, chose to pass over this first miraculous "healing" in silence and substitute the story about the governess's horrid little dog? Nor could Bertha's nocturnal discovery by her brother easily be made to pass for the kind of "psychic trauma" that Freud and Breuer had in mind in 1895. Not only that, the stocking symptom and its disappearance had an aspect of *literal* "capriciousness" that was altogether too obvious for Breuer even to think about parlaying this comical episode into the inaugural event of the cathartic cure.

In reality, the 1882 report shows clearly that Breuer was still quite far from theorizing about the Pappenheim case in terms of psychic trauma or memories dissociated from consciousness. Here, for instance, is what Breuer says about the "talking cure": "It was clear from this work as a whole that each product of her abnormal activity, whether it was a *spontaneous product of her phantasy* or derived from the diseased part of her psyche, acted as a psychic stimulus, and continued to act until it was narrated, but with this it completely lost its potency" [emphasis added]. And elsewhere, on the subject of a "whim" of Bertha's, which consisted of her asking for bread and then refusing to eat it, he writes: "this was a purely psychic inhibition proceeding from one of her phantasies, and when she *narrated the phantasy* the inhibition was discarded" [emphasis added]. . . .

Clearly, then, the theme of pathogenic memory was introduced into the Bertha Pappenheim case only later on, to make it fit the theory of traumatic hysteria put forward by Charcot and the Salpêtrière school, a theory that Breuer and Freud had adopted in the meantime. Freud, in the context of his squabble with Janet over who came first, was often to claim that Breuer had made his discovery "in 1881, independently of any outside influence"—that is, before Charcot's investigations into traumatic hysteria and the continuation of those investigations by Janet in *Automatisme Psychologique* (1889). But this statement is demonstrably false, at least if we consider the actual theoretical content of the "discovery," since no trace of the theory of the "mechanism of hysteria," as proposed by Breuer and Freud in the "Preliminary Communication" of 1893, can be found in the report of 1882. In fact, no theory can be found there at all: Breuer speaks rather vaguely about the elimination of "psychic excitation" due to "fantasies," and that's all. At any rate, there is no mention of "psychic trauma," "dissociation of consciousness," or "reminiscence."

The claim that it was Breuer who discovered the role of psychic trauma in hysterical neuroses is actually a total (and self-serving) anachronism on Freud's part, for the theory set out in the *Studies on Hysteria* comes straight from Charcot, as well as from other French works in this area. Breuer could not have known about these works at the time, for the simple reason that they were published only after the treatment of Bertha Pappenheim. . . .

. . . Only in 1895, when the Pappenheim case had to be made to fit in with other cases presented in the *Studies*, did Breuer systematically convert his patient's *"fantasies"* into "reminiscences" of traumatic and shocking events. The case of Anna O., far from being the empirical origin of Freud's and Breuer's new theory of hysteria, came to illustrate it after the fact, through a self-serving revisionism that was anything but innocent. What a fine example of *Nachträglichkeit* (Freud's "aftermath-effect"): modern psychotherapy, with its emphasis on the curative powers of narration and memory, has as its founding narrative the biased rewriting of an older narrative, one that tells only made-up stories. And what should we find but a false memory right at the heart of the modern myth of remembering.

2

Freud's Master Hysteric*

Peter J. Swales

This chapter is excerpted from an eighty-page article that deserves study in full as a classic of ingenious Freud scholarship. Until that article appeared in 1986, the identity of Freud's most important early patient, "Frau Cäcilie M.," had not been established, and historians had no means of weighing the cogency of his observations about her case in *Studies on Hysteria*. In passages omitted here, just before the juncture where our chapter starts referring to the patient as "Anna" (page 26 below), Peter J. Swales presents the clues indicating that "Cäcilie" had to have been the willful and eccentric Anna von Lieben of Vienna. That conclusion now stands beyond dispute.

Anna von Lieben, born in 1847 as the Baroness Anna von Todesco, was descended from wealthy financiers and industrialists, was reared in luxury, and married into still another fortune—a background that scarcely set her apart from most of Freud's other early patients. His daily treatment of Anna, lasting from 1887 through 1893, formed the very basis of his practice in those years; and, happily for the struggling physician and his family, there was no likelihood that she would be speedily cured of her "hysteria." Unlike Josef Breuer's "Anna O.," who eventually recovered, this Anna made a lifelong career of discommoding her relatives and subverting the equanimity of her doctors. By

* From "Freud, His Teacher, and the Birth of Psychoanalysis," in *Freud: Appraisals and Reappraisals; Contributions to Freud Studies*, Vol. 1, ed. Paul E. Stepansky (Hillsdale, NJ: The Analytic Press, 1986: 3–82).

the time of her death in 1900, "Frau Cäcilie" had kept the physicians pointlessly hopping for a full thirty-three years, and at the end she was no closer than ever to a normal existence.

Readers who have digested Chapter 1 will remark the points of affinity between the two Anna cases that decisively shaped the future course of psychoanalysis. Here again, in Anna von Lieben, we encounter a demanding hypochondriac who knows just how to garner what Freud would later call a "secondary gain from illness" and who shows the way in proposing her own diagnosis and treatment. Here, too, a latter-day mesmeric practitioner employs hypnotism and drugs to enforce some measure of control over the patient's outbursts. In both instances, the befuddled therapist neglects to ask himself whether his own interventions, including the administering of narcotics, may not be generating some of the symptoms and "memories" that he prefers to regard as emanations of the repressed. And both cases abound in symptom substitution, or the endless replacement of one affliction by another—the very fate that, according to the psychoanalytic Freud, would supposedly befall just those patients who *didn't* have their traumatic memories brought to the surface and "abreacted."

By 1887 Freud had already fastened his sights on making a breakthrough discovery from which fame and fortune would follow. Thus, as Swales shows, he was all too eager to swallow the poet Anna's romantic ideas about dreams and passion and to share her view of her symptoms as meaning-laden references to her past. She was indeed his "teacher," as he would always gratefully acknowledge. But she could hardly have led him to believe what he would brazenly claim in *Studies on Hysteria*: that cathartic procedures can actually cure hysteria. On the contrary, it was Anna's very intractability, combined with the incontinence of her imagination and her pathetic emotional attachment to Freud, that rendered her an ideal long-term research instrument for engendering protopsychoanalytic notions.

This chapter alludes briefly to a still earlier phase of Freud's professional life—namely, his period of fervid cocaine evangelism in the mid-1880s—that should have alerted the medical profession to his tendency to draw premature conclusions, to engage in salesmanship for untested panaceas, to disregard the welfare of patients, and to cover his tracks when forced to retreat. For a brief discussion, see Webster, 1995, pages 45–51.

Peter J. Swales is an independent Freud scholar and the author of numerous essays—highly influential among historians of psychoanalysis—
identifying Freud's early patients, exploring his personal and professional relations, and tracing the often obscure sources of his ideas. The
Swales entries in our "Works Editorially Cited" include the most
important of those essays.

For no fewer than thirty years, Frau Cäcilie M. had been afflicted with a
"chronic hysteria" featuring numerous psychic and somatic symptoms.
The latter included a severe facial neuralgia; pains in the feet such as
made walking impossible; and a penetrating pain in the forehead between
her eyes. Her psychological symptoms included lapsing into *absences* for
periods of time; she would complain of gaps in her memory; and, for
nearly three years during the course of her treatment, she was beset by
what would seem to have been an overwhelmingly moral dilemma—
specifically, fears of her own "worthlessness" based largely on an accumulation of self-reproaches from bygone times. The latter Freud presented as
a novel syndrome—viz., as "an hysterical psychosis for the payment of
old debts."

Influenced by the ideas of Breuer and Charcot, Freud understood all of
Frau Cäcilie's states and symptoms to be products of psychic traumas
dating from far back in her past. And, for nearly three years, she relived,
under his guidance, *all* of the many traumas of her past life—all of them
involving events long-forgotten but now vividly reawakened and reexpe-
rienced with the most intense suffering. While recapitulating her whole
life in this manner, apparently in reverse sequence, she exhibited one
by one all of the physical symptoms which, according to her testimony,
had accompanied each trauma when, long before, they had first been
experienced.

Interestingly, as Freud mentions, when sometimes he was unable to
attend, Frau Cäcilie would recollect these traumas for some or other depu-
tizing physician. But, in that event, she would describe them *without* all of
the associated emotions and their physical expression—such as might
assume the form of tears, cries of despair, and so on—which she would
reserve, and then enact, only for Freud. During nearly three years of this
reliving of all her former traumas, the woman "repaid" thirty-three years'

worth of "accumulated debts." This "purgation," then, was indeed a veritable "catharsis."

From all of the references to Frau Cäcilie M. found throughout the *Studies on Hysteria*, one can reconstruct a picture of the illness and treatment as these might present themselves daily. For some hours the patient would lapse into a pathological state of moodiness—involving anxiety, irritation, or despair—which she would regularly attribute to some more or less trivial recent event. Alternatively, or perhaps additionally, an obsessive and tormenting hallucination, a neuralgia, or some other physical symptom would begin seizing all her attention. And her mental capacity—that is to say, her alacrity, her capacity for reason, and her general mental "togetherness" (*Beisammenheit*)—would diminish in inverse proportion, to the extent that eventually her consciousness would become completely cloudy and she was dominated by her symptom to a point of total incapacitation, even "imbecility."

Then would regularly follow a hysterical crisis involving pains, spasms, hallucinations, long declamatory speeches, and the like. Immediately Freud would be sent for and, on arrival, he would rapidly induce a state of hypnosis and endeavor to abolish her symptoms by suggesting them away. After some time, however—and, thenceforth, for some three years following—he systematically made use of the cathartic method in seeking to dissolve these attacks. To invoke and thereby "abreact" the particular traumatic memory supposedly buried in the "unconscious" and directly responsible for the current symptom, Freud set himself to unravel many highly intricate and complex trains of thought—Frau Cäcilie's associations often involving pictures, symbols, and puns.

With the eventual reproduction of the sought-for traumatic memory, improvement followed very shortly afterwards. However, as Freud mentions, it was his regular custom to *hasten* the end of each attack by the use of some unspecified "artificial means." Frau Cäcilie's troubles having then disappeared "as if by magic," her mental lucidity and emotional stability were soon restored—until, that is, her *next* attack, just half a day later. Thus, Freud would be called upon twice a day: and, over a period of three or four years, he participated in "several hundred" such cycles. Thereby, as he asserts, he was able to gain the most instructive information on "the way in which hysterical symptoms are determined."

Particularly important for Freud, and especially significant about this particular patient, was her liability to that phenomenon named "hysterical conversion" by Freud, and which in her case involved an often almost comic mode of "symbolization." Sometimes some idea of hers would provoke a physical sensation, while at other times a physical sensation might produce a related idea. Thus, once upon a time when she had been a girl of fifteen, a grandmother had been viewing her with suspicion and had given her a "piercing look"—supposedly provoking a penetrating pain between her eyes that would then, thirty years later, be reproduced in treatment with Freud. Another time, at a stay in a sanatorium in a foreign country where she had been confined to bed for a time with pains in her feet, her pains were suddenly exacerbated by the idea that she might not "find herself on a right footing" with all the strangers in the place. . . . And one more example of this symbolic "conversion": Breuer had refused her request for a certain unspecified drug and so she had set her hopes on Freud, only to find him equally intransigent. So she had gotten furious—whereupon she hallucinated Breuer and Freud hanging together on a tree in the garden. The meaning: "There's nothing to choose between the two of them; one's the *pendant*"—in French, a pun meaning both "counterpart" and "hanging"—"of the other."

Freud states in the *Studies on Hysteria* that Frau Cäcilie M. was a "highly intelligent woman, to whom I am indebted for much help in gaining an understanding of hysterical symptoms"—"indebted," *nota bene,* almost as if to imply, then, that she had played a very active role in elucidating their mysteries. And there are several other instances in the book where both Freud and Breuer express their remarkably high esteem for this woman. Towards contradicting the French view that hysteria is a product of "degeneration" or "psychical insufficiency," Freud asserts that, early on, he and Breuer had learned from their observations of Frau Cäcilie M. "that hysteria of the severest type can exist in conjunction with gifts of the richest and most original kind." Frau Cäcilie was particularly gifted artistically, it is said, and her "highly developed sense of form was revealed in some poems of great perfection." But she was also very capable of rational thinking—she played chess so excellently she enjoyed playing two games at once. . . .

During these years, the 1870s and the 1880s, Anna (Frau Cäcilie) began to develop a number of other eccentricities. For long periods of time—possibly even with the idea in mind of combating her vastly increasing weight and size—she would exist solely on caviar and champagne. And then, while staying in the mountains, she would sometimes arrange for a few weeks or so at a time to have a man travel down each day especially from Vienna with a delivery of lamb cutlets—something she had grown to love having for breakfast while staying in England. Stricken with insomnia, she would hire a professional chess player to literally wait outside her room all night so that she could then play chess—or, one would presume, two games of chess simultaneously—if and when the fancy took her. And the games might go on all night. . . .

Occasionally it did happen that, for more or less protracted periods, Anna would leave her sickroom and live approximately normal hours. Sometimes she would even watch the children play and take some kind of an active interest in their education and upbringing. But, as often as not—and, in all probability, more often than not—the children would be kept away from her on account of her illness, and all they would ever hear of their mother would be the . . . sounds of her crying, screaming, and raving while she underwent her recurrent crises in another part of the house. . . .

Now, from certain points of view, to assign Freud to this case was a rather bold and adventurous step on the part of Breuer or Rudolf Chrobak, or perhaps the two of them. Following his 1886 lecture on hysteria before the Society of Physicians—and even more so following autumn 1888, when he began openly espousing hypnotic therapy—Freud became a controversial and somewhat marginal figure vis-à-vis the Viennese medical establishment. And it could very easily have been alleged—as, indeed, it is said was the case on the part of certain cynics within the von Lieben family's circle—that Freud was just an ambitious young upstart, if not actually a charlatan, eager to line his pockets with the large income to be gained from treating such a rich woman. . . . We have subsequent testimony of Freud's that his patient Anna von Lieben was handed over to him for treatment "because no one knew what to do with her"—as if to imply, then, that probably everything had been tried during the thirty or so years of her illness but that no one had had any success in curing her. . . .

We learn from *Studies on Hysteria* that an "old memory" suddenly returned to the patient—presumably some memory from long before that appeared to render intelligible the genesis of a particular symptom—whereupon "for nearly three years after this she once again lived through all the traumas of her life" under Freud's daily guidance. We would therefore suppose that, circa autumn 1889—about a year after he had apparently treated Anna with hypnotic suggestion—with her cooperation Freud began systematically employing the cathartic method. . . .

In his later works, Freud would represent that he had begun employing the cathartic method under the influence of what he had learned from Josef Breuer about the treatment of Bertha Pappenheim during the period 1881–1882. By 1889, however, such a mode of therapy was very much a product of the *Zeitgeist*—quite obviously, it was an idea whose time had come. . . . It had long been maintained by many that memories can be stored unconsciously and be liable to retrieval by artificial means. . . . There was only a short step involved in supposing that the medium of hypnosis might be used to retrieve long-lost memories. . . . In the particular case of Freud and Breuer, however, there was yet another powerful source of inspiration that would certainly have served to assure them that they were onto something big, also something very real. In his *Poetics*—wherein he conceives of drama, poetry, and music as being, fundamentally, modes of "imitation"—Aristotle interprets theatrical tragedy as a medium which, by invoking pity and fear, accomplishes a "catharsis of such emotions" among the audience. This passage was long understood to imply either a moral or an aesthetic purgation of the emotions; but, in 1857, the classical philologist Jacob Bernays had advanced a novel medical interpretation, arguing that Aristotle had conceived of tragedy as a catharsis of emotions which, if undischarged, would assume a noxious property.

Bernays's work had been republished in 1880, a year before his death; and this, together with a series of obituaries which then appeared in popular newspapers, would appear to have been responsible for stimulating a surge of interest in "catharsis" to the extent that it then became a very fashionable topic of discussion among the fin-de-siècle Viennese *haute bourgeoisie*. To our knowledge, it was not before 1892–1893 that Freud and Breuer would first use the terms "catharsis" and "abreaction." However, it is virtually inconceivable that, when formulating their joint theory, Freud and Breuer were not under the influence of Bernays's conception; and the same basic argument can be extended to apply to the very inception of Breuer's method while treating Bertha Pappenheim during the years 1881–1882. . . . Insofar as the essential concept of a "catharsis" being systematically undertaken to effect a psychological "purgation" precedes Freud's actual use of the method, probably his patient

Anna von Lieben would have subscribed to the beauty of the idea, would more or less have known what was expected of her, and would not have wished to disappoint her expectant and eager young physician. . . .

It is of great significance that, in personal communication with A. A. Brill, Freud attributed the very introduction of his "free association" method—and therefore the birth of psychoanalysis proper—specifically to his treatment of a woman whom we now know to have been Anna von Lieben. Up till now we have been concerned with Freud's introduction of the cathartic method, using it to replace straightforward hypnotic suggestion. But now, from Brill, we learn how Freud subsequently went on to dispense altogether with hypnosis, replacing it with the "association" technique. This method required the patient to lie on a sofa while Freud sat nearby. And the fact that Anna spent most of her time reclining on a *chaise longue* could well have been, therefore, a crucial factor in precipitating this development.

Like Freud himself, Brill connects Freud's innovation of the "association" method with his recollection of Bernheim's success in retrieving suggestions implanted during hypnosis. And, while it is possible that following the visit to Nancy Freud ceased altogether attempting to hypnotize Anna von Lieben, it may nevertheless have been the case that, in seeking to dissolve her hysterical attacks twice a day for some three years, it was only gradually that he relinquished hypnotism and, having to unravel the most intricate threads of her memory, allowed the "free association" technique more or less spontaneously to assert itself. And, presumably, in adopting this latter method Freud employed it in combination with his so-called "pressure technique," whereby, on the model of what he had watched Bernheim do towards retrieving hypnotic suggestions, he would lay his hand on his patient's forehead, or take the patient's head between his hands, assuring the person that this would stimulate the particular memory requiring recollection.

Now, there is an important detail absent from the fragments of the case history of "Frau Cäcilie M." as found in the *Studies on Hysteria*—specifically the fact that Anna von Lieben was a severe morphine addict. If we are to give significance to a reference to the drug found in a poem written during her period of illness in England, then possibly her use of morphine had begun during her youth and had since continued more or less sporadically. We do not know when she became actually dependent on the drug—however, one would assume this must have occurred at some time following 1882, the year when she gave birth to the last of her children. At any rate, Meja Ruprecht, the nurse and housekeeper, was put in charge of all of Anna's medicines—the morphine included. And now every day Freud would visit the nursery to give Meja instructions and fetch morphine from her. The drug was certainly, then, the "artificial means," referred to by Freud in one of the fragments of case history, which he used to "hasten the end" of his patient's hysterical attacks.

In my opinion, the absence of any reference to the morphine addiction of "Frau Cäcilie M." represents a serious omission from the *Studies on Hysteria*. From one fragment of her case history, we learn that Breuer and Freud once had occasion to refuse their patient "a drug she had asked for"; and, elsewhere in the book, Breuer makes reference in passing to an "acute hysteria" that "arose in association with a withdrawal of morphine" in a case where there was "already a complicated hysteria present." And these references prompt us to wonder why the two authors failed to clarify matters further. When referring to the "artificial means," Freud could as easily have stated "an injection of morphine"; and in referring to an acute hysteria accompanying a morphine withdrawal, Breuer identified the patient involved as merely "another case," when in all probability it was "Frau Cäcilie M." to whom he was referring.

There are a number of possible reasons for such an omission. During the years 1885–1887, Freud's scientific credibility had suffered damage following his incautious advocacy of cocaine as a means of curing morphine addiction; there are also certain indications that Breuer may have been somewhat hasty in dispensing morphine to his patients, on which basis he might well have incurred criticisms from certain of his colleagues. It is conceivable, then, that drugs represented for the two authors a somewhat sensitive issue. Possibly, too, the authors were concerned that critics might question whether it was not in fact the central effects of the morphine, rather than the cathartic treatment per se, which had been responsible for restoring the patient's clarity of mind and emotional stability. And possibly they were concerned to preclude another objection as well: was it not hazardous to generalize with respect to the psychological mechanism of hysteria on the basis of a woman addicted to morphine and therefore especially liable to alternating states of intense nervous excitation and sopor? . . .

Moreover, is Anna's penchant for turning pains into images and images into pains not to be directly related to her poetic bent and the flights of fantasy that these involved? Note how her hallucinatory conversion of the "counterparts" Breuer and Freud into two men hanging on a tree, by means of the pun contained in the French word *pendant,* is, besides being very "poetic," a symbolization produced contemporarily with the actual treatment—inviting the question, then, as to whether similar interpretations, involving mimetic relationships between symptoms and ideas that were supposedly forged on the occasion of events long forgotten, were not in fact *current* flights of mutual fantasy between patient and doctor in the manner of a *folie à deux.* . . .

It is to be supposed that Freud's commitment to treating Anna von Lieben twice a day for some three years would have entailed some restrictions on his own life and movements—but the treatment must have been a very lucrative one for him to undertake. And indeed, it can be said with certainty that Frau Anna was the "most important patient [*Hauptklientin*]" referred to by Freud in writing to his friend Wilhelm Fliess on August 1, 1890, partly on whose account he felt unable to visit his friend in Berlin because just then—as was so often the case—she was undergoing "a kind of nervous crisis, . . . and perhaps in my absence [she] might get well"— betraying, of course, the fact that Freud had a powerful vested interest in continuing her treatment. . . .

. . . These were the days when Freud was popularly conceived of in Vienna not as a regular physician but as a *magnétiseur.* A glimpse of just such a Freud we get from the biography of the legendary violinist Fritz Kreisler, born in 1875, who is quoted as reminiscing:

> Freud made a deep impression on me, even though [being so young] I was unable to grasp fully what he was discussing with my father [Dr. Samuel Kreisler, physician to Freud's parents and a friend of Freud's.] [. . .] He was then by no means the famous man he later came to be, but a practicing *magnétiseur.* He tried, in fact, to help my ailing mother [Anna Kreisler, born Reches] by suggesting [to her] that she really wasn't crippled at all but would be able to move about after hypnotic treatments. I never saw her walk, however!

And it is in this somewhat Mesmeresque context—that of Freud making use of what he called the "mystical" medium of hypnosis—that we must understand the young Lieben children's reaction upon seeing him constantly arriving at their home, or visiting the nursery to talk with Meja, twice a day for some years. They feared and detested him—for them he was *"der Zauberer,"* the "magician," come to put their mother into a trance yet again and to accompany her through her fits of ravings, screamings, and long declamatory speeches.

And indeed, the atmosphere in Anna's sickroom must have had something of the séance, something of black magic, about it, not to mention the decadent—what with the injections of morphine and possibly cocaine, the caviar and the champagne, and the opulence of the setting; also the passionate and perhaps on occasion somewhat lurid content of Anna's reminiscences as she lay there abreacting them on a *chaise longue;* also certain physical aspects of the treatment. . . . An entry from many years later in the diary of Sándor Ferenczi would indicate that Freud must have described to his pupil how, during his early years in practice, he had even lain on the floor, sometimes for hours at a time, accompanying a patient through hysterical crises—most surely a reference to his treatment of Anna von Lieben before any other of his patients.

It remains to be said that, according to descendants of the family, there existed some extraordinary kind of rapport—some extraordinary intensity of mutual "infatuation"—between Anna von Lieben and Freud. And, after all, who would really doubt as much when, half a century later, Freud would remember this woman out of *all* his many hundreds of patients as having been nothing less than his "teacher"—his *Lehrmeisterin?* From the published fragments of case history, it is clear that in treating "Frau Cäcilie M." Freud gained many of his earliest insights not only into the essential process of "abreaction" but also—particularly, no doubt, through their innovation of the "free association" method, although its use in her case is not explicitly stated—into so many of those mechanisms of mind postulated by him as being manifestations of the "unconscious." From the *Studies on Hysteria* it is evident that the phenomena of conversion and symbolization, counterwill, conflict and defense, even perhaps wit and superstition—all of these are to be found occurring in the treatment of this one patient; all of them presented themselves daily before Freud's eyes and ears. . . . Also, no doubt, since Anna's own understanding of her illness was that it was largely consequent upon earlier disturbances of passion, Freud was brought into direct confrontation with the realm of sexuality, blatant rather than latent. We may also venture to suppose that Anna, a woman hitherto concerned with dreams and their interpretation, would surely have been among those who encouraged Freud in his recognition of their significance. . . .

. . . It is of note, though, that the members of Anna von Lieben's family circle shared neither the enthusiasm of Freud nor the confidence of Breuer. Indeed, convinced of Anna's physician's impotence, they would have preferred to have no more of it and see him thrown to the dogs. According to descendants, the members of the family became ever more skeptical and had no confidence at all in what Freud was doing. In fact, they quite detested the man and kept on asking each other why he seemed powerless to really help her—to effect some permanent improvement in her condition—rather than going on month after month with all this "talking," which seemed to be leading nowhere at all. . . .

At some point before autumn 1893, the treatment ceased; in a letter to Fliess of November 27, 1893, Freud mentions having "lost" Frau von Lieben, and he says his head has since been missing the "usual overwork." The family's descendants are inclined to suppose that Freud was bound to end his treatment, as otherwise the woman would have devoured him— reportedly she talked so much that he instructed her to write everything down, but eventually even that got out of hand. Whether there is truth in that version of the finale, it is difficult to say. But I am myself inclined to the view that, having seen that the treatment was bringing no permanent improvement, the family intervened and, probably with Breuer's agreement, brought it to a halt.

3

Was Freud a Liar?*

Frank Cioffi

This influential BBC radio talk of 1973 was not the earliest modern challenge to the Freud legend, nor even the earliest by the Anglo-American philosopher Frank Cioffi (see, for example, Chapter 10 below). It did, however, trigger an intense debate that continues to this day, and it remains unmatched for its stark clarity and shrewdness.

Cioffi's talk deals with the crucial transition between Freud's "seduction theory" of 1896–97 (pages 4, 7 above)—his claim that people who become hysterical in adulthood must have been sexually molested as children—and his founding of psychoanalysis proper, with its central focus on "repressed fantasy." To be a good classical Freudian is to hold, first, that all children entertain highly explicit sexual designs on at least one parent and murderous designs on the other, and, second, that the repression of those desires, even though it occurs in everyone, can bring on hysteria many years afterwards. And to be a good modern Freudian, one must at least regard this scheme as a great improvement over "seduction," since, however erroneous its details might be, it pointed psychoanalysis toward its true domain of hidden wishes.

Some Freudian partisans have maintained that psychoanalysis was born at the moment when Freud, in a letter of September 21, 1897, to Wilhelm Fliess, privately backed away from his seduction theory (CLFF, pages 264–266). A rereading of the letter, however, unearths

* From "Was Freud a Liar?," a talk broadcast on BBC Radio 3, November 1973, and printed in *The Listener*, February 7, 1974, pages 172–174.

no sign of the famous oedipal breakthrough. Nor, in fact, did Freud really part company with his simplistic theory at that juncture. Rather, he kept hoping for corroborative evidence to turn up, meanwhile remaining publicly mum about his doubts. And understandably so, for he had already, in 1896, published three papers in which he had gone overboard for "seduction," claiming 100 percent diagnostic success and very substantial therapeutic success with a cohort of patients who, in reality, had failed to make therapeutic progress and in most cases had discontinued their treatment. Had Freud expressed his misgivings at once, alerting his colleagues to the inadvisability of dredging their patients' minds for memories of early abuse, he would have exposed himself as having committed scientific fraud in those papers.

When Freud finally did put forward a different etiology, shifting his emphasis from real-life victimization to guilty fantasy, it so happened that the proposed new cause of hysteria was so remote from observable data as to be immune to biographical refutation. Cioffi was the first observer to realize that this antiempirical quality was not an incidental drawback to Freud's oedipal "discovery" but rather its most essential feature. Lacking any demonstrable clinical evidence to support a sexual explanation of neurosis, Freud had to choose between honorably abandoning his favorite concept, repression, and relocating its operation in a safely inaccessible realm. His founding of the doctrine that would later captivate the modern world thus coincided with his definitive farewell to observation-based science.

Frank Cioffi is Honorary Senior Research Fellow in Philosophy at the University of Kent at Canterbury. He has also taught at the University of Essex. One collection of his essays, *Wittgenstein on Explanation and Self-clarification in Freud and Frazer*, is being published by Cambridge University Press in 1998, and a second collection, *Freud and the Question of Pseudoscience* (1998), has just been published by Open Court.

The story of how Sigmund Freud discovered the Oedipus complex and thus the main source of neurotic tribulation is a celebrated one, which has fired imagination and warmed hearts from the shores of Asia to the Edgeware Road. Let me remind you of how it goes.

In the mid-nineties of the last century, Freud, a Viennese physician who specialized in the treatment of nervous disorders, had a succession of patients who recalled an occasion in infancy in which they had been sexually molested, usually by one of their own parents. This came as a great shock to Freud, as he had no inkling of the pathogenic potency of sexual life and was, indeed, reluctant to credit it. Nevertheless, he believed his patients' stories, and when he had heard about a dozen or so he duly reported that he had discovered the specific cause of psychoneurotic disorder: a passive sexual experience before puberty. In other words, a seduction.

Let me continue the story in the words of Freud's biographer, Ernest Jones. "[Freud] found that several of the seduction stories were simply untrue, there had been no seduction. But he held fast to the fact that the patient had told him these stories . . . with the result that he discovered the importance of infantile fantasy life in the genesis of the neuroses."

How did Freud do this? How did he turn the seduction mistake into a discovery about the role of parents in infantile fantasy? Well, the story continues, Freud brilliantly penetrated the patients' false memories of being seduced by a parent and found concealed behind them their own infantile wishes for sexual relations with the parent.

Here I want to persuade you that with the exception of the claim that Freud was practising medicine in Vienna during the nineties, this story has about as much historicity as that of George Washington and the cherry tree or King Alfred and the cakes. The truth of the matter can be briefly stated, though not briefly documented. Freud did not base his seduction theory on stories of infantile seduction related by his patients. In any case, his patients did not tell him any fictitious seduction stories. And the seduction stories of whose truth they were eventually persuaded did not normally involve parents and so are unlikely to have been transformations of fantasies concerning parents. Further, Freud could not, for a variety of reasons, have been surprised by the discovery that his patients' illnesses had sexual causes. Rather it is likely that it was Freud's own preconceptions concerning the influence of sexual life that incited his patients to accept a sexual cause for their difficulties.

I think what really happened was this. At first Freud was exhilarated by the way in which his patients produced confirmation for his seduction theory. Then he discovered that some of the seductions had never happened. He had been warned by the reviewers of his first book on hysteria of the serious risk that his method produced false convictions in his patients as to the correctness of his explanations. And his critics, it seemed, were right. What a humiliation! Freud now put all his enormous resourcefulness into mitigating if not entirely evading it. When he finished he had persuaded himself that, in his own words, "not the analysis but the patient must . . . bear the responsibility for this unexpected disappointment." How did he manage it?

Freud had to account for the consistency with which he had arrived at the seduction scenes. They had to be fantasies, for the alternative was that they had been suggested by Freud, or worse, arbitrarily imputed by him. Freud's predicament can be presented in the form of a dilemma. Either the seductions were authentic or Freud's method of reconstructing the infantile past of his patients was invalid. But many of the seductions had proved fictitious, so it must have been Freud's method that was invalid.

Freud solved this dilemma by falsifying one of its horns. It then became "Either the seductions are authentic or my patients are self-deceived and their confessions false. But the seductions are fictitious; therefore my patients' confessions are false." He was now almost ready to face the world. But there was still a difficulty. Might not the alleged confessions of his patients be attributed to their suggestibility? Might the confessions not be the result of his own preconceived views as to the role of sexuality in nervous disorders? Freud resolved this difficulty by obliterating from his consciousness the fact that he had any preconceived views as to the influence of sexuality.

It is an established part of psychoanalytic folklore that Freud came slowly and reluctantly to an acknowledgement of the role of sexuality in the production of neurotic illness. And, like most psychoanalytic folklore, it derives directly from Freud's repeated assertions of it. But it is completely untrue. Freud was searching for the sources of neurotic disorders in the sexual life of his patients before he began practicing psychoanalysis even in its most primitive and rudimentary forms. And by the mid-nineties, when he put forward the seduction theory, he was already subjecting his patients to an aggressive cross-examination as to their sexual habits. . . .

So far I have merely shown that there is nothing extravagant in putting down Freud's grossly distorted account of the seduction episode to a failure of memory. But I have not yet shown that Freud's account was grossly distorted.

My first thesis is this: that the seduction stories were related by Freud to his patients, and not to Freud by his patients. First let me show that it is untrue to hold, as Freud later insisted, that his patients told him imaginary seduction stories. In the course of attempting to allay suspicions that his patients may have wilfully deceived him, Freud said of their attitude towards the seductions that "whilst calling these infantile experiences into consciousness . . . they still try to withhold belief by emphasizing the fact that they had no feeling of recollecting these scenes." So before Freud discovered that the seductions were imaginary, he was describing them as experiences which his patients had no feeling of recollecting. After he had discovered that the seductions had not occurred, he described them as "the deceptive memories of hysterics concerning their childhood." How can these two accounts be reconciled?

In the next sentence Freud went on to urge against the view that the seduction stories were fabrications the fact that "patients assure me . . . emphatically of their unbelief." This implies that not only were his patients not recollecting the seductions but that they were not even convinced that the seductions happened. And how is this to be reconciled with the active role Freud later assigned to his patients in statements like "hysterics trace back their symptoms to fictitious traumas," or patients "ascribe their symptoms to passive sexual experiences in early childhood." Was it not Freud himself who did the tracing and the ascribing? . . .

This brings us to another reason for holding that Freud unconsciously fabricated the patients' confessions. In his retrospective accounts, Freud tells us that the patients' delusions of seduction usually pertained to parents. But in the original seduction papers themselves the cast list includes nursemaids, governesses, domestic servants, teachers, tutors, older children and even brothers, but no parents. The claim that it is the parents who are the seducers is not only *not* made in the original seduction papers, it is inconsistent with them. Freud then says that in seven of the cases it was brothers who were the seducers, and since brothers are as identifiable as parents, the motive for this discrepancy can hardly be discretion.

By the way, even if the seduction beliefs of Freud's patients had uniformly pertained to the cross-sex parents, it is not obvious why this is a natural transformation of infantile fantasies about seducing that parent. Freud is very unforthcoming as to why this should be so. He merely asserts that the seduction memories are less wounding to the patient than the acknowledgement of his own incestuous infantile inclinations. But is the thought that you were sexually used by your mother really less disagreeable than the thought that you once desired her? I have not found anyone who felt so, but I am struck by the way in which people who gabble happily about the Oedipus complex are mildly affronted if you attempt to introduce a degree of particularity into the discussion. And since the imputed fantasies are unconscious in any case, why isn't that sufficient protection against self-reproach? Why the additional precaution of inverting them and giving the parents the active role actually taken by the child? You mustn't even ask.

Still, so far I have merely shown that Freud's patients *did not* relate stories of seduction and not that Freud *did*. My reasons for maintaining this are largely circumstantial. First there is the matter of Freud's tremendous confidence in his diagnostic powers, combined with the most unpsychological reluctance to credit the power of suggestibility. This is what he said in his book on hysteria, published in 1895, a year before the three seduction theory papers: "We need not be afraid of telling the patient what we think his next . . . thought is going to be. It will do no harm." Within a year of this remark he had stumbled into the seduction blunder.

One bit of evidence that it was Freud's practice to communicate his seduction suspicions to his patients comes from the analysis of one of his own dreams. In the dream Freud reproaches a patient for not accepting his explanations as to why she was ill and blames the persistence of her illness on this refusal. In his associations to this item, Freud says that the reproach in the dream was probably just a repetition of a reproach he had made to his patient in waking life. He adds: "It was my view at this time . . . that my task was fulfilled when I had informed the patient of the hidden meaning of his symptoms." But this was the dream of Irma's injection, and since we know the exact date of that dream, we can state that Irma was one of Freud's original batch of presumably seduced patients. Is it rash to infer that the "hidden meaning of the symptoms" about which Freud made it a practice to inform his patients at that time was a sexual seduction in infancy?

You may think this a bit thin. So let me see if I can do better. During the period when Freud thought he was receiving daily confirmation of his seduction hypothesis, a patient confessed to him that when a young girl she had been the victim of a sexual assault by her father. "Naturally," Freud wrote to the correspondent to whom he related the incident, "she did not find it incredible when I told her that similar and worse things must have happened to her in infancy." This was from a letter to his friend Fliess—and you can see why Freud wanted this correspondence destroyed!

One of the questions that the seduction story presents us with is this: How did Freud come by the discovery that the seduction theory was false? Once again Freud has a ready answer, and once again it is completely untrue. When Freud first publicly admitted the seduction error, nine years later, he explained it as follows: "I did not then know that persons who remain normal may have had the same experiences in their childhood. . . ." But he did know. In the original paper he wrote, "We have heard and acknowledged that there are many people who have a very clear recollection of infantile sexual experiences and yet do not suffer from hysteria." Why the discrepancy?

In this account Freud is explaining his discovery of the seduction error in terms of his realization that, as he put it, "persons who remain normal may have had the same experiences in childhood." This makes it sound as if the seduction error consisted only in the rashness of Freud's extrapolating to hysterics in general and not in attributing false histories of seductions to his own patients. The measure of Freud's inability to come to terms with the seduction error is to be found in the earlier portion of the sentence I quoted, which says, astonishingly, of the seductions, "I cannot admit that I exaggerated their frequency or their importance. . . ." It had taken Freud nine years to bring himself to publicly admit the seduction error, and when it came to the point he funked it. Why? From the same motive which led him to make the false assertion that his confidence in the reality of the seductions was based on his patients' confidence in them. This flatly contradicts what he said at the time, which was, "We adhere to the principle of not adopting the patients' belief without a thorough critical examination."

How then did Freud convince himself of the reality of the seductions? In his own words, "by letting the symptoms tell the tale." Far from basing his conviction on the patients' testimony, Freud argued that just as a physician can explain how a physical injury has been caused without any information from the injured person, so in hysteria the analyst can penetrate from the symptoms to their causes without the testimony of the patient.

Why should Freud have gone to such lengths to conceal from himself the real basis of his confidence in the reality of the infantile seductions? For a perfectly understandable reason. Freud could not bring himself to recognise the reasoning by which he had persuaded himself of the authenticity of the seductions because it was the same sort of reasoning which for the rest of his career he was to employ in his reconstruction of infantile fantasy life and of the content of the unconscious in general. This emerges clearly in one of the original seduction papers, in which Freud urges against scepticism concerning the seductions the fact that "patients appeared to live through it with all the appropriate emotions."

Let me sum up. Freud did not fall into the seduction error through believing his patients' stories; he did not fall into it through ignorance of the fact that persons sexually molested in infancy may, nevertheless, not succumb to neurosis; he did not fall into it through underestimating the frequency of seduction in the general population. Freud fell into the seduction error through the use of a procedure which to this day remains the basis of the psychoanalytic reconstruction of infantile life: the attribution to patients of certain infantile experiences because they appear to the analyst to be living "through them with all the appropriate emotions."

The lesson Freud ought to have learned from the discovery that the infantile seductions which he believed to be the specific cause of the psychoneurosis were often fictitious was not that infantile fantasy life is as important in the genesis of neurotic illness as actual infantile events, but that his method of eliciting from patients their infantile histories and, more important still, of interpreting these elicitations was an unreliable one which leads to mistaken reconstructions that deceive not only the physician but the patient himself. But instead of modifying his procedure so as to lessen the risk of mistaken inferences, Freud merely made the inferences themselves so indeterminate that the validity of his methods could never again be placed in jeopardy. Freud, like the emperor in the story, dealt with bad news by having the bearer executed.

Before you mechanically reject this blasphemous suggestion, ask yourself the following question: What could overthrow Freud's later theories of the infantile sources of neurotic illness, as the fictitious character of the seductions overthrew the seduction theory? The history of psychoanalytic disputes over the nature of infantile mental life is largely a history of mutual recrimination. What else could an orthodox Freudian say to Kleinian revisionists but that their nonsense didn't suit his nonsense?

The history of psychoanalysis is full of ironies. It seems that Freud, the apostle of self-knowledge, the relentless seeker after truth, was no better at detecting his own essays in self-deception than the rest of us. There is an aphorism of Nietzsche's which Freud quoted on several occasions to illustrate the affinity between Nietzsche's thought and his own: "I did this, says my Memory. I cannot have done this, says my Pride, and remains inexorable. In the end Memory yields." On several occasions in after years, Freud attempted to reconstruct the considerations which had led him to assert, first, that a sexual seduction and then that incestuous fantasy lay at the root of every psychoneurosis. I have tried to show that whenever he made this attempt, Freud's pride would not yield, and it was memory that lost.

Self-Seduced*

Mikkel Borch-Jacobsen

In Chapter 3 we presented one of the earliest critiques of Freud's historic shift from a "seduction" to a "fantasy" etiology of hysteria. The soundness of that critique has been confirmed by a number of more detailed studies (see, for example, Macmillan, 1977; Schimek, 1987; Schatzman, 1992; Israëls and Schatzman, 1993; Esterson, 1993; Powell and Boer, 1994, 1995), most of which have benefited from corroborating evidence in the unbowdlerized edition of Freud's letters to Wilhelm Fliess in 1985 (CLFF). Ironically, however, the editor of those letters, Jeffrey Moussaieff Masson, has proved to be a dissenter from the emerging consensus. In a popular book of 1984, Masson proposed that Freud's loss of faith in "seduction" was really a loss of nerve: Freud knew that his hysterical patients had been sexually abused, but he couldn't face the disapprobation of his colleagues, so he retreated to safer ideas about infantile sexuality and the Oedipus complex. Mikkel Borch-Jacobsen begins our current chapter by contemplating this thesis.

Scarcely any well-informed Freud scholars, whether pro- or antipsychoanalytic, support Masson's view (see, however, Balmary, 1982; Krüll, 1986). It is easy to see why not. Masson's argument collapses as soon as one learns, from Freud's own papers of 1896, that the tales of molestation were not volunteered by his patients but pieced together by Freud himself from "as-if" visualizations that he required the

* From "Neurotica: Freud and the Seduction Theory," *October*, 16 (Spring 1996): 15–43.

patients to produce. (For a definitive assessment of Masson's thesis, see Esterson, 1998.) Sadly, however, the Masson argument has proved perniciously influential; it forms one of the foundation stones of our current recovered memory movement, which is essentially a reversion to the "seduction theory" in all its accusatory recklessness (see pages x–xi above).

Because Freud offered Fliess a number of reasons for his own cresting doubts about the molestation etiology, we are left to surmise which factors weighed most heavily in his private recantation. The historians I have cited above differ among themselves on this point. In the essay below, Borch-Jacobsen provocatively advances the debate by suggesting that Freud was stymied by a surfeit, not an absence, of clinical support for his molestation etiology. That is, the very ease with which he was extracting visualizations (not memories!) of early sexual abuse made him realize that he himself was the principal author of those scenes.

Does it really matter, the reader may ask, why Freud abandoned a theory that nearly all knowledgeable observers consider to have been a grievous mistake? It matters a good deal, because classical psychoanalytic theory soon took the place of "seduction" as Freud's claim to scientific and medical distinction. At issue is whether Freud learned something new and powerful from his patients in 1897 (their shared experience of infantile sexuality) or merely covered the collapse of the seduction theory by turning his etiology inside out. Like Cioffi, Borch-Jacobsen favors the latter view, and he here makes the strongest case yet advanced for that interpretation. As he shows, Freud understood but could not own up to the role of therapeutic suggestion in prompting the trance visions that underwrote "seduction." As a result of his want of candor, he allowed exactly the same flaw—a peremptory dismissal of suggestion as a source of the patient's compliantly submitted "evidence"—to pervade psychoanalysis proper.

Jeffrey Masson attributes the abandonment of the seduction theory to two convergent facts: (1) Freud's desire to minimize Fliess's role in the bleeding of his patient Emma Eckstein, by attributing it to "wishes" and "fantasies" rather than to his friend's disastrous surgical intervention, and (2) Freud's no less pressing desire to reconcile himself with his male colleagues, who were scandalized by his allegations of incest and pedophilia.

The first reason invoked by Masson, which elaborates the classic explanation by the "transference" on Fliess, is not at all decisive, for Freud's remarks on Emma's "fantasies" could be easily reconciled with Freud's seduction theory. The notion of fantasy is in fact a first attempt at *rationalizing* the seduction theory, a way for Freud to account for the manifestly fantasist nature of certain "scenes," while allowing him to continue believing in the reality of the initial "scene." At the time he was proposing his remarks on Emma's fantasies, Freud was convinced that the fantasies were "protective fictions," destined to hide or "sublimate" the memory of the *real* trauma. So it is hard to see why Freud would have felt compelled to sacrifice his seduction theory on the altar of his friendship for Fliess, since in his mind the theory already sufficiently exonerated the latter.

As to Masson's second reason, which interests us more at this point, it would be plausible only if Freud's colleagues were actually repulsed by the idea of real incest and sexual perversion. But this is far from being the case: on this point. Masson is the victim (a quite willing one, to be sure) of the hardy "legend of the hero" forged by Freud and his biographers in regard to that episode. Not only did Freud not "suffer . . . intellectual isolation" during that period, as Masson claims, but he was not the first or the only one interested in sexuality, including perverse sexuality. As Frank Sulloway has expertly shown, Freud had been preceded along that path by the sexologists of the 1880s, notably Albert von Schrenck-Notzing, Richard von Krafft-Ebing, Leopold Löwenfeld, and Albert Moll. They had no a priori reason to be scandalized by the sexual theory of hysteria proposed by their young colleague. Krafft-Ebing, in particular, had himself mentioned numerous cases of child sexual abuse, including incest, in his *Psychopathia Sexualis* (1886), and his famous remark about Freud's lecture on "The Aetiology of Hysteria"—"It sounds like a scientific fairy tale"—could not possibly have the significance of offended indignation that Masson claims for it. In reality, the objections of Freud's colleagues to his new theory of hysteria had nothing to do with the content of the "scenes of seduction" alleged by Freud, but rather with the way that he obtained them from his patients.

Indeed, we tend to forget that those sexologists, like Freud himself, were theoreticians and practitioners of hypnosis. As a result, they were very sensitive to the role of suggestion in the treatment of hysteria, since they had all observed the collapse of Charcot's theory of *"grande hysterie"* under the criticism of Bernheim and the Nancy school. In all likelihood, this is what Krafft-Ebing meant when he spoke of a "scientific fairy tale": he knew the tendency of hysterics to make up stories in the sexual domain, but most especially, like everybody at the time, he tied that *pseudologia phantastica* to hysterical "suggestibility." In other words, the seduction theory was a "fairy tale," a hysterical lie, but above all, it was a "scientific" fairy tale, a fairy tale *suggested* by Dr. Freud. . . .

What Freud says in 1898 concerning his method for obtaining admissions of masturbation from his neurasthenics applies equally to the way he proceeded with his hysterical patients:

> Having diagnosed a case of neurasthenic neurosis . . . we may then boldly demand confirmation of our suspicions from the patient. *We must not be led astray by initial denials.* If we keep firmly to what we have inferred, we shall in the end conquer every resistance by emphasizing the unshakeable nature of our convictions [emphasis added].

This martial therapeutic voluntarism, which now appears again in the writings of current specialists in "trauma work," in no way prevented Freud from concluding two sentences further along: "Moreover, the idea that one might, by one's insistence, cause a patient who is psychically normal to accuse himself falsely of sexual misdemeanors—such an idea may safely be disregarded as an imaginary danger." We can rest assured.

This is no small matter. For, as Freud himself later rhetorically objected in reference to the transference, if the suggestion factor intervenes in analysis, "there is a risk that the influencing of our patients may make the objective certainty (*die Objectivität*) of our findings doubtful." Freud always maintained that suggestion, despite appearances, did not enter into analytical constructions and interpretations, and he repeats it again in 1925 concerning his seduction theory: "I do not believe even now that I forced the seduction-fantasies on my patients, that I 'suggested' them." This denial of the role of suggestion is constant in Freud, and it goes back to one of his most precocious and decisive theoretical choices. Indeed, behind all of it lies the quarrel between the Nancy and Salpêtrière schools concerning the suggested or nonsuggested nature of Charcot's *"grande hystérie,"* in which Freud took the position of the latter. Even though he used and advocated Bernheim's suggestive method quite early—first in a direct form and later, under the name of the "Breuer method," to act on the traumatic memory as Janet and Delboeuf had done before him—Freud never sided with Bernheim against Charcot on the problem of the "objectivity" of the hypnotic and hysterical manifestations observed at the Salpêtrière. . . .

This point is, indeed, extremely important, for it is this Charcotian—and, let me add, extremely naive—presupposition that allowed Freud to remain blind for so long to his own intervention in the phenomena that he observed in his patients. As long as hypnosis was identified with the hysterical "state," itself understood as a modality of self-hypnosis, there was no reason to worry about the suggestive influence that Bernheim warned against, since the hypnotic treatment was supposed to do nothing more than bring an internal, autonomous psychical determinism to the surface. Such was Freud's confidence in that psychical determinism that he thought it capable of "resisting" every external influence, even the therapist's most persistent pressure. As he continued to say in 1910, at a meeting of the Vienna Psychoanalytic Society, "if one wants to come up with anything, one cannot avoid asking some leading questions. Besides, the patient can be influenced only in a direction *that suggests itself to him*" [emphasis added].

Freud is often credited with liberating his patients from the "tyranny" of hypnotic suggestion and giving them back their status as speaking subjects. In reality, Freud's refusal to recognize the role of suggestion corresponds theoretically to a very profound *objectification* of the therapeutic relationship, as if his patients' speech were merely the reproduction of a "psychical mechanism" observable from the exterior. Even the fact, repeated over and over by Bernheim, Forel, and Delboeuf, that the hypnotized subject remains *aware* of the hypnotist's suggestions and *responds*, in every sense of the word, to them does not seem to have made Freud reflect on his own role in the relation—witness this stupefying letter of May 28, 1888, to Fliess: "I have at this moment a lady in hypnosis lying in front of me and therefore can go on writing in peace." Two paragraphs later: "The time for the hypnosis is up. I greet you cordially. In all haste, your Dr. Freud." With this sort of methodological presupposition, it is a wonder that the disaster of the seduction theory did not blow up long before it did! At any rate, for fellow travelers of the Nancy school like

Krafft-Ebing, Moll, and Löwenfeld, it must have been patently obvious that Freud was simply repeating the errors of his "Master," Charcot.

Objection: "But you are forgetting that at the time he was elaborating his seduction theory, Freud had already given up using hypnosis. How, then, can you claim that he was suggesting the scenes reported by his patients?"

True, the dates seem to contradict my thesis. Beginning in the autumn of 1892, Freud progressively gave up hypnosis in favor of "concentration" in the waking state and the "pressure technique" (*Druckprozedur*), a method consisting in pressing with the hand on the patient's forehead and asking him or her to evoke some idea or image. This abandonment of hypnosis corresponds, theoretically, to the accentuation of the role of repression in hysteria, to the detriment of the "hypnoid" mechanism of dissociation of consciousness. The final rupture with hypnosis seems to have been made in the early part of 1895, precisely at the moment Freud began to formulate his theory of the "aetiology of hysteria." But simply because he was no longer practicing direct hypnosis and suggestion, does this mean that Freud did not "suggest" in the larger sense of the word?

We must get rid of two false ideas here:

(a) Contrary to what Freud seems to imply most often by the term, hypnosis cannot be reduced to somnambulism followed by amnesia. There are, as Bernheim already asserted, many degrees of hypnosis, and it is impossible to quantify them rigorously. It is therefore difficult to say where hypnosis begins and where it ends, as Freud himself recognizes at several points in his *Studies on Hysteria*: "I told the patients to lie down and deliberately close their eyes in order to 'concentrate'—all of which had at least some resemblance to hypnosis." He also compares his "pressure-technique" to a "momentarily intensified hypnosis" and to the well-known hypnotic technique of crystal gazing. In *The Interpretation of Dreams*, Freud even goes so far as to say that his method of free association produces "a psychical state which . . . bears some analogy to the state of falling asleep—and no doubt also to hypnosis." Much later, the Wolf-Man would still recall how Freud jokingly compared psychoanalytic transference to hypnosis: "When I do what transference shows me, it is really like being hypnotized by someone. That's the influence. I can remember Freud saying, 'Hypnosis, what do you mean, hypnosis, everything we do is hypnosis too.' Then why did he discontinue hypnosis?" Excellent question: Where are we to place the famous Freudian "epistemic rupture" in such a continuum? If it is true, as Freud said in 1917, that "psychoanalysis proper began when I dispensed with the help of hypnosis," we might well wonder if such a pure psychoanalysis *ever* came into existence!

(b) Second false idea: the degree of suggestibility has to do with the depth of the hypnotic trance. On the contrary, it often happens that suggestibility is more pronounced in the so-called waking state than in a state of deep hypnosis. As Janet observed, "Suggestibility can be very complete outside of artificial somnambulism: it can be totally lacking in a completely somnambulistic state." This point had been forcefully made by Bernheim, who concluded quite logically in 1891 that "suggestive psychotherapy" would be just as effective, if not more effective, *without hypnosis proper.* Freud, who translated Bernheim's second book in 1892, was obviously aware of this, and we might well consider that by turning (like others), in that very year, toward a less directly hypnotic technique, Freud was only following Bernheim's example. Be that as it may, it is clear enough that the absence of deep hypnosis cannot be equated with the absence of suggestibility on the part of the patient (and thus of suggestion on the part of the therapist). As Freud himself admitted quite bluntly to Fliess in 1901, "My clients are sick people, hence especially irrational *and suggestible*" [emphasis added].

In short, just because at some point Freud stopped inducing somnambulic trances and using direct suggestion, it does not mean that the new "psychoanalytic" treatment was ipso facto nonhypnotic and nonsuggestive. In this regard, it is clear that the *Druckprozedur*, which Freud inherited from Bernheim (and perhaps more directly from Berger and Heidenhain), was a technique of the hypnotic type. Under Freud's insistent "pressure," his patients seem to have gone through an altered state of consciousness, characterized by visual "scenes" of a hallucinatory nature, a great emotional expressivity, and an increase in ideomotor and ideosensorial activity. As Freud says in "The Aetiology of Hysteria," "While they are recalling these infantile experiences to consciousness, [the patients] suffer under the most violent sensations."

It is no accident, then, that during this whole period, Freud speaks of *"reproductions"* of the infantile sexual scene, and not of "memories" or "reminiscences." In accordance with the "trance logic" of hypnosis, these scenes were actually experienced, *acted* in the present, rather than being truly recalled as memories (they were *Wiederholungen,* not *Erinnerungen,* to use Freud's later terminology). As Jean Schimek has judiciously noted, "The reproduction of the seduction scenes may have often been a kind of minor hysterical attack, with both verbal and nonverbal expression," which immediately brings them close to the "relivings" in *statu nascendi* previously obtained through the cathartic method. Read, for instance, the letter of January 24, 1897, to Fliess: "I was able to trace back, with certainty, a hysteria . . . to a seduction, which occurred for the first time at 11 months and [I could] hear again the words that were exchanged between two adults at that time! It is as though it comes from a phonograph." Clearly the whole "scene" was being played (mimed) here for the benefit of the fascinated therapist (you could call it the "scene of his Master's voice"). Or read the letter of December 22, 1897, apropos of a patient who identified with her mother, anally penetrated by the father during a scene allegedly observed by the child at age three: "The mother *now* stands in the room and shouts: 'Rotten criminal, what do you want from me? I will have no part of that. Just whom do you think you have in front of you?' Then she *stares* at a certain point in the room, her face contorted by rage, *covers* her genitals with one hand and *pushes* something away with the other," etc. [emphasis added]. . . .

In order to prevent a possible misunderstanding, I hasten to add that this hypnotic suggestibility is not the product of some mysterious power of the hypnotist, as Freud insisted too often in speaking of the "tyranny" of suggestion. Good hypnotists have always known that initially suggestibility is nothing but the sheer acceptance of the hypnotic contract: the subject must accept the hypnotic game, failing which the game cannot begin. . . . In this sense, suggestibility is not pure passivity or pure automatism (any more than hypnosis, of which suggestibility is one of the fundamental characteristics). On the contrary, it goes quite well with the inventiveness of the patients who play the hypnotic game with their therapists, sometimes even imposing new rules for it, as Bertha Pappenheim did with Breuer or Fanny Moser and Anna von Lieben with Freud. Hypnosis is always a matter of interaction—a "joint endeavor," says Milton Erickson. Thus, the history of psychoanalysis, insofar as it begins (and ends) with hypnosis, cannot be written solely from the point of view of Freud's theories, as if Freud simply "discovered" phenomena in his patients that had formerly been undetected. In reality, his patients did their best to confirm his theories, beyond his wildest expectations. Psychoanalysis is the product of this feedback, the magical fulfillment of its own prophecy. . . .

Why did Freud abandon his seduction theory? Innumerable explanations have been offered for that mysterious episode, but at least one thing is sure: Freud did not change his mind for lack of clinical "evidence." Quite the contrary, he had plenty of it, and it is simply not true, as two critics have proposed, that Freud was "not hearing enough seduction stories from his patients, and that the stories he heard did not fit the pattern the theory required." The reasons he advances in his letter of September 21, 1897, are merely reasons, themselves speculative, for *doubting* the authenticity of the alleged "confirmations" that he had obtained. I list them here in no particular order: an absence of infantile "scenes" in the psychoses, where they should have appeared spontaneously because of the lack of defense; a total absence of conclusive therapeutic results (whereas Freud had publicly claimed to have "completed" the analyses of eighteen cases!); the impossibility of distinguishing between the "truth and fiction that has been connected with affect"; and finally, the statistical improbability of the "paternal aetiology." But all of these reasons had been available to Freud before. So, if he decided to take them seriously at this point, it is likely that this was because the "influencing machine" that he had put in motion was working *all too* well, so well that he could no longer believe in the stories he had extorted from his patients. As he wrote in 1914: "This aetiology broke down under the weight of its own improbability."

Now, all this was bound to make Freud wonder about the way he had obtained these pseudomemories of sexual abuse. If the scenes were not real, where did they come from? Freud would say much later that they came from the oedipal fantasies of his female patients (note the feminine, as if he did not have male patients too). But in 1897, Freud had not yet come up with this handy excuse, so the only thing it could have been was this: the scenes *came from him*—which is precisely what his colleagues had believed and objected all along. That this is what Freud himself thought is indicated by a passage from the letter where, after having admitted the failure of his cures, he evokes "the possibility of explaining to myself the partial successes in other ways, *in the usual fashion*" [emphasis added]. In the context of the time this is a clear allusion to the elimination of the symptoms by suggestion and/or autosuggestion. Freud is here admitting that his famous "psychoanalytic" treatment is finally nothing but "suggestive psychotherapy" à la Bernheim. Twenty years later, in *An Autobiographical Study*, Freud would be even more explicit: "*Under the influence of the technical procedure which I used at the time,* the majority of my patients reproduced from their childhood scenes in which they were sexually seduced by a grown-up person" [emphasis added]. So after all, it was not the patients' oedipal unconscious that had forged these aberrant stories, but the *Druckprozedur* of Dr. Freud. . . .

"I shall not tell it in Dan, nor speak of it in Askelon, in the land of the Philistines": Freud never admitted his real reason for abandoning the seduction theory, for that would have been an admission, not only of the defeat, but of the dangers of his "psychoanalytic" method. On the contrary, he continued to support his theory publicly and even, for a certain time, cynically to apply it in his practice, all the while searching for a way to get himself out of the *cul-de-sac* he had gotten himself into. The rest is well known: the birth of "psychoanalysis proper." In the weeks that follow, Freud suddenly discovers in his "self-analysis" that he had been in love with his mother and jealous of his father, and then concludes, based on an analysis of Sophocles' *Oedipus Rex*, that this is a "universal event in childhood. . . . Everyone was once a budding Oedipus in fantasy." Was this, as is normally said, the dazzling "discovery" of the Oedipus complex? Not at all: the universality of the Oedipus complex is affirmed in a perfectly arbitrary fashion, with no supporting clinical material whatsoever (except for the particularly suspect "self-analysis"), in order to find an ad hoc explanation for his patients' constant stories of paternal seduction. The same goes for the Fliessian idea of infantile sexuality, to which Freud progressively gravitates in the months that follow: if the Freudian child is "polymorphously perverse," it is because Freud had to find an explanation for his patients' torrid stories of sodomy and fellatio, not at all because he had any empirical evidence of it.

In sum: the Oedipus complex, infantile sexuality, the wish-fantasies, all of Freud's self-proclaimed "discoveries" are arbitrary constructions designed to explain away his patients' stories of incest and perversion while simultaneously excusing the method that had provoked them. Freud never abandoned his seduction theory, nor hypnosis, nor suggestion. He simply denied them, attributing them to his patients' stories, to *their* unconscious wishes, and attributing the hypnotic-suggestive elements of the analytic cure to *their* "transference love." Masson, feminists, and child-abuse activists tell us that Freud covered up the despicable actions of pedophile fathers. Not so. He covered up the hypnosis that allowed him to obtain the stories, while leaving the astonished world with an oedipal unconscious. The Oedipus complex is a hypnotic myth, superimposed on the no less hypnotic myth of "infantile seduction," and it serves no purpose whatsoever to oppose the one myth to the other, for they are intrinsically bound together. True, we are all obsessed with incest, but do we know that it is because we are living in a world fashioned by the hypnotic pact between Dr. Freud and his patients? . . .

5

The Rhythm Method*

Frank J. Sulloway

A specter haunts the reputation of Sigmund Freud, and its name is Wilhelm Fliess. Freud airbrushed Fliess—his intimate friend from 1887 until the turn of the century—out of his autobiography (SE, 20: 7–74), destroyed Fliess's letters to him, and tried unsuccessfully to get his own letters to Fliess burned as well. When those letters were finally issued by Anna Freud and two other analysts (Freud, 1950), it was in an abridged "damage control" edition whose omitted passages, later restored by a psychoanalytic rebel (Masson, 1985), proved to be as revealing as its content. The complete letters show, first, an extreme credulity on Freud's part toward the Berlin neurologist's bizarre notions about such topics as numerology, male sexual periodicity, and the intimate relation between nasal and genital disorders; second, collusion with Fliess in submitting a patient of Freud's, Emma Eckstein, to a pointless and disfiguring operation whose aftermath, once known, shattered the myth of Freud's diagnostic astuteness and objectivity; and third, a significant "Fliessian" component to ideas that Freud would eventually appropriate as his own discoveries from "clinical experience."

The Eckstein case (glancingly mentioned in Chapter 4 above) could not be kept permanently under the rug, since Freud's personal physician, Max Schur, had sketched the outlines of the drama in an article of

* From *Freud, Biologist of the Mind: Beyond the Psychoanalytic Legend* (1979; Cambridge: Harvard University Press, 1992).

1966 and a subsequent posthumous book (Schur, 1972). Freud had decided that his "hysteric" Emma must be suffering from Fliess's imagined syndrome, the "nasal reflex neurosis," and in February 1895 he allowed Fliess to address her sexual dysfunction by removing the middle left concha of her nose. After the superfluous operation, Fliess immediately returned from Vienna to Berlin, leaving Eckstein on the verge of bleeding to death from a half meter of iodoform gauze that he had carelessly left within her nasal cavity. Freud's subsequent letters show him gradually shifting the blame for her hemorrhaging from Fliess to Emma herself and, in the process, adjusting his theoretical orientation from real-world trauma to fantasy. Eckstein was bleeding not because of her ruptured veins but as an unconscious love call to Freud himself! (For details of the case, see Wilcocks, 1994, pages 91–97.)

The Freud legend, we have seen, reluctantly includes Fliess, but only as a symptomatic figure in the "neurotic" phase of the hero's development that would end triumphantly with his self-analysis and his discovery of the Oedipus complex. But the supposed antithesis between Fliess's influence and Freud's self-exploration is utterly false. Freud kept Fliess continually informed about his cocaine-influenced dreams and hallucinations, and his visions of himself as a toddler intent upon incest coincided with, and obviously owed much to, speculations that he and Fliess had been sharing for at least two years about the erotic strivings of the very young. It was the spontaneous penile erections of Fliess's tiny son Robert (born in 1895), zealously recorded by the hovering, peeping Fliess and misconstrued by both thinkers as evidence of the newborn's lecherous stirrings toward his mother, that inspired Freud to "remember" his copulatory designs on his own mother at the scarcely less preposterous age of two.

The book that finally enabled scholars to begin confronting the Freud-Fliess relationship in its true lineaments was Frank J. Sulloway's *Freud, Biologist of the Mind*, which is now justly considered one of the classics of Freud studies. In 1979, Sulloway still lacked access to the complete correspondence between the two would-be scientific revolutionaries, and as a consequence, his assessment of both Freud and Fliess was more indulgent than it has subsequently become (see Sulloway, 1991, and the revised preface to Sulloway, 1992). The reader of the following excerpts should be prepared, then, to find Fliess's ideas repeatedly characterized as "pioneering." But Sulloway never meant to imply that those ideas were correct. Rather, his point was that whether or not we subscribe to the psychoanalytic outlook, we need to understand that it emerged in deductive collaboration with Fliess.

Sulloway's book demonstrates that Freud, instead of liberating himself from Fliess when he turned his interest from repressed memories of sexual abuse to repressed sexual fantasies, removed the last barrier to full acquiescence in the Fliessian worldview. Fliess had already been pushing Freud to adopt a theory of innate infantile sexuality, a concept that comported much better with a "fantasy" etiology of hysteria than with a "seduction" etiology. Now the blame for adult symptoms could be placed largely on the tumultuous but remote childhood psyche (and masturbatory practice) of the sufferer herself; vulgar contention over the exposing of "perpetrators" could subside; huge evolutionary vistas could form the backdrop for psychodynamic theory; and analytic therapy could evolve toward becoming an instrument of prolonged self-inquiry, more akin to a religious than a forensic discipline.

Although Sulloway does not make this point below, he now understands the cardinal liability that Freud incurred when he "transformed the Fliessian id" to his own ends. For all its faults, the molestation etiology at least paid homage to the commonsense principle that something distinctive must have happened to people who fall ill. But Fliessian developmental theory, by making everyone's passage to adult normality look like the perilous traversing of a fixed obstacle course laid down by evolution, vastly complicated the question of pathogenicity. Why does one child cross the oedipal minefield successfully while another does not? Neither Fliess nor Freud could produce a satisfactory answer. Some of the more fanciful flights of later psychoanalytic theory, from the repetition compulsion through the death instinct to phylogenetic memory traces of the primal crime, can be understood as attempts to escape from this most fundamental of explanatory defects.

Frank J. Sulloway is a Research Scholar in Brain and Cognitive Sciences at the Massachusetts Institute of Technology. He is the author, most recently, of *Born to Rebel: Birth Order, Family Dynamics, and Creative Lives* (1996).

Amidst all the provocative and multifarious scientific ideas championed by Wilhelm Fliess in the mid-1890s, there is one additional aspect of his scientific repertoire that was bound to have aroused Sigmund Freud's interests. I am referring to Fliess's systematic and, in many respects, pioneering investigations concerning the existence and the causes of childhood sexuality. . . .

There can be no mistake. Fliess's whole theory of vital periodicity implied the necessary existence of spontaneous infantile sexuality. According to this theory, both the 23-day male and the 28-day female cycle were present in each sex throughout the course of life. The mother's two sexual periods were transmitted to the child in earliest embryonic life and were supposed to determine the sex of the offspring and to regulate its further maturation and overall vital activities until the day of its death. Growth to Fliess was therefore just another form by which sexual chemistry expresses itself in a wider, asexual mode of biological reproduction. "Each sex and every age of life," so Fliess claimed in his 1897 monograph, "is subject to them [the male 23-day and female 28-day sexual rhythms]. The development of individual tissues . . . and functions . . . is linked to their temporal exactness."

It was to show that his two periodic rhythms were biochemically *sexual* in nature that Fliess was drawn to the problem of infantile sexuality. To begin with, his claims as to the sexual regulation of major developmental milestones in life—the appearance of teeth or first attempts at walking and speech, etc.—according to cycles of 23 and 28 days were contentions with absolutely no proof. Indeed, his pansexualist unification of biorhythms, sexual chemistry, and a theory of the entire human life cycle seemed to contradict contemporary scientific belief in the absence of sexual phenomena before puberty. And so it was that Fliess seized eagerly upon the little-recognized evidence of spontaneous infantile sexuality, and particularly for the periodicity of its manifestations, as a major corroboration of his overall system of ideas. . . . Fliess ascribed 23-day male and 28-day female sexual cycles to earliest infancy, as his theory demanded he do. Accordingly, his average infant was not just sexual, it was doubly so—*bisexual!*

Thus, when Sigmund Freud later wrote in *An Outline of Psycho-Analysis* that one of "the most unexpected" findings of all his psychoanalytic researches has been the discovery that "sexual life does not begin only at puberty, but starts with plain manifestations soon after birth," he was in fact echoing one of Wilhelm Fliess's equally pioneering insights.

Fliess set forth his provocative views on spontaneous infantile sexuality at a time when Freud, obsessed by his faith in a traumatic (seduction) theory of psychoneuroses, was intent on minimizing just such a possibility. Further, when Freud finally did give up his seduction theory, he replaced it with an etiological conception that was considerably more Fliessian in scope. Indeed, Freud's own later theory of human psychosexual development reveals the impact of Fliess's influence at five important points, which alone justify a complete reappraisal of Fliess's scientific relationship with Freud during the origins of psychoanalysis.

I. FLIESS'S "ORGANOLOGICAL" EMPHASIS: THE COMPONENT NATURE OF INFANTILE SEXUALITY

Wilhelm Fliess perceived sexuality to be a highly variegated phenomenon in childhood, in both its basic chemical nature and its various forms of possible "organological" expression. His fundamental conception of sexuality as having two dominant component impulses, the male and female bisexual drives, is merely the most prominent illustration of his multiform conception of human sexuality. Like Freud, Fliess was concerned with what is commonly known in psychoanalytic parlance as *erotogenic zones*— that is to say, those parts of the body (including the nose) that are capable of contributing to sexual excitement in its wider, nongenital sense. Indeed, Fliess published his views on this aspect of the later Freudian libido theory even before Freud; and it is also interesting to note the peculiarly psychoanalytic mode of argumentation (that is, the use of etymologies) that Fliess himself adopted in making such claims about childhood sexuality:

> I would just like to point out that the sucking movements that small children make with their lips and tongue on periodic days . . . the so-called "*Ludeln*," as well as thumb-sucking, must be considered as an equivalent of masturbation. Such activity likewise brings on anxiety, sometimes combined with neurasthenia, just as does true masturbation. It comes on impulsively and is, on this account, so difficult to wean children from. . . . The role which the word "sweet" [*süss*] later plays in the language of love has its initial physiological root

here. With lips and tongue the child first tastes lactose [*Milchzucher*] at his mother's breast, and they provide him with his earliest experience of satisfaction. "Sweet" [*süss*] is related to the French *sucer* (to suck) and to *Zucker, suggar, sugere*.

Thus, not only did Fliess seem to accept the idea of an "oral" component in childhood sexuality, but he also believed that such activity could induce a childhood neurosis! . . .

In addition to discussing oral masturbatory activities in childhood, Fliess did not fail to connect the various *excretory* organs with potential expressions of sexuality in young children. Speaking, for instance, of bed-wetting in childhood, Fliess asserted:

> The enuresis of children (and urticaria [skin rash]) also appears only at periodic intervals. Childhood enuresis resembles the urge to urinate by which so many women are tormented and which also in fact occurs at periodic intervals among adults. Its relationship with sexual processes was apparently already known to the ancients (*castus raro mingit* ["the chaste rarely urinate"]). But only if one knows its exact periodic relationship can one understand why among older people, following the extinction of the sexual function, the bladder becomes less "retentive" and how it might come to be that in some men, directly after castration and in an often mysterious way, that incessant impulse to urinate suddenly disappears, which at times can make life miserable for those with prostate disorders.

Freud, I might add, could not have expressed better what was to become his own psychoanalytic position on the sexual nature of childhood bed-wetting.

Fliess's views did not stop with enuresis. He was equally convinced of a close physiological tie between the *anal* excretory function and the sexual manifestations of children. Witness his careful documentation of periodic patterns of bowel functioning in childhood. So, too, he stood on Freudian ground when he drew a connection in his sexual theory between hemorrhoids in adults and those "reflex-neuroses" associated with the reproductive system.

When Freud later laid psychoanalytic claim to the discovery of infantile sexuality, he stressed two aspects of his innovations that are particularly relevant to Fliess's pioneering views on this subject—namely, the *polymorphously perverse* nature of infantile sexuality and its specific association with the doctrine of infantile *erotogenic* zones. That Fliess indeed played a part in these two related insights is underscored by the correspondence between him and Freud. More than once in letters to his friend, Freud alluded to such ideas about sexuality as being part of Fliess's "organological" approach to the human sexual function. Freud accordingly described one of his case histories to Fliess in early 1897 as being of special "organological interest" on account of the patient's use of "oral sexual organs," while just six months later he acknowledged his deference to Fliess in this area of the latter's expertise with the words: "The organological side is waiting for you, I have made no progress with it."

II. LATENCY, SUBLIMATION, AND
REACTION FORMATION AS FLIESSIAN CONCEPTS

It was Wilhelm Fliess whom Freud credited in the *Three Essays on the Theory of Sexuality* as his source for the term *period of sexual latency*. Freud scholars have been content to let the whole matter go at that: Freud's linguistic debt to Fliess. Fliess's monograph of 1897 shows most clearly that his influence upon Freud was by no means confined to the term alone. Behind Fliess's use of it lay a sophisticated and, above all, dynamic-genetic conception of human sexual development—one that encompassed the basic Freudian notions of *sublimation* and *reaction formation*.

But, first, I must briefly explain how Freud envisioned the latency period in psychoanalytic terms. In the *Three Essays on the Theory of Sexuality*, he placed this developmental process between the fifth year and puberty and described it as follows:

> It is during this period of total or only partial latency that are built up the mental forces which are later to impede the course of the sexual instinct and, like dams, restrict its flow—disgust, feelings of shame [i.e., reaction formations] and the claims of aesthetic and moral ideas [sublimations]. One gets an impression from civilized children that the construction of these

dams is a product of education, and no doubt education has much to do with it. But in reality this development is organically determined and fixed by heredity, and it can occasionally occur without any help at all from education.

One should not be misled by the term itself into thinking that Freud saw the latency period as devoid of sexual activity. Rather, he envisioned a partial muffling of childhood sexual impulses during this interval and did not rule out occasional resurgences of the unruly infantile id. "Thus the activity of those [infantile] impulses," he emphasized in 1905, "does not cease even during this period of latency, though their energy is diverted, wholly or in great part, for their sexual use and directed to other ends."

Freud held two key processes, sublimation and reaction formation, responsible for diverting libido into other physical channels during the latency period. It is these two psychical mechanisms, not the seeming cessation of sexual activity, that constitute the essence of "latency" in Freud's later theory. What is more, this highly dynamic conception of sexual latency is fundamental to Freud's mature conception of human psychosexual development.

Although Fliess did not employ the same language as Freud—that is, "sublimation" and "reaction formation"—he nonetheless clearly endorsed the basic concepts behind these terms in his sexual theory of 1897. Fliess was dedicated to discovering the basic *Entwicklungsmechanik* ("developmental mechanics") of life. As an unflinching reductionist in such matters, he sought to derive the higher achievements of human development, including the psychical ones, from their lower, physiological determinants. In his mind, these physiological determinants were sexual substances, a circumstance that logically entailed his endorsement of the sublimation concept, especially as it applied to the prepubertal period of human development. For the period from conception to puberty in Fliess's scheme of human development was dominated by sublimated sexuality in the service of growth. "During childhood," he wrote of his two sexual-chemical rhythms, "they accumulate the energies [through physiological growth] that the human being is in a position to spend from puberty on and with which he preserves the species." Once this accumulation was finally exhausted through sexual reproduction—that is, at the time of menopause—Fliess held that the organism's biorhythms "alter their prognostication and cause the body to decay in just as wavelike a manner as they have built it up."

Was Freud influenced by Fliess's bioenergetic-developmental thinking about human sexuality? Indeed he was! In his first published reference to the existence of a sexual life in the child, Freud espoused Fliess's bioenergetic conception of the latency period:

> We do wrong to ignore the sexual life of children entirely: in my experience, children are capable of every psychical sexual activity, and many somatic sexual ones as well. . . . Nevertheless it is true that the organization and evolution of the human species strive to avoid any great degree of sexual activity during childhood. It seems that in man the sexual instinctual forces are meant to be stored up so that, on their release at puberty, they may serve great cultural ends. (W. Fliess.)

Three years later, in the "Dora" case history, Freud referred to this same process by the formal term *sublimation*. There, in almost identical wording, he wrote that the child's sexual impulses, "by being suppressed or by being diverted to higher, asexual aims—by being sublimated— are destined to provide the energy for a great number of our cultural achievements." Thus it was in full scientific cooperation with Fliess's ideas that Freud extended the economic (energy-dependent) point of view in psychoanalysis to encompass a developmental perspective on human psychosexuality. . . .

III. LIBIDINAL DEVELOPMENT: ITS PERIODIC EBB AND FLOW

Without recognizing its possible conceptual tie to Wilhelm Fliess, Richard Wollheim has given us the following synopsis of Freud's theory of libidinal maturation: "The most general feature of infantile sexual development, as recounted by Freud, is that it is *periodic* or *oscillatory,* the oscillations being explained partly in terms of the waning and reinforcement of the sexual impulse, partly in terms of the building up of mental forces opposed to sexuality [. . .]." . . .

Not only did Freud accept the periodic nature of childhood sexual development à la Fliess, but he also endorsed Fliess's medical extension of this conception to include the periodic nature of childhood anxiety neuroses. While discussing the sexual nature of adults' anxiety dreams in *The Interpretation of Dreams*, Freud went on to comment along just such Fliessian lines: "I should have no hesitation in giving the same explanation of the attacks of night terrors accompanied by hallucinations (*pavor nocturnus*) which are so frequent in children. In this case too it can only be a question of sexual impulses which have not been understood and which have been repudiated." To this conclusion there is appended the following indirect but patent reference to the theories of Wilhelm Fliess: "Investigation would probably show a periodicity in the occurrence of the attacks, since an increase in sexual libido can be brought about not only by accidental exciting impressions but also by successive waves [*schubweise*] of spontaneous developmental processes."

Freud's use of the German expression *schubweise* in the preceding passage is particularly worthy of commentary. *Schub* ("push," "shove," "thrust," etc.) and *schubweise* ("by thrusts") were developmental terms Fliess used throughout his monograph of 1897 in order to express the periodic ebb and flow that he personally attributed to all developmental processes in human beings. As such, these terms were unique to his writings in this scientific and biophysical context. Freud adopted these terms from Fliess and introduced them into his correspondence with his friend soon after reading the latter's monograph of 1897. In English translation, this linguistic tie between Fliess and Freud has largely been lost. Thus, Eric Mosbacher's English rendition of these terms in Freud's letters to Fliess (e.g., *Entwicklungsschübe* as "progressive steps of development" and *Schübe* as "steps" of development) has unfortunately obliterated both the precise scientific meaning of these terms in German, where *Schub* is specifically used in physics to mean "thrust," and their peculiarly Fliessian, biorhythmic significance.

In short, both Freud and Fliess had in mind a truly *thrust*like conception of infantile sexual development—a conception directly linked to Fliess's two periodic laws. Freud acknowledged this Fliessian tie more explicitly in 1913 when he admitted that the problem of pathological "fixations" of libido lies partly in developmental biology. "Since Wilhelm Fliess's writings have revealed the biological significance of certain periods of time," Freud added to his assertion in a footnote, "it has become conceivable that disturbances of development may be traceable to temporal changes in the successive waves of development [*Entwicklungsschüben*]."

It was likewise Fliess's *Entwicklungsschubmechanik* that helped Freud to rationalize in biochemical-developmental terms the extreme frequency of childhood (anxiety) neuroses. "Anxiety hysterias are the most common of all psychoneurotic disorders," Freud asserted in 1909. "But, above all, they are those which make their appearance earliest in life; they are *par excellence* the neuroses of childhood."

There were, of course, many physicians who immediately denied the sexual nature of such childhood neuroses. But just as quickly, Freud fell back upon the rationale provided by Fliess's own *Entwicklungsschub-mechanik*. Responding to Carl Gustav Jung, who like so many others balked at accepting the sexual nature of childhood neuroses, Freud counterclaimed: "Only the sentence about child hysteria struck me as incorrect. The conditions here are the same, probably because every thrust of growth [*jeder Wachstumsschub*] creates the same conditions as the great thrust of puberty (every increase in libido, I mean)." . . .

We should not be too surprised, then, that Freud, actively engaged as he was in applying Fliess's theories to himself, his patients, his wife, and even his children, also found Fliess's *Entwicklungsschubmechanik* most useful for the understanding of infantile psychosexual development. True, Freud eventually came to question the extreme rigidity with which Fliess himself was wont to apply his periodic laws, but he seems never to have questioned Fleiss's central premise that life, sexual as well as otherwise, is governed by a periodic ebb and flow.

IV. BISEXUALITY, NEUROSIS, AND THE NATURE OF THE UNCONSCIOUS MIND

It was Wilhelm Fliess who first convinced Freud that all human beings are bisexual and that this physiological fact is of major relevance for the theory of the neuroses. . . . What is not perhaps sufficiently appreciated by most historians of psychoanalysis is just how extensively this notion of bisexuality served to link Freud's psychoanalytic conception of human development to the biological theory championed by Fliess. In his thinking on the bisexual nature of man, Fliess sought to interconnect the following four scientific problems: the etiology of homosexuality, the mechanism of repression, the etiology of psychoneurosis, and the nature of the unconscious mind. I shall briefly review these four ideas in sequence in order to show how they influenced Freud.

A natural corollary to Fliess's views on the embryonic bisexuality of the human fetus was his interpretation of hermaphrodites and homosexuals as victims of a disturbance or inhibition in the normal course of sexual development. Spurred on as he was by his contact with Freud, Fliess approached this whole issue in a protopsychoanalytic fashion and developed, in the process, an ingenious psychobiological solution to the problem of repression. Although Freud eventually rejected certain of Fliess's specific suggestions on this problem, he was nevertheless inspired by them and continued to praise their "attractive" nature and their "bold simplicity."

In Fliess's view, as Freud later explained it, "The dominant sex of the person, that which is the more strongly developed, has repressed the mental representation of the subordinated sex into the unconscious. Therefore the nucleus of the unconscious (that is to say, the repressed) is in each human being that side of him which belongs to the opposite sex."

Fliess apparently communicated his bisexual theory of repression to Freud during their Nuremberg congress in April 1897, and it was certainly known to Freud by October of that year, when he briefly alluded to it in a letter to Fliess. Although Freud was more inclined at the time to view the masculine side as the primary target of repression in both sexes, he was nevertheless quite intrigued throughout the late 1890s by Fliess's dynamic, psychobiological approach to the whole problem. It was in this same context that Freud came to accept Fliess's clinical assertion that all neurotics exhibit unconscious fixations of the libido upon members of their own sex. This last insight, communicated by Fliess during their Nuremberg congress (April 1897) or possibly during their subsequent Breslau congress (December 1897), was taken over by Freud without further qualification and is specifically credited to Fliess in the *Three Essays on the Theory of Sexuality*.

Three further and equally permanent psychoanalytic corollaries may be traced to Fliess's theory of bisexuality in man. First, Fliess's biological framework subsequently allowed Freud to attribute homosexuality—a perversion—to insufficient repression of the embryonic bisexual disposition. Freud did much to improve upon this idea after 1900, but the general point of view provided by bisexuality theory was never outmoded by his later psychoanalytic thoughts on this subject. Second, Fliess's claim about the unconscious homosexual complexes of all neurotics demanded a conceptual link between Freud's theory of psychoneurosis and the problem of perversion. If neurotics are homosexuals but have *repressed* their homosexuality, then such afflictions could be seen broadly as a "negative" state of perversion. This last idea constitutes one of Freud's most fundamental psychoanalytic insights within his later theory of psychosexual development. Third and last, Fliess's theory suggested a general paradigm by which sundry forms of psychoneurosis might be conceived, like repressed homosexuality, as inhibitions in the development of specific libidinal component impulses. This particular insight, developed and perfected by Freud, was to become a bulwark of the psychoanalytic theory of neuroses.

In summing up the various implications of bisexuality theory for the understanding of psychoneurosis, Freud called it "the decisive factor" in 1905, adding that "without taking bisexuality into account I think it would scarcely be possible to arrive at an understanding of the sexual manifestations that are actually to be observed in men and women."

V. CHILDHOOD ONANISM AND THE ETIOLOGY OF NEUROSIS

The fifth and last point of theoretical agreement between Freud and Fliess constitutes more a conceptual overlap than an instance, like the previous four, of Fliess's direct influence upon Freud. Both of their theories of human psychosexual development were formulated at a time when medical views on the supposed evils of masturbation were undergoing dramatic change. An all but universal medical diagnosis in the 1870s and 1880s, the attribution of neuroses and even insanity to "masturbatory excesses" had virtually vanished by the 1930s and early 1940s. This change was effected largely by the pioneering medical efforts of Havelock Ellis, Albert Moll, and other contemporary sexologists, who, by systematically collecting information on the problem, found healthy and mentally disturbed individuals to differ little in their autoerotic practices.

Freud, for all his progressive views on sexuality, remained a partisan of the old school, as did Fliess. Freud's second son Oliver once came to his father with adolescent worries about masturbation, only to receive a stern warning about the many dangers inherent in this practice. As a result of this painful incident, Freud's son reports that he was never able to enjoy the sort of close relationship with his father that his older brother Jean-Martin had achieved.

What is also not appreciated about Freud is how integral his medical views on masturbation were to his overall theory of the neuroses. After his abandonment of the seduction theory in 1897, his theory of the neuroses became, in significant part, a theory about infantile sexual masturbation. It was childhood masturbation that he later blamed for the neurotic phantasies that had misled him in the first place. Such phantasies, Freud wrote, "were intended to cover up the auto-erotic activities of the first years of childhood, to embellish it and raise it to a higher plane." Speaking before the members of the Vienna Psychoanalytic Society in 1912, Freud summed up his medical views on the deleterious effects of masturbation: "*A priori,* one is forced to oppose the assertion that masturbation has to be harmless; on the contrary, there must be cases in which masturbation is harmful. Since the etiology of the neuroses is given by way of the conflict between infantile sexuality and the opposition of the ego (repression), masturbation, which is only an executive of infantile sexuality, cannot *a priori* be presented as harmless."

Freud and Wilhelm Fliess were united in their endorsement of the harmful consequences of such onanistic activities by their toxicological conception of the whole problem. Included in this toxicological analysis was the assumption of permanent organic alterations (by reflex action) in disparate parts of the body. Freud even appealed to Fliess's nasal reflex theory in this physiological context. Of his famous patient Dora and her complaints about gastric pains, Freud had maintained along such Fliessian lines: "It is well known that gastric pains occur especially often in those who masturbate. According to a personal communication made to me by Wilhelm Fliess, it is precisely gastralgias of this character which can be interrupted by an application of cocaine to the 'gastric spot' discovered by him in the nose, and which can be cured by the cauterization of the same spot." How fortunate it was for Dora that she did not live any closer to Berlin—and to Fliess!

Finally, during the late 1890s, Freud was able to extract from Fliess's theories a general physicalist rationale as to why sexual activity in childhood, either onanistic or induced, should pose a pathological threat to the developing organism. After citing Fliess's idea in 1898 that "the sexual instinctual forces" are meant to be stored up so that they may serve, after puberty, "great cultural ends," Freud added: "Considerations of this sort may make it possible to understand why the sexual experiences of childhood are bound to have a pathogenic effect." In spite of many emendations, Freud's mature theory of the neuroses continued to support this toxicological-bioenergetic conception of sexual pathology that had bound him to Wilhelm Fliess in the 1890s.

To sum up, Fliess's whole theory of human development provided (1) a novel and compelling biological justification for the observed facts about spontaneous infantile sexuality, (2) a dynamic account of how such early sexual manifestations undergo step-by-step (*schubweise*) development and differentiation, accompanied by repression in the unconscious, and (3) a sophisticated logic for sexuality's intimate medical ties to the neuroses. While Fliess's ideas do not by any means constitute a complete Freudian theory, they certainly rank as a not-too-distant intellectual relative. It is because of such manifold proto-Freudian aspects of Fliess's scientific thinking that I would designate Fliess's theory of psychosexual development as an important anticipation of Freud's own notion of the id. For as we have seen, Wilhelm Fliess, like Sigmund Freud, assumed the unconscious mind to be the repository of those biologically innate and repressed sexual impulses that have proved incompatible with the normal adult psychosexual organization. . . .

There is perhaps no better testimony to the convergence of Freud's and Fliess's respective ideas on human psychosexual development than the fact that in 1901 Freud, in a deliberate effort to win back Fliess on the brink of their personal estrangement, was willing to let him be coauthor of his forthcoming book on the sexual theory. This planned work, Freud informed Fliess at the time, was to be called "Bisexuality in Man." It was another four years before that seminal work eventually came out—minus Fliess's cooperation—under the better-known title *Three Essays on the Theory of Sexuality*. Although Fliess's acknowledged influence upon this later Freudian book is limited to the two specific notions of bisexuality and the undercurrent of homosexuality in every neurotic, it would not be too much to say that behind Freud's *Three Essays* there lurks the long-unrecognized specter of Fliessian sexual biology.

II

THE ILLUSION
OF RIGOR

"We have our own science."

—Freud

OVERVIEW

With this set of chapters, we shift our focus from the origins of psycho-analysis to its essential knowledge claims. The reader must understand that those claims reside at a deeper level than psychoanalytic propositions about the mind. Like the Hydra of the *Odyssey* that could always grow two new heads when one was lopped off, Freudian theory has been end-lessly resourceful in replacing discredited notions with fresh ones. But the key question we need to ask is always the same: On what grounds are we to believe what is being asserted? If, as we will see, there are no credible warrants for preferring Freudian claims to rival ones, and if the psycho-analytic means of gathering evidence is demonstrably circular, then the whole system of thought stands fatally compromised.

We have already, in Part I, been accumulating substantial doubts about Freud's trustworthiness as a gatherer and transmitter of knowledge. From his cocaine evangelism in the 1880s (see Freud, 1974) through *Studies on Hysteria*, and continuing through his 1896 "seduction" papers, Freud projected an absolute confidence in ideas that he was actually finding to be unworkable and potentially destructive. And beginning with his rec-ommendation of cocaine injections as a cure for morphine addiction and his appropriation of Breuer's failed Anna O. case, he habitually misstated the therapeutic results that supposedly underwrote those ideas. He was setting a pattern of behaving less like a scientist than like an overeager salesman, concealing his doubts about questionable merchandise while privately casting about for something better.

Moreover, Freud's loss of confidence in an early tool of inquiry—first hypnosis, then the "pressure technique"—hadn't prompted any corresponding admission that the conclusions he had reached by using it were therefore invalid. His "seduction" etiology was conceived and announced, privately repudiated, publicly reaffirmed, and finally dropped in silent embarrassment without his ever facing up to the real problem: therapeutic suggestion. And when he eventually admitted to having been wrong about childhood molestation and hysteria, he placed all the blame on his patients' alleged "stories" and none on his investigative method, which he was continuing to employ with the same hectoring adamancy as before.

Biographically, then, a miasma of suspicion hangs about Freud's knowledge claims. But fairness and logic require an exercise of caution here. Even while being mistaken in his assumptions and foolish in his conduct, Freud could have happened upon truths about the mind. It is the quality of his arguments, then, not the quirks of his personality, that must occupy us in this set of chapters.

The first three chapters of Part II all touch upon free association, a patient's uttering of any and all phrases that come to mind in connection with a given symptom (Chapter 6), dream (Chapter 7), or slip (Chapter 8). This remains the basis of psychoanalytic method even today, though the knowledge claims surrounding it have become far more modest. Once Freud had used the analysis of free associations to glean insights from such sources, he felt ready to reconstruct specific childhood events or fantasies that had actuated an etiologic chain issuing in the patient's adult disorder. Words alone, then, spoken in a therapist's consulting room, could supposedly put the psychic investigator onto an unbroken causal trail leading back twenty, thirty, or more years.

Malcolm Macmillan has shown that Freud's remarkable confidence in the capacity of free associations to reveal the repressed past stemmed from his belief in a "bulletlike determinism," ensuring that "a train of thought could terminate only in an idea that shared experiences and pathways with the starting idea" (Macmillan, 1997, page 108). If the human mind doesn't operate according to such a cortical row of dominoes extending through the decades, then Freud's trust in the power of free association to unearth early causes was ill-advised. But so, as we will see, was his more modest faith in free association as an identifier of *imme-*

diate causes, such as the conflictual elements that lay behind the manifest content of a reported dream.

Does the fact that a patient thinks about topic X when asked to associate to a dream mean that topic X *caused* that dream? Or might the patient have mentioned topic X anyway, simply because it was a preoccupation on that day? Moreover, if unintentional therapeutic suggestion is the besetting peril of "clinical knowledge," we must ask whether free association typically helps to prevent that defect or to magnify it. We will see that free association, precisely by virtue of its open-endedness, gives the analyst ample scope to highlight "evidence" that suits his preconceptions and to blur the line between the patient's mental contents and his own. Like such concepts as repression, resistance, and denial, free association thus serves as a wild card in the analyst's hand.

Freud called *The Interpretation of Dreams* his masterpiece; he revised it often; and he never backed away from his pretension to have unlocked the innermost secrets of dream meaning. His faith, moreover, has been contagious: dream interpretation remains a staple of the typical analytic hour, and Freudian dream theory has undergone little alteration in nearly a century. Yet agreement among analysts about the meaning of a given dream is notoriously rare (see, for example, Fine and Fine, 1990)—a fact that acquires a certain grimness when we realize that dreams are once again being taken to prove the existence of forgotten sexual abuse in childhood (see, for example, Prozan, 1993, 1997).

Freud asserted that dreams are the guardians of sleep; by granting the repressed a furtive venting, he said, they allow the sleeper to keep from being awakened by his clamorous unconscious. That claim was backed by no evidence at all, and it is undermined by what we now know about REM (rapid eye movement) sleep, the condition in which dreams occur (see Hobson, 1988). Such sleep is universal among our fellow mammals, none of whom are likely to be suffering from Viennese-style repressed childhood memories or castration complexes. Our own dreams assuredly contain meaningful as well as nonsensical elements, but Freud's particular dream theory, with its strict delimitation between "manifest" and "latent" content and its rules for reconstructing the disguised "dream thoughts," remains entirely speculative.

We will find that the same must be said of his theory of slips, expounded in the most popular of all his works, *The Psychopathology of Everyday Life* (1901). That "Freudian slips," as most people casually conceive of them, are sometimes committed seems plausible enough; a speaker with some sexual or aggressive thought in the back of his mind might allow that thought to alter an utterance in an embarrassing way. Consider, for example, the hapless radio announcer, doing a bakery commercial, who blurted out, "Always demand the breast in bed." Just such instances have convinced millions of people that Freud really did unveil the repressed unconscious. But are they right?

To begin with, how do we know that the announcer's interest in female anatomy was *repressed*—and why, after all, should it have been? Do men usually banish all such thoughts from their conscious minds? And second, the slip could well have been caused by an innocent similarity between two printed words in close sequence. The Freudian interpretation is more entertaining but not necessarily more probable. Indeed, it is distinctly less so, because lexical mix-ups of this kind occur with great frequency when no erotic meaning is apparent. Unfortunately for Freud's ultimate stature, this example is all too typical of the ones he actually proffered. His failure, throughout the *Psychopathology*, to consider "banal" sources of error or to offer a single indisputable instance of repression left his theory of mind not only unproven but, strictly speaking, unillustrated in that book.

Once we have realized that Freud's method of gathering and assessing clinical data allowed him to find his presuppositions reinforced by literally anything a patient might say or do, we can understand why psychoanalytic theory as a whole is so riddled with unresolvable disputes and contradictions. And that untidiness is worth pondering in its own right. A would-be scientific body of thought reveals its deepest tendency through its means of handling doubts and alternative explanations. Freud ignored the latter, but he was continually expanding and hedging psychoanalytic doctrine to make it more hospitable to recalcitrant facts pointed out by his adversaries. Although subsequent Freudians have cited such recasting as proof of an austere methodological rigor, they fail to realize the cardinal difference between putting one's theory at empirical risk and blunting that very risk through ad hoc rescue maneuvers. Such tactics can postpone refutation indefinitely, but in the long run they heap up so many escape clauses and ambiguities that the doctrine becomes self-canceling. In Chapters 9 and 10 we will see how such clutter compares to the requirements of a well-conceived, logically coherent, empirically responsible theory.

Theoretical clutter, however, is not the main drawback to ungoverned psychological speculation. Insofar as it impresses the world, it brings tangible human consequences in its wake—generally negative ones. Nowhere is this point more strikingly manifested than in the realm of Freudian female psychology, which we will review in Chapter 11. Although we cannot measure the suffering inflicted on women by Freudian condescension, misdiagnosis, and blame, we can at least show how unnecessary it has been. As we will find, it was not just Freud's famous misogyny that caused him to represent women as second-class humans, but also his entrapment in the labyrinth of his own gratuitous premises. Women just didn't fit into a "castration-based" account of the mind, but Freud had no choice but to *make* them fit—with results from which we are still attempting to recover.

Made-to-Order Evidence*

Adolf Grünbaum

In his monumental study of 1984, *The Foundations of Psychoanalysis: A Philosophical Critique,* Adolf Grünbaum exhaustively demonstrated that the "clinical evidence" cited by Freud and his successors cannot yield reliable inferences about the causation of neuroses, dreams, or slips. Not even the psychological causation of last night's dream, he showed, to say nothing about the pathogenicity of a possibly fictitious infantile trauma, can be ascertained by exercising rules of interpretation that are saturated in the presuppositions of an uncorroborated doctrine about repression, psychosexual development, and the production of overt behavior through conflictual "compromise formation."

Grünbaum has also searchingly examined Freud's claim that his alleged cures of neuroses serve to provide a warrant for asserting that free associations really do lead to the correct identification of pathogenic repressed material (SE, 5: 528). Whenever the patient emerges from the treatment durably liberated from symptoms, Freud maintained, the right hunches and hypotheses must have been followed. This is what Grünbaum has famously dubbed Freud's "tally argument," whereby lasting therapeutic success is taken to prove, by means of a dubious postulate, that the analyst's reconstructions must "tally with what is real" (SE, 16: 452) in the patient's history and makeup. Yet Freud was eventually compelled to admit that he hadn't been pro-

* From *The Foundations of Psychoanalysis: A Philosophical Critique* (Berkeley and Los Angeles: University of California Press, 1984).

ducing cures after all (see page 144 below). Moreover, Grünbaum has shown that the tally argument is empirically ill-founded even when, as sometimes happens in the course of an analysis, enduring symptom removal actually occurs. The happy outcome could have been wrought by causes other than psychoanalytic insight and the lifting of repressions—namely, by placebo or "hand-holding" factors shared by other regimens or even by factors extraneous to the entire treatment process.

The following excerpt from Grünbaum's *Foundations* begins by querying Freud's belief in the uncontaminated nature of free associations. Are those utterances "suggestion proof"? To be sure of that, Grünbaum shows, one would have to be satisfied that the psychoanalytic dialogue in general is immune to subtle transmission of the therapist's expectations to the patient. A tall order, especially since, as Grünbaum mentions, Freud himself emphasized the "intellectual help" that passes from analyst to analysand. Grünbaum goes on to indicate that the "memories" produced in such a contest are no more shielded from suggestion than are free associations. If so, there can be no hope of validating the authenticity of the associations by referring to the early recollections that they seemingly trigger.

Grünbaum's view of psychoanalysis is not unrelievedly negative. He countenances some of the lesser Freudian defense mechanisms such as rationalization, projection, and reaction formation, and he does not rule out the possibility that future experimental or epidemiological studies may show some major tenet in the theory of repression to have been well founded. But nothing in Grünbaum's examination of Freud's clinical theory leads one to expect any such result. Meanwhile, he consigns the entire Freudian theory of psychopathology, dream production, and slips to a scientific limbo, devoid of any demonstrated basis in sound evidence.

Adolf Grünbaum is the Andrew Mellon Professor of Philosophy, Research Professor of psychiatry, and Chair of the Center for Philosophy of Science at the University of Pittsburgh. His twelve books include the recent successor volume to his *Foundations*, *Validation in the Clinical Theory of Psychoanalysis* (1993). The objections of Freudians to his arguments against psychoanalysis are examined and rejected in that study; in Grünbaum, 1986; and in Erwin, 1993, 1996. For his most recent overview of the standing of psychoanalysis, see Grünbaum, 1997.

Freud's method of free association has been hailed as the master key to unlocking all sorts of repressed ideation. Its products have been claimed to be uncontaminated excavations of buried mentation precisely because the flow of associations generated when the patient adheres to the governing "fundamental rule" is allegedly "free." As Freud maintains, it was "confirmed by wide experience" that the *contents* of all the associations that flow in the patient's mind from a given initial content do stand in an *internal causal connection* to that initial content. By avowedly being purely internal, this causal relatedness rules out the mediation of externally injected content in the strictly deterministic linkages that Freud postulates to exist between the initial mental content and the ensuing associations. And if there actually is no such external mediation, then the patient's flow of associations is indeed immune to contamination by distorting influences emanating from the analyst's suggestions! Thus, the analyst could then be held to function as a neutral catalyst or expeditor of the flow of his patient's free associations, even when he prompts the analysand to continue them after he suspects that they are being censored by internal resistances. In this way, the chain of the patient's associations is purported to serve as a pathway to the psychoanalytic unmasking of his repressions. . . .

Does the patient's adherence to the fundamental rule of free association indeed safeguard the causally uncontaminated emergence of actually existing repressed wishes, anger, guilt, fear, etc.? Or is the process of association contaminated by the analyst's injection of influence of one sort or another? Clearly, the answer will depend, at least partly, on just what the analyst does while the patient is busy fulfilling his share of the analytic compact. This answer is also likely to depend on the antecedent beliefs that patients going into analysis bring into the analytic situation, for many an intelligent analysand is consciously aware of the sort of material that his Freudian therapist does expect from his free associations. For example, male patients are expected to have repressed castration anxiety, and females are to have unconscious penis envy. While dealing with our question, we shall need to be mindful of another, since it likewise pertains to the epistemic effects of the analyst's intervention: if a plethora of unconscious thoughts surface, by what criteria does the analyst decide when to call a halt to the surfeit of associations, while investigating parapraxes [slips] and dreams? Hence, let us canvass in what respects overt and subtle interventions by the analyst affect the data yielded by the patient's associations.

The limitations of the analytic hour alone require that the patient's associations not be allowed to continue indefinitely. But suppose that one were to disregard the epistemically irrelevant expedient of this hour and allow the patient to continue unimpeded, even if he pauses off and on. If the intelligent and imaginative analysand is permitted to associate in this way long enough, his unfettered ruminations will, in due course, presumably yield almost any kind of thematic content of which he had at least recently not been conscious: thoughts about death, God, and indeed cabbages and kings. But, if so, how does the analyst avoid an antecedently question-begging selection bias in the face of this thematic elasticity of the associations, while unavoidably limiting their duration?

Thus, if the associations do flow apace and the analyst somehow interrupts them at a certain point, he is interfering in their spontaneous causal dynamics. By what criterion does he do so? But in the case of, say, a parapraxis or a given element of manifest dream content, when the associations are faltering and the analyst demands their continuation, how does he manage not to load the dice by ever so subtly hinting to the patient what kind of material he expects to emerge? After all, his demand for continuation will convey his suspicion that it was censorial resistance to a related repressed content that brought the flow of associations to a halt at that particular point, and his attempt at overcoming that resistance may well convey his expectation. . . .

Thus the clinical use of free association features epistemic biases of selection and manipulative contamination as follows: (1) the analyst selects thematically, from the patient's productions, partly by interrupting the associations—either explicitly or in a myriad more subtle ways—at points of his or her own theoretically inspired choosing; and (2) when the Freudian doctor harbors the suspicion that the associations are faltering because of evasive censorship, he uses verbal and also subtle nonverbal promptings to induce the continuation of the associations until they yield theoretically appropriate results; for surely not any and every previously repressed thought that emerges will be deemed a relevant repression for the purpose of etiologic inquiry, dream interpretation, or the analysis of a slip.

Experimental studies by L. Krasner, G. Mandler, W. K. Kaplan, and K.

Salzinger, which are summarized by the analyst Judd Marmor, do bear out empirically the actual contamination of the products of free association by the analyst. Freud had credited free association by saying: "it [free association] guarantees to a great extent that [. . .] nothing will be introduced into it by the expectations of the analyst." Commenting on precisely this statement of Freud's, Marmor writes: "Clinical experience has demonstrated that this simply is not so and that the 'free' associations of the patient are strongly influenced by the values and expectations of the therapist." He then cites an earlier article of his, where he had written:

> In face-to-face transactions the expression on the therapist's face, a questioning glance, a lift of the eyebrows, a barely perceptible shake of the head or shrug of the shoulder all act as significant cues to the patient. But even *behind* the couch, our "uh-huhs" as well as our silences, the interest or the disinterest reflected in our tone of voice or our shifting postures all act like subtle radio signals influencing the patients' responses, reinforcing some responses and discouraging others. That this influence actually occurs has been confirmed experimentally by numerous observers. . . .

Indeed, recalling a finding from that earlier article, Marmor concludes:

> As a result, depending on the point of view of the psychoanalyst, patients of every psychoanalytic school tend, *under free association,* "to bring up precisely the kind of phenomenological data which confirm the theories and interpretations of their analysts! Thus each theory tends to be self-validating."

This report derives added poignancy from the studies marshaled by A. K. Shapiro and L. A. Morris as support for claiming that therapists may subtly and unwittingly "communicate information to patients, such as hypotheses, expectations, attitudes, cultural values, and so on." They emphasize how this state of affairs issues in the spurious clinical confirmation of psychological hypotheses via the effects of suggestion: "The returned communication is then regarded as an independent confirmation of the therapist's theory. This increases the credulity and suggestibility of both." This epistemological difficulty is, of course, compounded by the operation of those phenomena that Freud termed "counter-transference" phenomena after shrewdly discerning them: the distorting effects of the therapist's feelings toward the patient on the accuracy of the former's perception of the latter's behavior. . . .

One wonders how Freud could have persuaded himself to put much stock in patient resistance as insurance against adulteration by suggested compliance. For he himself maintained that when the patient's transference toward the analyst is positive, "it clothes the doctor with authority and is transformed into belief in his communications and explanations." Interestingly, Freud's aforecited reliance on patient resistance is introduced by the following tribute to the analyst's purported ability to winnow the bona fide memories from the fancied ones: "Any danger of falsifying the products of the patient's memory by suggestion can be avoided by prudent handling of the technique." But this particular assurance is especially unconvincing. Clearly, the clinical authentication of the etiologically relevant early history in the lives of psychoneurotics must largely rely on the adult patient's memories of *infantile* and *childhood* experiences, and such early memories are surely more fragile epistemically than ordinary recollections from adult life!

This is so especially since the analyst is doing exactly what a cross-examining attorney is forbidden to do in the courtroom: leading the witness. Freud makes no bones about this particular feature of analysis:

> The treatment is made up of two parts—what the physician infers and tells the patient, and the patient's working-over of what he has heard. The mechanism of our assistance is easy to understand: we give the patient the conscious anticipatory idea [the idea of what he may expect to find] and he then finds the repressed unconscious idea in himself on the basis of its similarity to the anticipatory one. This is the intellectual help which makes it easier for him to overcome the resistances between conscious and unconscious.

Freud does not specify just how the "prudent handling of the technique," which he claims to have exercised in the psychoanalytic quest for the recovery of repressed memories, actually provided a safeguard against the suggestive elicitation of pseudomemories ("paramnesias").

It can be granted, of course, that requirements of consistency or at least overall coherence do afford the analyst some check on what the patient alleges to be bona fide memories. But Freud's own writings attest to the untrustworthiness of purported adult memories of early childhood episodes that had presumably been repressed in the interim and then retrieved by analysis. And he conceded that even reliance on the slender reed of the patient's recall is sometimes disappointingly unavailable: "The patient cannot remember the whole of what is repressed in him, and what he cannot remember may be precisely the essential part of it." To fill just this lacuna, the patient simply has to take the analyst's word for the soundness of the reconstruction of his past. Indeed, the malleability of adult memories from childhood is epitomized by a report from Jean Piaget, who thought he vividly remembered an attempt to kidnap him from his baby carriage along the Champs-Élysées. He recalled the gathered crowd, the scratches on the face of the heroic nurse who saved him, the policeman's white baton, the assailant running away. However vivid, Piaget's recollections were false. Years later the nurse confessed that she had made up the entire story, which he then internalized as a presumed experience under the influence of an authority figure.

Yet, writing about Leonardo da Vinci's memories from childhood, Freud declared, "What someone thinks he remembers from his childhood is not a matter of indifference; as a rule the residual memories—which he himself does not understand—cloak priceless pieces of evidence about the most important features in his mental development." The early Freud had even been sanguine enough to declare that if he ever were to alter or falsify the reproduction of memories or the connection of events, "it would inevitably have been betrayed in the end by some contradiction in the material." Hence, he concluded insouciantly: "We need not be afraid, therefore, of telling the patient what we think his next connection of thought is going to be. It will do no harm"! . . .

Apparently the analyst cannot justly claim to be a mere neutral expeditor or catalyst for the recovery of memories that can be intraclinically certified as authentic by virtue of his "prudent handling of the technique." Indeed, the help-seeking patient may well sense that the analyst expects confirmation of a conjecture by a memory, and the knowledge, authority, and help-giving potential he attributes to the analyst may well serve to make him compliant, no less than his desire to gain the analyst's approval qua parental surrogate. Such approval or disapproval manifests itself through the myriad subtle nonverbal cues present in human communication.

That psychoanalytic treatment ought not to be regarded as a bona fide memory-jogging device emerges more generally as a corollary of at least three sets of recent research findings elaborated by Elizabeth Loftus: (1) the remarkable extent to which human memory is malleable, (2) the interpolative reconstruction and bending of memories by theoretical beliefs or expectations, and (3) the penchant, under the influence of leading questions, to fill amnesiac gaps by confabulated material. As for the first point, people have pseudomemories for events that never occurred. For example, under the influence of racial stereotypes, some experimental subjects who were shown a picture of several people on a subway car—including a black man with a hat and a white man with a razor in his hand—claimed to remember seeing the razor in the hands of the black man.

The tendency characterized under the second point arises from taking various fragments of experiences and filling in details under the guidance of all sorts of suppositions, so as to create a new distorted or even fictitious "memory." As Loftus summarizes the evidence:

> Human remembering does not work like a videotape recorder or a movie camera. When a person wants to remember something, he or she does not simply pluck a whole memory intact out of a "memory store." The memory is constructed from stored and available bits of information; any gaps in the information are filled in unconsciously by inferences. When these fragments are integrated and make sense, they form what we call a memory.

Finally, Loftus's discussion of confabulation in response to leading questions is likewise germane. For example, when people are asked to point out a previously seen culprit in a police lineup, worthless identifications can result from this recognition test unless care is taken not to steer them suggestively to a particular individual in the lineup. I claim that such pitfalls of memory-based recognition tests lurk even more when an analytic patient is asked to draw on his memory to test an interpretation offered him by his analyst. Such a memory test normally does not match the features of a well-designed police lineup recognition test, for the therapist tends to favor his own interpretations of the analysand's past, and this attitude will typically not be lost on the patient. . . .

The epistemic adulteration I have documented seems to be ineradicable in just those patient responses that are supposed to lay bare repressions and disguised defenses after resistances have been overcome. Yet Freud attributed pride of place to these very data in the validation of his theory of repression. Thus, generally speaking, clinical findings—in and of themselves—forfeit the probative value that Freud had claimed for them, although their potential heuristic merits may be quite substantial.

Manifestly Fallacious*

Rosemarie Sand

Do dreams, in spite of their bizarre and inexplicable elements, tell us something about our conscious daily preoccupations? Virtually everyone feels that it is so. Dream interpretation of a simple but intuitively plausible kind is regularly conducted over the breakfast table: "I had a nightmare about giant spiders because of that horror film we saw last night"; "Jane phoned yesterday and boasted about her fancy new job; I put her in her place by dreaming that she was cleaning sewers." And on this point the folk wisdom turns out to be correct. Quantitative studies have established what one scholar calls "striking continuities between dream content and waking life, making possible accurate predictions about the concerns and interests of the dreamers" (Domhoff, 1996, page 2).

As Rosemarie Sand shows below, however, this discovery can hardly be credited to Freud. Many of the ancient and modern authorities whom he *rejects* in his introductory chapter to *The Interpretation of Dreams* (1900) considered dreams to be pictorial representations of thoughts, including selfish ones. Freud's rival view was far more problematic. Pictorial representation—indeed, the entire manifest dream—was exactly what he wanted to brush aside as mere disguise, a ruse intended to trick the mind's sleep-lulled "censor" into allowing

* From "On a Contribution to a Future Scientific Study of Dream Interpretation," in *Philosophical Problems of the Internal and External Worlds: Essays on the Philosophy of Adolf Grünbaum*, ed. John Earman et al. (Pittsburgh: University of Pittsburgh Press, 1993), pp. 527–546.

shameful unconscious desires to get indirectly expressed. Thus even the dream about Jane's cleaning sewers, which clearly does embody a wish, departs from the Freudian pattern by virtue of its straightforwardness. Far from having "discovered the secret of dreams," Freud proves to be the odd man out among history's prominent interpreters—the one authority who failed to realize that manifest dream content can be a direct, unmediated clue to the dreamer's concerns.

Rosemarie Sand is a retired psychoanalyst whose view of her profession is more sanguine than that of most other contributors to this volume. As her final paragraph below attests, she takes some hope from the gradual erosion of Freudian dogma and the tacit reintroduction of common sense about dream meaning. She is at work on an ambitious book showing that, despite Freud's assertion to the contrary, there was a flourishing pre-Freudian tradition of dream interpretation emphasizing unconscious aspects of the mind.

Psychoanalysts typically rely not on one, but on two different theories when they interpret dreams. One of these theories is Freud's. The other is an ancient hypothesis which has increasingly made its way into psychoanalytic practice over the decades.

Freud's theory has been repudiated by scientific dream researchers because they regard its method as yielding pseudoevidence. Aspects of the old hypothesis, on the other hand, have been well accepted by some experimenters. I suggest, therefore, that if psychoanalysts will eschew the Freudian method and rely entirely upon the ancient technique, they will thereby remove a major roadblock which has prevented cooperation between dream researchers and clinicians. In this essay, I hope to contribute to future understanding by first reviewing once again the fallacy in Freud's method which has been pointed out by many critics and then by describing the merits of the old, or classical, technique.

When Freud presented his theory, in 1900, he specifically rejected what he called the "popular, historic and legendary" method of interpretation. He made it plain that he was breaking with the past by distinguishing between what he called the "manifest" and the "latent" dream. Every previous attempt to solve the problem of dreams, he averred, dealt with the manifest dream, meaning the dream as recalled and reported by the dreamer. "We are alone," he asserted, "in taking something else into account." This "something else" was the latent, or hidden, content of the dream which he believed could be uncovered by the process of free association.

The manifest dream, according to Freud, was not to be interpreted directly, as it had been in the past, because it was merely a facade, a deliberate disguise which hid the real meaning of the dream. The manifest dream was to be split into segments and then free associations were to be obtained for each of these separate segments. In this way, the latent thoughts, the real meaning of the dream, would emerge.

It has often been remarked that, in spite of his own careful instructions, Freud did not always segment the manifest dream before interpreting it. A perusal of his work shows that not only did Freud often rely upon the manifest dream in practice, but it was also incorporated into his theory, in which it appears in many guises. Thus, Freud's new theory and the old hypothesis, as well as the methods associated with them, coexisted from the start and have continued to coexist. . . .

Freud's basic hypothesis was as follows: A dream is produced when an unacceptable, repressed, infantile wish becomes active during sleep. Repression being weakened during sleep, the unacceptable wish threatens to break through into consciousness and to disturb sleep. However, a process which safeguards sleep intervenes. Instead of being wakened by the wish, the sleeper dreams of it, but not in its disturbing form. A transforming process, the "dream work," distorts it so that the wish appears in the dream in an unrecognizable guise. The dream which the dreamer recalls, the "manifest dream," therefore does not picture the real wish but masks it. The essential cause of the dream, the trigger which sets the process in motion, is the hidden, unacceptable wish.

Modern science has cast grave doubts upon Freud's hypothesis that wishes are the causes of dreams. Dream research received a powerful impetus when, in 1953, Aserinsky and Kleitman at the University of Chicago discovered that people rapidly move their eyes at intervals during the night, that this rapid eye movement, or REM period, coincided with specific brain activation patterns and that, during these periods, dreams were in progress. This discovery strongly suggested that the neural mechanisms which caused the REM state also caused the dream. It has since been learned that dreams also occur outside of the REM state, but it still remains likely that neural mechanisms, and not repressed infantile wishes, trigger the dream.

Meanwhile, Adolf Grünbaum has cogently argued on other grounds that Freud's theory is false. Freud stated that the dream was related to neurotic symptoms because both dreams and symptoms were caused by unacceptable wishes which were repressed and unconscious. He also asserted that symptoms disappear when repression is removed during psychoanalytic treatment because undoing the repression enables unconscious wishes to become conscious, after which they can no longer produce symptoms. It seems necessary to conclude, therefore, that once unconscious wishes become conscious they will no longer be able to cause dreams either. If Freud's theory were true, Grünbaum suggested, then psychoanalytic treatment ought to at least reduce the frequency of dreaming as treatment progressed and as repressions were removed. He has concluded that in the case of long-term psychoanalytic patients, "either their free associations are chronically unsuccessful in retrieving their buried infantile wishes, or, if there is such retrieval, then Freud's account of dream generation is false."

Although wishes do not cause dreams, they may still be pictured in dreams, just as anything else may be pictured. In that case, a wish may be regarded as a *source* of the dream. It is useful to distinguish the *cause* of a dream from its *sources*. The cause is the trigger of the dream; the cause makes the dream happen. Scientists suggest this is a neural mechanism. The dream's sources determine the contents of the dream. So, for instance, if an image of my Aunt Mildred appears in a dream, then a previous perception, a memory, of this aunt is the source of the image. My wish to see my aunt did not cause me to dream, but my wish to see her may be pictured in the dream. The source of a dream is a kind of cause also, in fact, a necessary cause, because if I did not have a memory of my aunt, her image would not appear in my dream. However, the use of the word "cause" in two senses, one as trigger of the dream and the other as a determinant of dream content, has proven confusing. Therefore, when I refer to the latter, I will use the word "source." The source is pictured, or displayed, in the dream.

Thus, a wish, as well as any other mental state, can be a source of a dream. That we often see our wishes come true in dreams is one of humankind's oldest convictions. Freud, however, insisted that the wish which produced the dream was *not* displayed in the dream. He averred that his method could show that the real wish was hidden and that only its disguised derivatives appeared in the manifest dream.

This claim was rejected by critics long before the REM state was discovered, based on a fallacy located in Freud's method. Freud thought he could prove that a hidden wish produced the dream because free association to segments of the dream would bring to light the "background thoughts" of the dream and these would be related to the dream-engendering unacceptable wish. He put it this way: If "I put the dream before him [the dreamer] cut up into pieces, he will give me a series of associations to each piece, which might be described as the 'background thoughts' of that particular part of the dream."

How so? Freud's critics asked as soon as *The Interpretation of Dreams* appeared, and they have continued to ask this question ever since. Why should a series of associations to pieces of the dream give you the "background thoughts" of those pieces? How can you assume that a series of thoughts which *follow* a dream will lead you to the thoughts which *preceded* the dream? No doubt, a series of thoughts will lead you *somewhere,* but you cannot justifiably assume that you have been led to the background thoughts which produced the dream.

When persons are asked to free associate "to" an element of a dream, as psychoanalytic parlance has it, they are instructed to relax their critical faculty and to express "everything that comes to mind," regardless of whether it seems to them inapplicable, nonsensical or embarrassing. This entails *not* focusing on the element which is the takeoff point for the associations but rather letting the mind wander from one thought to the next, perhaps in a long series. The assumption is that if conscious control is abandoned, the liberated, or "free," associations will be guided by unconscious motivational forces which, supposedly, are the same forces which produced the dream. This is the much-criticized assumption. Granted that free associations are influenced by some force or other, what licenses the supposition that this is the force responsible for the dream?

I will refer to this erroneous supposition as the "free association fallacy," not because all free association provides misleading information but because a particular error occurs when free association is used to discover specific determinants of symptoms, dreams and parapraxes. The fallacy occurs, for instance, when it is assumed that something—a thought, a feeling, a motive—which turns up during free association to a dream, merely because it turns up, must be a background thought of the dream. In other words, to put it most succinctly, the free association fallacy is that, given a dream A, if I associate from A to B, then B must have been a determinant of A. This is the reasoning which Freud's critics condemned. . . .

An example of the free association fallacy as committed by Freud is the dream known as "Otto was looking ill." Freud had dreamed that "my friend Otto was looking ill. His face was brown and he had protruding eyes." This was the manifest dream. Freud then free associated to this dream and after a long series of thoughts arrived at what he considered to be the latent dream, two wishes, one that he might become a professor and the other that he might live a long life. The subject matters of the manifest and the supposed latent dreams are entirely different, and there is no apparent meaningful connection between them. The assumption that the supposed latent dream, the wishes for a professorship and a long life, gave rise to the manifest dream about Otto's appearance is based solely on the fact that a string of associations connected them. That is, it is assumed that B is a determinant of A because B occurred in the series of associations.

This conclusion seems entirely unjustified unless it is simply *presupposed* that ideas which emerge in association to a dream preceded it and produced it. It must be remarked that the possibility that such a presupposition could be true cannot be absolutely ruled out, because one cannot predict what the science of the future may bring. Perhaps in the near or in the distant future it may be possible to show that even long strings of associations which emerge in association to a dream really are "dream thoughts" which went into the production of the dream.

However, with no such development perceptible on the immediate horizon, psychoanalysts would do well to eschew the claim that they have discovered the source of a dream by means of association of this sort. Psychoanalysts are not being asked to depreciate free association; they are only being requested to recognize one of its limits. It is important to note that the general capacity of free association to provide information about the dreamer is not in question here. When people free associate, to dreams or at other times, expressing their thoughts as they let their minds wander, there is no reason to doubt that they will provide data about *themselves*. The analyst is likely to learn something about the patient and on that account may justly value free association. But the analyst is mistaken if she believes that whenever a patient free associates to a dream, the patient is necessarily on a trail which leads to the source of the dream.

For many psychoanalysts, the usefulness of free association in the clinical situation has likely obscured the fallacy which may occur in it. The patient associates to a dream and during the course of the association important thoughts and feelings may emerge, some perhaps previously unrecognized. The analyst is then likely to attribute any discovery to "analysis of the dream." The conviction that all of the thoughts uttered by the patient following the dream report can be taken to be "associations to the dream" is not uncommon. Indeed, the analyst may even suppose that she is justified in accepting that everything the patient said and did *before* reporting the dream during the session is an "association to the dream." . . .

The manifest dream should be recognized as possessing an independent theory with its own structure, its own concept of the dream-creating process, and its own interpretative rules. According to this theory, the dream can reveal circumstances, attitudes and motives of the dreamer by displaying them in the dream content.

This is an ancient theory which for many centuries coexisted with, but was often overshadowed by, the supposition that dreams revealed the future. For instance, in the second century after Christ, the celebrated oneirocritic, Artemidorus of Daldis, whose profession was to predict, assumed that many dreams did not foretell the future but simply revealed the hopes and fears of the dreamer. He stated that "it is natural for a lover to seem to be with his beloved in a dream and for a frightened man to see what he fears." Centuries earlier, Zeno, founder of the Stoic philosophy, recommended the use of the dream to study progress attained by the dreamer in the pursuit of the Stoic ideal. . . .

In the nineteenth century it was widely believed that the dream could picture the life, including the inner life, of the dreamer. In the chapter which introduces *The Interpretation of Dreams* Freud stated that "the preponderant majority of writers" on the subject hold that dreams are related to the dreamers' interests, and he quoted several of these. One stated that "the content of a dream is invariably more or less determined by the individual personality of the dreamer, by his age, sex, class, standard of education and habitual way of living, and by the events and experiences of his whole previous life." Another noted that "we dream of what we have seen, said, desired or done." It stands to reason, therefore, that a perusal of a dream may teach us something about the dreamer. In this connection, Freud quoted what he called a "familiar saying," "Tell me some of your dreams and I will tell you about your inner self."

Modern dream science strongly supports these opinions. Researcher Milton Kramer, surveying experimentation, concludes that "the dream is indeed signal rather than noise. The dream is a structured product and reflects meaningful psychological differences among subjects. The dream responds to or reflects emotionally charged influences, and the domains of waking and dreaming are significantly and straightforwardly related." Seymour Fisher and Roger P. Greenberg, after summarizing results of a number of dream studies, arrived at a similar estimate and noted that "the manifest dream content carries a great deal of meaning. [. . .] [T]he weight of the evidence argues against viewing the manifest content as a largely meaningless conglomeration of camouflage devices, such as Freud spelled out."

That the theory which relies solely upon the manifest dream for purposes of interpretation, the classical, or traditional, theory, is an independent theory which can be sharply distinguished from Freud's is demonstrated by a comparison of the basic principles of these two hypotheses. These principles are not merely different, for three of them are directly contradictory:

1. *Freudian theory:* The manifest dream is not to be interpreted directly.
   Classical theory: The manifest dream is to be interpreted directly.
2. *Freudian theory:* The manifest dream *disguises* the origin of the dream.
   Classical theory: The manifest dream does *not disguise* the origin of the dream. It pictures, or displays, it.
3. *Freudian theory:* The dream-producing process is structured to produce a disguise.
   Classical theory: The dream-producing process is not structured to produce a disguise; it is structured to create a picture, or display.

Moreover, there are other important differences between the two theories. According to Freud's theory, an unconscious infantile wish *causes* the dream. The "background" thoughts of the dream may include any other mental state.

According to the classical theory, psychological states of all kinds are *displayed* in the dream. Historically, there is a diversity of opinion about dream causation, with unanimity, however, that psychological states are *at least* displayed. There is no particular emphasis on wishes. Other states, perceptions, intellectual puzzles, memories, intentions, fears, worries, and so on are equally important dream sources.

The Freudian interpretative technique is *free association* to segments of the dream. Classical interpretation depends upon the *discovery of a pictorial relationship* between the dream and a state of the dreamer. If no such relationship can be found, the dream cannot be interpreted. . . .

In spite of its great age, the traditional theory has been insufficiently tested. Dream researchers, when they have been occupied with psychoanalytic theory, have focused on Freud's hypotheses. Psychoanalysts, although relying on it, have in the past treated the classical theory as something of a stepchild, employing it ambivalently because of Freud's strictures against interpretation of the manifest dream. Yet, in spite of the paucity of the evidence garnered so far, the traditional dream theory is clearly superior to Freud's for the simple reason that the former does not depend upon free association and consequently, not being involved in the free association fallacy, escapes the charge that it systematically leads to erroneous conclusions. Relinquishing the hypothesis that free association provides a sure passage from a manifest dream to a latent dream concealed beneath it removes a major roadblock to mutual endeavors on the part of experimenters and clinicians. The traditional theory promises to open doors. Researchers are already focused upon it; clinicians are coming to understand its full significance. Perhaps these two groups, so often at odds in the past, may yet be tempted to work together. If they did so, then this hypothesis, whose roots are ancient, could be examined in an unprecedented manner. We might expect that, whatever the outcome of such joint research, the result would be the healing of the breach which, with a few notable exceptions, has separated these disciplines. The study of the dream could only benefit from their collaboration.

8

Error's Reign*

Sebastiano Timpanaro

Although the formidably complex *Interpretation of Dreams* (1900) took a while to find a wide audience, the game of seeking "Freudian meaning" everywhere caught on immediately through the most enduringly entertaining of Freud's works, *The Psychopathology of Everyday Life* (1901). What made both of those early books alluring wasn't just the keys they offered to finding low motives in unexpected places but also the image they projected of Freud himself as a master sleuth, very much in the mold of his favorite literary character, Sherlock Holmes (see Welsh, 1994). These are indeed works of detective fiction, featuring a hero who is every inch Holmes's equal as a tracer of the faintest clues and an infallible solver of puzzles that would daunt any ordinary mortal. And our awe is redoubled by our impression that we are *not* reading fiction but rather science in agreeably narrative form.

Freud himself, it appears, was taken in by his own pretense: he believed that if he could supply a "dynamic" explanation for virtually every reported dream or error, the soundness of his method would thereby be demonstrated. He thus overlooked the most fundamental requirement of investigative prudence, mistaking the mere thematic coherence produced by his method for proof that it was the single *reliable* method. We begin to approximate empirical rigor only when we ask whether some rival set of assumptions might make plausible sense of

* From *The Freudian Slip: Psychoanalysis and Textual Criticism*, 1974; trans. Kate Soper (London: NLB, 1976).

the same data while levying fewer demands on our trust; but Freud never did so, either in error analysis or in any other domain.

It was precisely in the spirit of comparing and weighing alternative explanations that the Italian linguist and textual critic Sebastiano Timpanaro examined Freud's theory of errors in the middle 1970s. Timpanaro's starting point was his awareness of the kinds of mistakes that typically result in the corruption of texts. In transcription, for example, scribes would often "banalize" an unusual word or phrase by replacing it with a more familiar expression or "disimprove" a term through an inadvisable attempt to correct it. Such emendations strikingly resemble many of the slips for which Freud provided "deep" psychodynamic explanations. *The Freudian Slip* shows that a psychoanalytic account of any error can be overmatched by a mere listing of alternatives that draw upon common sense, not on the postulates of a contested doctrine. Timpanaro's point is not that a given commonsense account has to be true but that its superior probability of being true robs the Freudian version of certainty.

Our selection begins after Timpanaro has summarized the second of two "specimen slips" that Freud employed at the outset of his *Psychopathology* to dazzle us with his interpretive acuity, just as he had done with a "specimen dream" in *The Interpretation of Dreams* (Glymour, 1983). In Timpanaro's summary:

> A young Austrian Jew, with whom Freud strikes up a conversation while travelling, bemoans the position of inferiority in which Jews are held in Austria-Hungary. . . . He becomes heated in discussing this problem, and tries to conclude his "passionately felt speech" . . . with the line that Virgil puts in the mouth of Dido abandoned by Aeneas and on the point of suicide: *Exoriare aliquis nostris ex ossibus ultor* (*Aeneid,* IV 625). ("Let someone arise from my bones as an Avenger" or "Arise from my bones, o Avenger, whoever you may be.") But his memory is imperfect, and all he succeeds in saying is *Exoriare ex nostris ossibus ultor:* i.e., he omits *aliquis* and inverts the words *nostris ex* (Timpanaro, 1976, pages 29–30).

To Timpanaro's eye, this appears to be a likely case of "banalization." Virgil's line is vexingly ambiguous—is, indeed, a famous crux for Latinists. But a young Austrian of average culture, for whom Dido's words were no doubt little more than a distant memory from grammar school, was led unconsciously to banalize the text, i.e., to assimilate it to his own linguistic sensibility. The unconscious elimination of *aliquis* corresponds precisely to this tendency: *exoriare ex nostris ossibus ultor* is a sentence which can be transposed perfectly into German without any need to strain the order of words (Timpanaro, 1976, pages 33–34).

Yet Freud, as we will see, discounted any such routine explanation and instead launched into a minipsychoanalysis of his compatriot, inferring triumphantly that the forgetting of *aliquis* must have been determined by the young man's fear that a certain lady may have become inconveniently pregnant.

Unlike most readers, who are awed by Freud's cultural sophistication and eager to bask in his cleverness, Timpanaro is not impressed by the string of multilingual puns that Freud "reconstructs" as the young man's chain of associations from pregnancy to *aliquis*. The textual scholar looks askance at agile leaps among several languages—so characteristic of Freud's idiosyncratic mind but so uncharacteristic of the way most of us think. And in fact, Timpanaro notes, key "associations" were fed directly to the young man and then analyzed as if they had been his own.

Above all, Timpanaro shows that any other word in Virgil's line besides *aliquis* could be connected, if one cared to try, to the same preoccupation with pregnancy that allegedly blocked *aliquis* from memory. Whereas Freud boasts that so many linked items surrounding *aliquis* could not have come together by chance, Timpanaro devastatingly counters that if you permit yourself *so many* steps to get from a slip to your hypothesized cause of it, jumbling your own associations with those of the subject, the "success" of your procedure is a foregone conclusion.

Although Timpanaro removed all persuasiveness from the *aliquis* episode in the 1970s, he at least considered it to be biographically genuine. Freud, however, was not above inventing such tales to embellish his theories; he had even confessed as much in one of his "seduction" papers (SE, 3: 196–197). There is now good reason to suspect that his encounter with the young Austrian never occurred at all.

(See Swales, 1982a.) If so, it is all the more striking that Freud couldn't assemble even a *fictitious* case that would logically justify his method of interpretation.

Now retired, Sebastiano Timpanaro trained in classical philology at the University of Florence before pursuing a career as a secondary school teacher, editor, and prolific author. His areas of interest have included eighteenth- and nineteenth-century cultural history and Marxist thought. *The Freudian Slip* was recently followed by a related study, as yet untranslated into English (Timpanaro, 1992).

With the young Austrian's consent, Freud subjects him to a miniature "analysis." Obviously, it cannot be considered as a real psychoanalytic session—just as in general *The Psychopathology of Everyday Life* is not concerned with real neuroses but with those "microneurotic" mechanisms that reveal themselves even in basically healthy people. However, the technique employed to go back to the cause of the young man's memory disturbance is, even in this case, that of "free association." Freud says: "I must only ask you to tell me *candidly* and *uncritically* whatever comes into your mind if you direct your attention to the forgotten word without any definite aim." Thus it happens that the young Jew, starting with the thought of *a-liquis,* and opportunely guided by Freud's . . . method, associates this word in succession with *Reliquien—Liquidation—Flüssigkeit—Fluid.* Then with St. Simon of Trent, the child whose murder was calumniously attributed in the fifteenth century to the Jews, and whose relics in Trent have been visited not long before by the young Jew. Then—through a succession of saints—with San Gennaro (St. Januarius) and the miracle of the clotted blood that liquefies, and the excitement that grips the more superstitious people of Naples if this liquefying process is retarded, an excitement expressed in picturesque invective and threats hurled at the saint. Finally, with the fact that he was himself obsessed with the thought of an "absent flow of liquid," since he was afraid he had made pregnant an Italian woman with whom he had been—among other places—in Naples, and was expecting to receive confirmation of his worst fears any day.

But there is more: one of the saints the young man thinks of after

St. Simon is St. Augustine, and Augustine and Januarius are both associated with the calendar (August and January), i.e., with expiry dates that
must have had a sinister ring for a young man afraid of becoming a
father. . . . Yet again: St. Simon was a child saint, another unpleasant idea.
He had been killed while still a baby: this connects with the temptation
of infanticide—or abortion as equivalent to infanticide. "I must leave it
to your own judgment," Freud concludes with satisfaction, "to decide
whether you can explain all these connexions by the assumption that they
are matters of chance. I can however tell you that every case like this that
you care to analyse will lead you to 'matters of chance' that are just as
striking."

Is the chain of associations linking the young Jew's forgetting of *aliquis*
in that line from Virgil with his confession of the fear afflicting him at the
time as cast-iron as it seemed to Freud—and, so far as I can make out,
seems today to all, or at least a majority of Freudians? I would answer no;
indeed, I am of the opinion that, beneath the brilliance of the intellectual
fireworks, few procedures can be reckoned so antiscientific as the one followed by Freud in this and so many other analogous cases.

The "associations" that Freud, in accordance with his well-known
method, allows his patient to generate spontaneously are of various kinds.
There are phonic similarities between words having quite different meanings or even belonging to different languages (e.g., between *aliquis* and
Reliquien). There are affinities between the meanings of phonically dis-
similar words (and here again it is irrelevant whether they belong to
the same language or not—e.g., the affinity between *Liquidation* and
Flüssigkeit-Fluid). There are also all sorts of factual and conceptual connexions (Simon, Augustine, and Januarius were all saints; St. Januarius—
San Gennaro—is connected with Naples, and the miracle of San Gennaro
concerns the liquefying of blood, etc.). Now we are not concerned to
deny, in the abstract, the possibility of all these forms of association
(except in one case: the excessive ease with which translation from one's
mother tongue into other languages is employed). Rather, our concern is
to point out that by passing through so wide a range of transitions, one
can reach a single point of arrival from any point of departure whatever.

If there really did exist a causal relationship between the young Austrian's forgetting of *aliquis* and his fear of the Neapolitan woman's pregnancy, . . . then one would have to conclude that the young man had to
disturb *that* word and no other—either by forgetting it, or remembering it

in an altered form, or introducing it in a context where it was not needed. Stretching the point a little, one might go so far as to admit that a single unpleasant thought, if consciously repressed, might give rise to diverse symptoms—in this particular case, the forgetting of various words. But one certainly could not admit that the imperfect recall or outright forgetting of *any* word in the line from Virgil could equally well be counted as a symptom. In that case, with the one cause producing any number of effects, the concept of causal relationship would lose all significance. So we should expect that if we take a series of counterexamples—i.e., if we suppose that some other word in that line from the *Aeneid* was forgotten—then the chain of associations will break down, or will be less convincing than in the "authentic" case narrated by Freud.

Very well, then, let us suppose that instead of forgetting *aliquis,* the young Austrian slipped up on *exoriare,* "arise." He would have had no difficulty in connecting the idea of "arising" with that of "birth" (*exoriare* can have both meanings): the birth, alas, of a child—so feared by him. Next let us suppose that he forgot *nostris:* the Latin adjective *noster* would have brought to mind the Catholic *Pater noster,* . . . and he could easily connect God the Father with the saints, and—passing from saint to saint—eventually with San Gennaro and the feared failure of the woman to menstruate; or more directly, the thought of the Father in heaven would have aroused in the young man his fear of soon becoming a father on this earth. Now let us suppose he forgot *ossibus:* bones are typical relics of Catholic saints, and having once reached the thought of relics of various kinds, the way was again wide open to San Gennaro; or the well-educated young man's mind might have connected *os* "bone" with *os* (pronounced with a long ō) "mouth," and thence with the passionate kisses between himself and the woman, and with all the compromising events that followed the kisses (perhaps Freud would at this point have added one of those polyglot digressions he loved so much, on the euphemistic use of the verb *baiser* in French). Finally, what if he forgot *ultor?* In this case several itineraries were possible. *Ultor* does not sound too different from *Eltern* ("parents" in German), and this word would have led our young man back to the painful thought of himself and the woman as parents of the child that was perhaps already conceived. . . .

Are these connexions that I have amused myself thinking up (and which could be varied and expanded at will) grotesque ones? Of course they are. But are the connexions via which Freud explains, or rather makes his interlocutor explain, the forgetting of *aliquis* any less grotesque or less "random"? . . .

The "interpretative mechanism" of psychoanalysis, rightly observes Gilles Deleuze, "can be summarized as follows: whatever you say, it means something else." In compliance with this norm, Freud asks the young man to "attend all the same to the associations starting from *exoriare,*" and he is given the word *Exorzismus.* This reply, we may note, should scarcely come as any surprise, for if one consults a German dictionary, one finds that, apart from *Exordium* and *Exorbitanz,* both rare words, the only German word beginning with *exor-* is precisely *Exorzismus.* But Freud at once sees in the word *Exorzismus* a harking back to the names of the saints (insofar as they were endowed with the power to exorcize the devil), with once again the possibility of connecting with San Gennaro and everything that follows.

Later, in an addendum to this same footnote written in 1924, Freud refers to the opinion expressed by P. Wilson, who attributed even more significance to the idea of exorcism but interpreted it in yet another way, without passing via San Gennaro: "Exorcism would be the best symbolic substitute for repressed thoughts about getting rid of the unwanted child by abortion." Here is Freud's unruffled comment: "I gratefully accept this correction, which does not weaken the validity [literally: the rigorous, inexorable character, *Verbindlichkeit*] of the analysis." Thus, provided one eventually succeeds in establishing a causal link between the unfortunate young man's quotation from Virgil and his fear of the woman's pregnancy, it is irrelevant whether one takes as the revealing symptom his forgetting of *aliquis* or his particularly intense recollection of *exoriare* (explained in turn, as we have seen, in two different ways)! The curious thing is that Freud sees this profusion of competing explanations as confirmation of his method's validity, without ever asking himself whether this superabundance, this unlimited supply of explanations, might not be an indication of the weakness of his construction, or without asking himself whether this might not demonstrate the "nonfalsifiability," and hence absence of any probative value, of the method he employs.

I have used a term, "falsifiability," which may legitimately give rise to interminable epistemological disputes—arguments between "verificationists" and "falsificationists"; arguments over the so-called *experimentum crucis,* to which strong objections have been made and whose validity is now generally denied; arguments over the distinction between "verification" and "confirmation" and over the priority of the latter. However, I would maintain that the counterexamples given here and others developed later are pertinent at a much more modest and artisanal level, and for that very reason are valid irrespective of rarefied epistemological debates. . . . It will always be true that a theory, or a particular explanation that claims to be scientific, must not be such as to elude all forms of control. One must be able to conceive of an empirical fact that, if it were true, would disprove the theory or explanation in question. If this is not possible, if the explanation for one determinate fact could with equal facility explain any other fact, then one must conclude that this explanation has no scientific value. Such an objection is being more and more frequently levelled at psychoanalysis; and to my knowledge it has not yet been answered. . . .

We may also note the "suggestive" character of many of Freud's interventions in the dialogue. The method of "free association" (*free* from external interferences and from critical interpellations by the subject himself, and precisely for that reason conforming to a strict causal concatenation), which the person under analysis is requested to respect, ought, as we know, to be matched by a corresponding method of "suspended attention" on the part of the analyst: up till the moment of interpretation, the analyst, like his patient, should abstain from any critical filtering of the discourse that would prematurely privilege certain of its elements at the expense of others. Adherence to this norm is difficult, if not impossible, and this is known to be one of the main reasons—there are others—why it remains an issue of contention among Freud's successors, many of whom have abandoned it.

On the other hand, in very few accounts of cases of analysis does it appear to be so openly flouted as in the episode currently engaging our attention. . . . For example, when the young Austrian says that he recalls a companion he encountered on a journey the previous week by the name of Benedict, Freud intervenes to say that this name, like those previously recollected, Simon and Augustine, is that of a saint, and thus puts the sequence of remembrance "back on the track" from which it had threatened to go astray. Indeed, since this Benedict was described by the young man as *ein wahrer Original* ("a real original"), Freud adds, with apparent indifference, that "There was, I think, a Church Father called Origen"; the remark is not followed up directly then, but it represents a kind of "card up the sleeve" whose value is by no means negligible, be this because

Origen's principal claim to fame lies in his self-castration, or because the second element of the name, derived from the Greek root designating generation or birth, can summon forth various associations of a sexual nature, should there be a need of these. . . .

More significant, however, than Freud's particular interventions in the dialogue is the generally suggestive atmosphere in which the young Jew found himself immersed from the beginning of the conversation. Though he had only once met Freud in person before, on an earlier holiday trip, he was acquainted with Freud's writings on psychology—as Freud himself tells us. . . . He knows he is face to face with the fearsome Doctor Freud, who, they say—and it seems true from what he has read himself—is able to extort confessions even of what is least confessable. He is intrigued as to whether Freud will succeed in this respect with him, too, though he is already half convinced that he will; and he is further confirmed in this belief because Freud cheats a little: whereas in the past he has admitted that analyses have failed because the resistances were too strong, on this occasion he boasts a complete confidence, claiming that the analysis "should not take us long." Before the analysis has proceeded very far, the young man asks: "Have you discovered anything yet?" It is the creation of this sort of fatalistic conviction—that "one cannot oppose Freud"; that no matter how strong one's resistance, one's secret will certainly be extracted—which, more than any of the specific promptings we have noted, is the most powerful means of suggestion at Freud's disposal.

This is even more true of the present case, where the secret is not concealed in the depths of the unconscious: the young man's anxiety about the Italian woman's possible pregnancy was actual and present, and not a repressed thought. . . . It is precisely because the fear of becoming a father was the secret "dominating" the young man's thoughts that it was also the idea which he found the most unpleasant to disclose, and yet, whether consciously or not, most drawn to confess. If this was the situation, it matters little that what gave rise to the interrogation was the forgetting of *aliquis.* Some other "slip," some other parapraxis, some more trivial manifestation of nervousness, could have functioned just as well as the starting point for an analysis which in each case would have led to the same conclusion. . . .

Yet Freud still induced his interlocutor not only to confess his anxiety but also . . . to grant the correctness of Freud's explanation of his "slip." We touch here on a problem which Freud dealt with explicitly in the third of his *Lectures* of 1915–16, where he speculates on the possibility of a psychoanalytic explanation being rejected by the person who committed the "slip." Whom ought we to believe in such an event? According to Freud, the analyst. But, he goes on to say, his audience will object: "So that's your technique [. . .] When a person who has made a 'slip of the tongue' says something about it that suits you [i.e., admits to the repressed thought responsible for its production] you pronounce him to be the final decisive authority on the subject. [. . .] But when what he says doesn't suit your book, then all at once you say he's of no importance— there's no need to believe him." Freud then replies: "That is quite true. But I can put a similar case to you in which the same monstrous event occurs. When someone charged with an offence confesses his deed to the judge, the judge believes his confession. If it were otherwise, there would be no administration of justice, and in spite of occasional errors we must allow that the system works." Thus to the question he then imagines put to him: "Are you a judge then? And is a person who has made a 'slip of the tongue' brought up before you on a charge? So making a 'slip of the tongue' is an offence, is it?" He replies. "Perhaps we need not reject the comparison," and proposes to his audience (my emphasis) "*a provisional compromise,* on the basis of the analogy with the judge and the defendant. I suggest that you shall grant me that there can be no doubt of a parapraxis having sense if the subject himself admits it. *I* will admit in return that we cannot arrive at a direct proof of the suspected sense if the subject refuses us information, . . . and equally, of course, if he is not at hand to give us information."

The comparison between the relationship of judge and defendant and that of analyst and patient reveals a generally authoritarian conception of psychiatry and medicine; moreover, even within the framework of such a conception, the psychological criteria to which it appeals are extraordinarily short-sighted. One is inclined to say that this investigator of the many complexities of "depth psychology" was possessed of an oddly simplistic vision when it came to certain mechanisms of "superficial psychology," with which even a bourgeois judge of not particularly retrograde tendency or a moderately enlightened teacher is familiar—and would have been in Freud's day also. The truthfulness of any confession is accepted by Freud without question, and the judge (and the psychologist and the teacher) is thereby exempted from any further need to verify it. The possibility that, even apart from any violent form of coercion, an accused (or patient, or pupil, or child) might be induced by the suggestions of an interrogation to "confess" to things which he had not done—taking "things" to include not only actions themselves but at least as much thoughts, intentions, motivations of acts—is blithely ignored.

Furthermore, when Freud speaks of "the admission of the sense of a parapraxis" here, he conflates two very different facts. We have already remarked on the difference between them in our treatment of the forgetting of *aliquis:* on the one hand there is the fact—this, to be sure, is undeniable—that the young Austrian feared news of the Italian woman's pregnancy; on the other hand, there is the presumed causal chain which is supposed to link this fact with the forgetting of *aliquis.* Now, confronted with a Freud already possessed of a theory of "slips" who is in a position (by way of the acrobatics and "unfalsifiable" links we have noted) to conjoin everything with everything, and who responds to a doubt expressed by the young Austrian as to the relationship between two thoughts with brusque authority: "You can leave the connexion to me," the patient is in an obviously inferior situation because he has no alternative explanation at his disposal. He is therefore inevitably induced to believe that if Freud, who has taken his cue from a true fact (the forgetting of *aliquis*), has managed to make him "blurt out" another true fact whose confession is unpleasant (the fear of the woman's pregnancy), then the procedure adopted must have been scientifically correct. However, the counterexamples I have already given show us that things are not as straightforward as that.

Moreover, for Freud any denial of the charge by the defendant, or of the explanation of the "slip" by the patient, though it is certainly regarded as a complicating factor in the work of the judge or the analyst, cannot be allowed as much weight as attaches to the conviction that the charge or the explanation is justified. Let us take heed of those words we have just stressed: "provisional compromise." Freud contents himself with this formula because he cannot hope in a single lecture to overcome the scepticism and, above all, the "resistances" of his audience. But the word "compromise" clearly indicates that, in his opinion, the real solution is something other than this: the patient is always, or nearly always, wrong when he makes a denial, because every negation on his part is in reality a manifestation of resistance, and thus an involuntary confession. . . .

A teacher notices some breach of discipline, and asks: "Who did that?" A young pupil, either because he knows he is already under suspicion for his misbehaviour on other occasions or because he sees, or thinks he sees, the teacher's gaze fixed on him, hastens to answer: "It wasn't me!" If the teacher (though the same applies, with minor modifications, to the officer of the law or the psychoanalyst) concludes: "So he was the one," he will err in a very high percentage of cases. Thus once again we register the way in which his zeal for his own theses rendered the master of depth psychology extraordinarily unaware of any of the subtleties of "superficial psychology."

9

Can Intuitive Proof Suffice?*

Barbara Von Eckardt

If Freud remained confident that psychoanalysis was on the right track even while his patients went uncured and his theory kept bumping against contradictions, it was because he possessed an ultimate faith in what Barbara Von Eckardt here calls "explanatory power," or the feeling of congruence and closure that he gained from finding thematic connections everywhere. This chapter shows how far short of adequacy such a criterion falls. Drawing from philosophers of science as disparate in perspective as Ernest Nagel (1959), Karl Popper (1962), and Adolf Grünbaum (papers preceding his *Foundations*, 1984), Von Eckardt upholds a cardinal principle to which all of those thinkers subscribe: a good scientific theory must be not only coherent in itself but also demonstrably superior to its competitors.

Freud, however, dealt with nonpsychoanalytic ideas not by actually weighing them but by stigmatizing their proponents as too cowardly to face the hard truths of his own doctrine. Meanwhile, as Von Eckardt shows, his belief in the all-sufficiency of "clinical evidence" meant that other explanations than his own never troubled him. Why, when his puzzle pieces always fell right into place, should he bother with experiments that might test the comparative merits of rival theories?

Von Eckardt's critique of this position gains strength from its scrupulous impersonality. She joins Grünbaum (1984, 1993) and

* From "The Scientific Status of Psychoanalysis," in *Introducing Psychoanalytic Theory*, ed. Sander L. Gilman (New York: Brunner/Mazel, 1982), pp. 139–180.

Edward Erwin (1996) in setting aside Freud's actual conduct, which was often alarmingly opportunistic, and instead taking at face value his announced methodological standards. Such generosity is not motivated by any softness toward psychoanalysis. On the contrary: if Freudian truth claims *at their best* remain empirically inadequate, that point is more devastating than any evidence that Freud failed to practice what he preached.

Barbara Von Eckardt is Associate Dean of the College of Arts and Sciences at the University of Nebraska-Lincoln; she was formerly Chair of the Department of Philosophy. Her writings include the book *What Is Cognitive Science?* (1993).

The scientific status of Freudian psychoanalysis has been challenged with respect not only to its theories, but also to its methodology. However, despite the repeated presentation by critics of certain features of Freud's methodology as problematic, the challenge to Freud's method has never been as clearly formulated as the challenge to his theory. The difficulty is, of course, that if such a challenge is to assume the same logical structure as Karl Popper's and Ernest Nagel's challenge with respect to psychoanalytic theory, then something must be said about what makes a research methodology scientific. And this is a notoriously difficult and controversial topic. Nevertheless, to get a clearer picture of the scientific status of the Freudian methodology, I shall attempt to tackle this difficult question. I shall try not only to identify those aspects of Freud's methodology that are troublesome, but also to indicate *why* they are troublesome in the light of standard scientific practice. . . .

That a theory or hypothesis can explain some set of relevant data is a minimal condition of its acceptability. But more than this is required because, given any set of data, there is always more than one possible explanation. The role of the second property, thus, is to distinguish among these possible explanations. Popper's notion of a risky prediction permits us to distinguish between explanations that follow from our background beliefs and those that follow from the theory under consideration. But this is not enough, for there may be more than one *new* way of explaining the data. Thus, a good scientific test distinguishes, in principle, between the theory in question and rival theories (both old and new) to as great an extent as possible. . . .

A number of aspects of Freud's methodology are troublesome when compared to this scientific ideal. First, Freud restricted himself to clinical observation as the basis for confirming his theories. This emphasis on clinical observation was, undoubtedly, initially the result of his interest in using his theories as a basis for therapy, but the restriction was more than just a practical one. As we have seen, Freud made it a matter of principle.

The difficulty with this restriction to clinical data is not that it makes prediction impossible, as some have thought, but that, for the most part, it makes prediction on the basis of a good scientific test impossible. The reason is this. A good scientific test is one that *discriminates* between the theory under consideration and rival theories. It is a test which, if successful, significantly cuts down the class of hypotheses compatible with the data. . . . Rival theories often make similar predictions over a wide range of circumstances. To distinguish between them one must be able to isolate that one circumstance which will make a difference. But this is precisely what is impossible if one bars the use of experimental manipulation in principle. A reliance on data acquired by observation rather than experimental control is a reliance on data determined by circumstances as they *happen to occur* rather than as they are required by the demands of a good scientific test.

In fact, for the most part, Freud did not even avail himself of the predictive possibilities that exist within the clinical setting. He seems to have believed that a theory could be justified solely on the basis of its explanatory power. If we take a close look at how Freud came to adopt his various theories, we see that he typically proceeded in the following way. First, he starts with various background assumptions—either inherited from other thinkers or determined by those of his own theories to which he is already committed. These, in conjunction with various observations, give rise to certain questions. Next, he attempts to formulate an answer to these questions, and this answer constitutes his tentative hypothesis. He then attempts to justify his hypothesis by seeking further observations explainable by the hypothesis. If he finds such additional observations, he takes the hypothesis to be confirmed. However, if he comes upon evidence which does not fit his hypothesis, then the original hypothesis is frequently revised. The revised version is then tentatively accepted until such time as further recalcitrant data are found. Note that at no time in this process is the tentatively accepted hypothesis—either original or revised—subjected to rigorous predictive tests. As long as it can explain all relevant data at hand, Freud regards it as acceptable. . . .

Freud was so impressed with the explanatory value of his repression hypothesis vis-à-vis the phenomenon of resistance that he reported the following in his "Five Lectures on Psycho-analysis": "I gave the name of 'repression' to this hypothetical process, and *I considered that it was proved by the undeniable existence of resistance*" (emphasis added). Now, why did he consider it proved? The only possible answer is that he regarded it as proved because of its *explanatory value*. And this was so because he regarded a high degree of explanatory power as sufficient for the justification of a scientific theory. But, as we have seen, according to the standard scientific methodology this is not enough. A theory is not sufficiently justified unless it has been submitted to a variety of good scientific tests. And here Freud's methodology systematically falls short.

There is an additional requirement for assessing a theory or hypothesis in a scientific way—whether in terms of its explanatory power or in terms of its success on good scientific tests—and that concerns the nature of the data against which the assessment is made. The traditional way of putting this requirement is to say that data must be *objective*. But what do we mean by this?

Naively, to say data are objective is to say that they reflect the way things really are (in the object) rather than something in the person (subject) gathering the data. . . . Drawing largely on work in the psychology of perception, however, such critics as Norwood R. Hanson and Thomas Kuhn have suggested that observation always involves interpretation and that such interpretation is relative to a person's conceptual apparatus, beliefs, expectations. Observation is—as the slogan goes— "theory-laden.". . .

But it is possible for observation to be both theory-laden and theory-neutral in all the ways that matter: theory-laden in a way that satisfies the demands of empirical findings in the psychology of perception, yet theory-neutral in the sense that what one observes is not influenced by the *particular* theory undergoing assessment. That the scientific theories and hypotheses to which we are committed *can* and often do influence our perception of the world does not entail that they *must* do so. The ideal of objective data is possible at least to this extent: that data relevant to a given theory T can be collected by someone whether or not he or she believes in T or even, in fact, whether or not he or she has knowledge of T. Ronald N. Giere puts the point this way: The prediction of a good scientific test "must be a statement that can reliably be determined to be true or false using methods that do not themselves presuppose that the hypothesis in question is true." . . .

We have seen that the data Freud relied on most heavily for the justification of his mature etiological hypotheses were data concerning the meaning or significance of his patient's dreams, slips of the tongue, jokes, and symptoms. All were regarded by Freud as expressions of the unconscious, and all thus could be used to make inferences concerning the character of a person's repressed unconscious states. The procedure Freud developed for getting at these unconscious states consisted in eliciting from the patient descriptions of thoughts, feelings, and memories, reports of dreams, unconscious verbal slips, plus associations to each of these, and then subjecting this "clinical material" to a process of interpretation. The results of this process were *interpretations* which then constituted the evidential basis for his theoretical claims.

We have argued that a necessary condition of a research methodology being scientific is that the data it uses as the basis for accepting or rejecting a candidate hypothesis must be objective. The question now before us is this: Does the psychoanalytic method satisfy this requirement of objectivity? I shall argue that it does not—at least in its original Freudian form. It does not because the process Freud used to arrive at interpretations he took to be correct was theoretically biased in an unacceptable way.

To make our case, we should first examine how Freud himself describes the method of interpretation at various points in his career. Initially, he appears to have regarded the process of interpretation as a rule-governed procedure whose correct utilization insured that the practitioner would sooner or later arrive at a correct interpretation. In 1904, he described the method thus:

> Freud has developed [. . .] an art of interpretation which takes on the task of, as it were, extracting the pure metal of the repressed thoughts from the ore of the unintentional ideas. This work of interpretation is applied not only to the patient's ideas but also to his dreams, which open up the most direct approach to a knowledge of the unconscious, to his uninten-

tional as well as to his purposeless actions (symptomatic acts) and to the blunders he makes in everyday life (slips of the tongue, bungled actions, and so on). The details of this technique of interpretation or translation have not yet been published by Freud. According to indications he has given, they comprise *a number of rules, reached empirically, of how the unconscious material may be reconstructed from the associations,* directions on how to know what it means when the patient's ideas cease to flow and experiences of the most important typical resistances that arise in the course of such treatments [emphasis added].

By 1923 his picture is quite different. The process of interpretation is now no longer seen as a rule-governed procedure. Rather, Freud conceives of it as a process of insightful problem-solving. Assigning an interpretation to a dream is like finding the solution to an extremely complicated jigsaw puzzle. The solution is not obtained by following rules, but by trial and error coupled with creative insight.

Despite Freud's altered conception, however, this view has something important in common with the rule-governed procedure. In both cases, the method of interpretation is regarded as a *discovery procedure,* such that if the procedure is carried out correctly, discovery of the actual meaning of the phenomenon being interpreted will result. What insures the correct outcome on Freud's first picture of the procedure are the rules themselves: what insures the correct outcome on the insightful problem-solving view are a number of *constraints* which must be satisfied for something to count as a solution to the problem. When an analyst considers whether or not a given interpretation is correct, according to Freud:

> What makes him certain in the end is precisely the complication of the problem before him, which is like the solution of a jigsaw puzzle. A coloured picture, pasted upon a thin sheet of wood and fitting exactly into a wooden frame, is cut into a large number of pieces of the most irregular and crooked shapes. If one succeeds in arranging the confused heap of fragments, each of which bears upon it an unintelligible piece of drawing, so that the picture acquires a meaning, so that *there is no gap anywhere in the design and so that the whole fits into the*

frame—if all these conditions are fulfilled, then one knows that one has solved the puzzle and that there is no alternative solution [emphasis added].

Freud is clearly assuming that "gestalt" constraints analogous to those for a jigsaw puzzle apply in an interpretation, and that if these constraints are satisfied, a given interpretation will be correct.

He is not always this confident about the reliability of his procedure, however. As early as the 1917 lectures, he acknowledges that the physician may infer something "wrongly." But he does not seem to regard the problem as a serious one, for "anything that has been inferred wrongly by the physician will disappear in the course of the analysis; it must be withdrawn and replaced by something more correct." What he means, of course, is that any mistaken interpretations will be corrected in the course of a *successful* analysis, that is, one in which the patient succeeds in overcoming inner resistances and achieving positive inner change.

This point is discussed at length twenty years later. Distinguishing between "interpretation," which applies to "some single element of material, such as an association or a parapraxis," and "construction," when one "lays before the subject of the analysis a piece of his early history that he has forgotten," Freud now compares construction to an archaeologist's excavation of some dwelling place that has been destroyed and buried. The new metaphor allows him to recognize that constructions, like archaeological hypotheses, are subject to "difficulties and sources of error." That is, no *discovery procedure* can guarantee the correctness of the proposed construction or hypothesis. This recognition gives rise to the following question: "What guarantee [do] we have while we are working on these constructions that we are not making mistakes and risking the success of the treatment by putting forward some construction that is incorrect?" His answer, in short, is that "only the further course of the analysis enables us to decide whether our constructions are correct or unserviceable"—in particular, what further associations the proposed construction gives rise to in the patient, whether the analysis is therapeutically successful, and whether the patient comes to accept the truth of the construction.

This last picture of the method of interpretation does not so much undercut the insightful problem-solving view as force a revision in it. Individual interpretations (that is, interpretations of elements of the manifest content of a dream, single slips of the tongue, single symptoms, etc.) are arrived at by insight. To be correct, however, such interpretations must satisfy two sets of constraints: internal and external. The internal constraints are the gestalt constraints mentioned previously. Roughly, individual interpretations are correct only if they fit together into a meaningful whole—a "construction" in Freud's mature terminology—that makes sense of all the clinical material. But this is not sufficient, for Freud now admits that such an internally coherent construction might be false. Thus, as a further guarantee of its correctness, it must satisfy an external constraint: It must be a construction that, roughly speaking, plays a central role in a successful analysis.

If we assume this amalgamated picture to reflect fairly closely both Freud's mature view and his practice, we can now understand why Freud devotes so little time to *defending* the sample interpretations he gives us in his writings, especially in the context of the case studies. Explicit defense is not required, for what justifies a given interpretation in his view is given implicitly. The case studies present individual interpretations as part of a *whole construction;* furthermore, they are, presumably, case studies of *successful* (at least, in Freud's mind) analyses. In other words, that any given interpretation satisfies both internal and external constraints is implicit in the context in which these interpretations are given to the reader.

We are now in a position to evaluate Freud's method of interpretation as good scientific method. Precisely, what is it about Freud's use of the method of interpretation which raises questions about its scientific status? . . . Freud claimed his theories to be empirically well supported primarily on the basis of claims arrived at by the method of interpretation. These interpretative claims constituted his "data." The issue, then, is whether they were arrived at independently of the theory they were designed to support. The answer is clearly "no," but there are both simple-minded and more complex accounts that lead to this answer.

First, the simple-minded account. If we look carefully at the interpretations Freud offers us in his various case studies, it becomes readily apparent that his theoretical commitments strongly influence the kind of interpretations he comes up with. This happens in two ways. First, he often either actively solicits key associations (the material upon which interpretations are based) from his patients or actually supplies them himself. Second, in arriving at interpretations that satisfy the gestalt constraints, the fundamental guiding principle that Freud seems to employ is "closeness of fit" with his theory. That is, what makes the separate interpretative pieces fit together is no more than that they all fit the theory.

However, that his theory plays a significant role in the *generation* of interpretative claims is not alone sufficient to undercut the objectivity of Freud's interpretative data. . . . The problem arises only given the "theory-ladenness" of the Freudian interpretations coupled with a second fact, namely that *the external constraint that Freud relies on to insure the correctness of his interpretations is inadequate to do the job.* This, then, is the complex account of why Freud's method of interpretation fails the requirement of objectivity.

Adolf Grünbaum has recently discussed in considerable detail the pitfalls associated with using claims of therapeutic success as empirical support for Freudian theory. . . . Showing that the therapeutic success of psychoanalysis exceeds the spontaneous remission rate is not sufficient. . . . It must further be shown that the relative success is due to features of the analytic situation *characteristic* of the psychoanalytic method, such as the use of the method of interpretation. But this is precisely what has not been shown. In fact, outcome studies suggest (a) that the success of psychoanalytic therapy may be due to *incidental* features of the situation, such as the establishment of a trust relationship between two people, and (b) that nonanalytic therapeutic techniques can be equally effective. . . .

In summary, assessment of the Freudian research methodology requires that we say something about what makes a research methodology scientific. Two requirements are the so-called requirement of a good scientific test and the so-called requirement of objectivity. The way Freud typically went about justifying his theoretical claims fails both of these requirements. His research methodology fails the requirement of a good scientific test because of his reliance on the clinical setting for gathering data and because of his reliance on explanatory power as a sufficient mark of truth. It fails the requirement of objectivity because the sort of data he relied on most heavily, interpretative data, was typically arrived at by assuming the truth of the very theories it was intended to support. . . .

Is psychoanalysis scientific? We can summarize our findings in this way: Freudian theory is perfectly scientific in the sense of being a *candidate* for scientific testing, so long as we do not restrict ourselves to Freud's methodological assumptions. However, since Freud's own research methodology was seriously deficient from a scientific point of view, the *orthodox* grounds for regarding the theory as empirically well founded are not acceptable. Neither Freudian interpretations that appear to support the theory nor the success of analysis as a therapeutic technique provide scientifically acceptable evidence for the truth of the theory. Thus, although the theory can be considered scientific in the minimal sense, whether it will prove to be *good* science remains to be seen.

10

Claims Without Commitments*

Frank Cioffi

This essay of 1970 by Frank Cioffi (see also Chapter 3) was the first
of our selections to see print, near the outset of the "Freud revolution." In some respects, however, it constitutes the boldest of all brief
challenges to classical psychoanalysis. As his original title indicated—
"Psychoanalysis and the Idea of a Pseudo-Science"—Cioffi is here concerned with the features that place Freudianism outside the circle of
authentic empirical endeavor. A pseudoscience, on Cioffi's reckoning,
betrays itself as such by its proponents' consistent record of flight from
criticism. By this criterion, he argues, psychoanalysis qualifies as the
paradigmatic modern pseudoscience.

According to Cioffi, the telltale signs of pseudoscientific practice are,
first, a liberality in adding ambiguities and escape clauses to the doctrine's claims, so that no seeming disconfirmation can ever be decisive;
second, a weakening of the very idea that self-contradiction is a sign
of trouble; third, an appeal to the proviso that only practitioners of
the doctrine's special method of knowledge acquisition are entitled to
evaluate its results; fourth, recourse to quasi-physical terminology
that creates an impression of precision while actually allowing "the
quantitative factor" to serve as an excuse for the failure of predicted
effects to materialize; and finally, the maintenance of a pretense,
despite all evidence to the contrary, that independent validation has

* From "Freud and the Idea of a Pseudo-Science," in *Explanation in the Behavioural Sciences*, ed.
Robert Borger (Cambridge: Cambridge University Press, 1970): 471–499.

already been demonstrated. The great merit of Cioffi's perspective, as applied to psychoanalysis, is that it reaches beyond specific claims and assesses the haphazard, opportunistic character of the total Freudian system. Freud, he shows, left a telltale paper trail of incompatible claims, each of which answered in its moment to the pseudoscientist's immediate need to fend off counterevidence, but all of which, taken collectively, bespeak a fundamental break with empiricism. And the record of his successors in brushing aside challenges has only compounded that evasiveness.

The references to pyramidology, numerology, and so forth found in Cioffi's concluding paragraph are fully explained in an omitted portion of the essay. The general drift, however, should be clear: psychoanalytic interpretation is made up of arbitrary acts of conjecture that fashion a kind of coherence instead of discovering it within the person or text being studied.

A successful pseudoscience is a great intellectual achievement. Its study is as instructive and worth undertaking as that of a genuine one. In this paper I shall maintain that psychoanalysis is such a pseudoscience; that the character of this claim has often been misunderstood; and that when it is understood its intractability is less surprising.

Psychoanalysis may be described as an attempt to determine the historicity and/or pathogenicity of episodes in a person's infantile past, and the character of his unconscious affective life and its influence over his behaviour, by the manner in which he responds to assertions or speculations concerning these—not however, just *any* attempt, but a particular, historically identifiable one which issued in a body of aetiological and dynamic theses, the abiding core of which is Freud's claim that "only sexual wishful impulses from infancy are able to furnish the motive force for the formation of psycho-neurotic symptoms." In attempting to assess the genuinely empirical character of such an enterprise, the statements we must subject to scrutiny are not merely those in which the claims that are the ostensible object of investigation are advanced, but also those that describe, or enable us to infer, what the procedures of investigation are. A pseudoscience is not constituted merely by formally defective theses but by methodologically defective procedures. . . .

For an activity to be scientific it is not enough that there should be states of affairs that would constitute disconfirmation of the theses it purports to investigate; it must also be the case that its procedure should be such that it is calculated to discover whether such states of affairs exist. I use the word "calculated" advisedly. For to establish that an enterprise is pseudoscientific it is not sufficient to show that the procedures it employs would *in fact* prevent or obstruct the discovery of disconfirmatory states of affairs but that it is *their function* to obstruct such discovery. To claim that an enterprise is pseudoscientific is to claim that it involves the habitual and wilful employment of methodologically defective procedures (in a sense of wilful that encompasses refined self-deception).

It is characteristic of a pseudoscience that the hypotheses that comprise it stand in an asymmetrical relation to the expectations they generate, being permitted to guide them and be vindicated by their fulfilment but not to be discredited by their disappointment. One way in which it achieves this is by contriving to have these hypotheses understood in a narrow and determinate sense before the event but a broader and hazier one after it on those occasions on which they are not borne out. Such hypotheses thus lead a double life—a subdued and restrained one in the vicinity of counterobservations and another, less inhibited and more exuberant, one when remote from them. This feature won't reveal itself to simple inspection. If we want to determine whether the role played by these assertions is a genuinely empirical one, it is necessary to discover what *their proponents* are prepared to call disconfirmatory evidence, not what *we* do.

An example of this is provided by what Freud calls his "Libido Theory" of the neuroses. Freud makes many remarks whose bearing seems to be that the sexual nature of the neuroses is an inference from the character of the states that predispose towards them, or of the vicissitudes that induce them, i.e., that their causes are to be found "in the intimacies of the patient's psychosexual life." The importance of this claim for our present purpose is that it would relieve our doubts about the validity of the psychoanalytic method if the inferences to which it leads as to "which the repressed impulse is, what substitutive symptoms it has found, and where the motive for repression lies" were corroborated by independent investigation of the patient's sexual life, as, for example, Freud's aetiology of the actual neuroses was (presumably) corroborated. But the claims that constitute Freud's libido theory are only apparently assessable by an investigation of the relation between the patient's sexual life and his accesses of illness.

Here are some assertions of Freud's by means of which the impression that they are so assessable is produced:

> Whenever a commonplace emotion must be included among the causative factors of the illness, analysis will regularly show that the pathogenic effect has been exercised by the ever present sexual element in the traumatic occurrence.

> In the ensuing remarks, which are based on impressions obtained empirically, it is proposed to describe those changes of conditions which operate to bring about the onset of neurotic illness in a person predisposed to it. The following view [. . .] connects the changes to be described entirely with the libido of the person concerned.

> Human beings fall ill when [. . .] the satisfaction of their erotic needs in reality is frustrated.

> Patients fall ill owing to frustration in love—(owing to the claims of the libido being unsatisfied [. . .]).

> People fall ill of a neurosis when the possibility of satisfaction through the libido is removed from them. . . .

These statements certainly look like hypotheses. But our hopes that Freud might be placing a limit on the kinds of events or states that are conducive to the onset of neurosis, and that he might then go on to tell us what these are, are dashed when we read: "We see people fall ill who have hitherto been healthy, to whom no new experience has presented itself, whose relation to the outer world has presented no change.[. . .]" Though they rise again when Freud goes on to say:

> Closer scrutiny of such cases shows us nevertheless that a change has taken place [. . .] the quantity of libido in their mental economy has increased to an extent which by itself

sufficed to upset the balance of health and establish the conditions for a neurosis [. . .] this warns us never to leave the quantitative factor out of consideration when we are dealing with the outbreak of the illness.

But what are these changes in the mental economy that "closer scrutiny" reveals? Once again Freud keeps the word of promise to our ears and breaks it to our hopes: "We cannot measure the amount of libido essential to produce pathological effects. We can only postulate it after the effects of the illness have manifested themselves."

For instance, this is how the apparent counter-examples constituted by the war neuroses are assimilated to the libido theory. Freud says that those who had observed "traumatic neuroses, which so often follow upon a narrow escape from death, triumphantly announced that proof was now forthcoming that a threat to the instinct of self-preservation could by itself produce a neurosis without any admixture of sexual factors," but that "any such contradiction has long since been disposed of by the introduction of the concept of narcissism, which brings the libidinal cathexis of the ego into line with the cathexis of objects and emphasises the libidinal character of the instinct of self-preservation.[. . .]" In any case, "Mechanical concussions must be recognized as one of the sources of sexual excitation."

Consider in this connection Freud's account of the relation of neurosis to the perversions: "Neuroses are related to perversions as negative to positive. The same instinctual components as in the perversions can be observed in the neuroses as vehicles of complexes and constructors of symptoms." And elsewhere: "The path of perversion branches off sharply from that of neuroses. If these regressions do not call forth a prohibition on the part of the ego, no neurosis results; the libido succeeds in obtaining a real though not a normal satisfaction."

We might take this to imply that Freud is ruling out the occurrence of a condition in which perverted sexual impulses are being gratified and the pervert is nevertheless suffering from neurotic symptoms. But no. Freud tells us that we are not to be surprised at the existence of such states of affairs: "Psycho-neuroses are also very often associated with manifest inversion." The symptoms may then express the patient's repressed conviction of the unacceptability of his perverted practices. And this is how Freud reconciles his view that delusional attacks of jealousy are due to surplus libido with the fact that he came across a case in which the attacks "curiously enough appeared on the day following an act of intercourse": "after every satiation of the heterosexual libido the homosexual component likewise stimulated by the act forced for itself an outlet in the attack of jealousy."

Freud also maintains that "homosexual tendencies [. . .] help to constitute the social instincts": "It is precisely manifest homosexuals and among them again precisely those that struggle against an indulgence in sensual acts who distinguish themselves by taking a particularly active share in the general interests of humanity." Does it follow that homosexuals indulge their tastes at the expense of their philanthropic impulses? That Casement would have been more solicitous on behalf of the exploited natives of Putomayo and the Congo had he been more chaste? Or does it not follow? The following formula could cope with either contingency: "In the light of psychoanalysis we are accustomed to regard social feeling as a sublimation of homosexual attitudes towards objects. In the homosexual person with marked social interests, the detachment of social feeling from object choice has not been fully carried out."

But on occasions on which counter-observations are too vividly present to him, Freud's claim that the neuroses have sexual causes takes this form:

> It did not escape me [. . .] that sexuality was not always indicated as the cause of neurosis; one person would certainly fall ill because of some injurious sexual condition, but another because he had lost his fortune or recently sustained a severe organic illness [. . .] every weakening of the ego from whatever cause must have the same effect as an increase in the demands of the libido; viz., making neurosis possible [. . .] the fund of energy supporting the symptoms of a neurosis, in every case and regardless of the circumstances inducing their outbreak, is provided by the libido which is thus put to an abnormal use.

And on a later occasion, in connection with the case of a businessman in whom "The catastrophe which he knows to be threatening his business induces the neurosis as a by-product," Freud says that nevertheless "the dynamics of the neurosis are identical" with those in which "the interests at stake in the conflict giving rise to neurosis are [. . .] purely libidinal.[. . .] Libido, dammed up and unable to secure real gratification, finds discharge through the repressed unconscious by the help of regression to old fixations."

It is fair to conclude that though the introduction of the term "libido" permits Freud to give the impression that claims are being advanced as to the nature of the vicissitudes that precipitate, or the states that predispose to, the development of neurotic disorders, in fact a convention has been adopted as to how these vicissitudes and states are to be described. "Sexual trauma" has been extended in the direction of pleonasm; "nonsexual conflict" no longer has a use. . . .

Our confidence in Freud's reconstructions of his neurotic patients' infantile sexual life, and therefore in his claim that adult neuroses are continuations or recrudescences of infantile ones, might be justified by the endorsement of the validity of psychoanalytic method afforded by the accuracy of those portions of the reconstructions that are held to characterise childhood in general and that can thus be confirmed by the contemporary observation of children. That Freud recognizes that at least some of their significance resides in this latter fact is indicated by this remark in the *Three Essays on Sexuality*: "I can point with satisfaction to the fact that direct observation has fully confirmed the conclusions drawn from psychoanalysis and thus furnished good evidence for the reliability of the latter method of investigation." And on many occasions Freud does say that his clinically derived theses regarding the infant's sexual life could be tested by systematically observing the behaviour of children. In the case history of Hans he refers to the observation of children as a "more direct and less roundabout proof of these fundamental theories," and he speaks of "observing upon the child at first hand, in all the freshness of life, the sexual impulses and conative tendencies which we dig out so laboriously in the adult from among their own debris." He even implies that the facts to which he has called attention are so blatant that one must take pains to avoid noticing them. . . .

But on occasions when Freud is under the necessity of forestalling disconfirmatory reports, he forgets the so-easily-confirmable character of his reconstructions of infantile life and insists on their esoteric only-observable-by-initiates status. In the preface to the fourth edition of *Three Essays on Sexuality* we are told that "none, however, but physicians who practise psychoanalysis can have any access whatever to this sphere of knowledge or any possibility of forming a judgment that is uninfluenced by their own dislikes and prejudices. If mankind had been able to learn from direct observation of children these three essays could have remained unwritten." This retreat to the esoterically observable in the face of disconfirmatory evidence is a general feature of psychoanalytic apologetic. . . .

Freud's peripheral awareness of this would account for a lack of candour in his expositions. The expression "direct observation" alternates with "direct analytic observation" as if they were synonymous, so that it only becomes clear after several rereadings that when Freud speaks of "the direct observation of children" he is referring to the psychoanalytic interpretation of infantile behaviour. That is, Freud in attempting to dispel our doubts as to the validity of psychoanalytic method by appeals to "direct observation" proffers us a copy of the same newspaper, this time with his thumb over the banner.

But there is apparently another way of testing the validity of psychoanalytic method. It might seem that there can be no question of the genuinely empirical-historical character of those clinical reconstructions that incorporate references to the external circumstances of the patient's infantile life, such as that he had been threatened with castration or been seduced, or had seen his parents engaged in intercourse. These at least are straightforwardly testable, and their accuracy would therefore afford evidence of the validity of psychoanalytic method; for if the investigation into the infantile history of the patient revealed that he had had no opportunity of witnessing intercourse between his parents (the primal scene), or that he had not been sexually abused, or not been threatened with castration, this would cast doubt on the validity of the interpretative principles employed and on the dependability of the anamnesis that endorsed them.

But Freud occasionally manifests a peculiar attitude towards independent investigation of his reconstructions of the patient's infantile years. In "From the History of an Infantile Neurosis" he writes: "It may be tempting to take the easy course of filling up the gaps in a patient's memory by making enquiries from the older members of the family: but I cannot advise too strongly against such a technique.[. . .] One invariably regrets having made oneself dependent on such information. At the same time confidence in the analysis is shaken and a court of appeal is set up over it. Whatever can be remembered at all will anyhow come to light in the course of further analysis." In the same paper he even expresses misgivings about the value of child analysis: "the deepest strata may turn out to be inaccessible to consciousness. An analysis of childhood disorder through the medium of recollection in an intellectually mature adult is free from these limitations."

This preference is expressed as early as *The Interpretation of Dreams*, where Freud remarks of the death wish of children against the same-sexed parent: "though observations of this kind on small children fit in perfectly with the interpretation I have proposed, they do not carry such complete conviction as is forced upon the physician by the psycho-analysis of adult neurotics." (This is as if Holmes, having concluded from the indentation marks on his visitor's walking stick that he was the owner of a dog smaller than a mastiff and larger than a terrier, instead of glancing with interest in the direction from which the animal was approaching, were to turn once again to a more minute inspection of the stick.) Finally, Freud makes assurance double sure by dispensing with the patient's anamnesis altogether. In the case history of the Wolf Man he says: "it seems to me absolutely equivalent to a recollection if the memories are replaced [. . .] by dreams, the analysis of which invariably leads back to the same scene, and which reproduce every portion of its content in an indefatigable variety of new shapes [. . .] Dreaming is another kind of remembering.[. . .]"

However, if, by some chance, circumstances from the patient's infantile past that were at variance with Freud's reconstructions did come to light, the validity of his interpretative principles would not thereby be imperilled. This is how Freud deals with the fact that according to his clinical experience "it is regularly the father from whom castration is dreaded, although it is mostly the mother who utters the threat": "We find that a child, where his own experience fails him, fills in the gap in individual truth with prehistoric truth; he replaces occurrences in his own life with occurrences in the life of his ancestors. Wherever experiences fail to fit in with the hereditary schema they become remodelled in the imagination. We are often able to see the schema triumphing over the experience of the individual."

Nor does Freud restrict this device to paternal castration threats. He extends it to "memories" of seduction and of the primal scene as well. "These primal phantasies [i.e., of seduction, castration, and witnessing parental intercourse] are a phylogenetic possession.[. . .] If they can be found in real events, well and good; but if reality has not supplied them they will be evolved out of hints and elaborated by phantasy [. . .] the individual, where his own experience has become insufficient, stretches out beyond it to the experience of past ages." If "memories" of infantile events that prove never to have occurred are to be taken as due to an "analogy with the far-reaching instinctive knowledge of animals," how could Freud ever discover that the discrepancy between his reconstruction of the patients' infantile life and the independently ascertained facts of his infantile history was not an instance of "the phylogenetically inherited schema triumphing over experience," but was due to the invalidity of his reconstructive procedures?

Freud sometimes offers a therapeutic rationale for his conviction as to the authenticity of his reconstructions, asserting that it rests on the fact that anamnesis of the reconstructed scenes, fantasies, impulses, or whatnot dissipates the symptoms that are held to be the distorted manifestations of their repression. . . . But we are also told that "marked progress in analytic understanding can be unaccompanied by even the slightest change in the patient's compulsions and inhibitions." . . . So that as well as patients who do not recall their infantile sexual impulses and retain their symptoms and patients who do recall their infantile sexual impulses and relinquish their symptoms, we have patients who do not recall their infantile sexual impulses but nevertheless relinquish their symptoms, and patients who do recall their infantile sexual impulses and nevertheless retain them. And since this is just what we might expect to find if there were no relation between the anamnesis of infantile sexuality and the remission of the neurotic symptoms, it is fair to conclude that there is no support from this source for the authenticity of Freud's reconstructions. . . .

Consider Freud's account of how inevitable it was, given the character of Dostoyevsky's father, that he should have come to possess an over-strict super-ego:

> If the father was hard, violent and cruel, the super-ego takes over these attributes from him, and in the relations between the ego and it, the passivity which was supposed to have been repressed is re-established. The super-ego has become sadistic, and the ego becomes masochistic, that is to say, at bottom passive in a feminine way. A great need for punishment develops

in the ego, which in part offers itself as a victim to fate, and in part finds satisfaction in ill-treatment by the super-ego (that is, the sense of guilt).

This is not at all implausible. But neither is this:

> The unduly lenient and indulgent father fosters the development of an over-strict super-ego because, in the face of the love which is showered on it, the child has no other way of disposing of its aggressiveness than to turn it inwards. In neglected children who grow up without any love the tension between ego and super-ego is lacking, their aggressions can be directed externally [. . .] a strict conscience arises from the co-operation of two factors in the environment: the deprivation of instinctual gratification which evokes the child's aggressiveness, and the love it receives which turns this aggressiveness inwards, where it is taken over by the super-ego.

That is, if a child develops a sadistic super-ego, either he had a harsh and punitive father or he had not. But this is just what we might expect to find if there were no relation between his father's character and the harshness of his super-ego.

As a final illustration of the use Freud makes of the indefiniteness and multiplicity of his pathogenic influences and of the manner in which they enable him to render any outcome whatever an intelligible and apparently natural result of whatever circumstances preceded it, consider the contrast between his accounts of two children—Hans, who was almost five, and Herbert, who was four. Herbert figures as a specimen of enlightened child-rearing in a paper of 1907, "The Sexual Enlightenment of Children," where he is described as "a splendid boy [. . .] whose intelligent parents abstain from forcibly suppressing one side of the child's development." Although Herbert is not a sensual child, he shows "the liveliest interest in that part of his body which he calls his weewee-maker," because "since he has never been frightened or oppressed with a sense of guilt, he gives expression quite ingenuously to what he thinks."

On the other hand, the unfortunate Hans was a "paragon of all the vices"—his mother had threatened him with castration before he was yet four, the birth of a younger sister had confronted him "with the great riddle of where babies come from," and "his father had told him the lie about the stork, which made it impossible for him to ask for enlightenment upon such things." Thus, due in part to "the perplexity in which his infantile sexual theories left him," he succumbed to an animal phobia shortly before his fifth year.

We learn from Jones's biography that Hans and Herbert are the same child, the account of Hans written *after* and that of Herbert *before* he had succumbed to his animal phobia (but not before the events to which Freud later assigned pathogenic status). Freud even decides as an afterthought that Hans's/Herbert's "enlightened" upbringing would naturally have contributed to the development of his phobia: "Since he was brought up without being intimidated and with as much consideration and as little coercion as possible, his anxiety dared to show itself more boldly. With him there was no place for such motives as a bad conscience or fear of punishment, which with other children must no doubt contribute to making the anxiety less." This belongs with Falstaff's account of why he ran away at Gadshill. . . .

The explanation of these equivocations, evasions, and inconsistencies is that Freud is simultaneously under the sway of two necessities: to seem to say and yet to refrain from saying which infantile events occasion the predisposition to neuroses. To seem to say, because his discovery of the pathogenic role of sexuality in the infantile life of neurotics is the ostensible ground for his conviction that the neuroses are manifestations of the revival of infantile sexual struggles and thus for the validity of the method by which this aetiology was inferred; to refrain from saying, because if his aetiological claims were made too explicit and therefore ran the risk of refutation, this might discredit not only his explanations of the neuroses but, more disastrously, the method by which they were arrived at. Only by making these prophylactic and pathogenic claims can his preoccupations and procedures be justified, but only by withdrawing them can they be safeguarded. So the "quantitative factor" to which Freud invariably alludes in his exposition of the aetiology of the neuroses, and his insistence on the importance of the inherited constitution, are not examples of scientific scrupulousness. They are devices for retaining a preoccupation long after any reasonable hope of enhancing one's powers of prediction and control by means of it have been exhausted. . . .

Examination of Freud's interpretations will show that he typically proceeds by beginning with whatever content his theoretical preconceptions compel him to maintain underlies the symptoms, and then, by working back and forth between it and the explanandum, constructing persuasive but spurious links between them. It is this which enables him to find allusions to the father's coital breathing in attacks of dyspnoea, fellatio in a *tussis nervosa,* defloration in migraine, orgasm in an hysterical loss of consciousness, birth pangs in appendicitis, pregnancy wishes in hysterical vomiting, pregnancy fears in anorexia, an accouchement in a suicidal leap, castration fears in an obsessive preoccupation with hat tipping, masturbation in the practice of squeezing blackheads, the anal theory of birth in an hysterical constipation, parturition in a falling cart-horse, nocturnal emissions in bedwetting, unwed motherhood in a limp, guilt over the practice of seducing pubescent girls in the compulsion to sterilize banknotes before passing them on, etc.

In this paper I have assembled reasons for concluding that whatever Dante was doing when he found a trinitarian allusion in the date of Beatrice's death; whatever the cleric encountered by Macaulay was doing when he demonstrated Bonaparte's identity with the Beast mentioned by St. John; whatever pyramidologists are doing when they discover allusions to mathematical and scientific truths in the dimensions of the Great Pyramid; whatever St. Augustine was doing when he expounded the significance of St. Peter's catch of 153 fish; whatever Newton was doing when he identified the subdivisions of the Western Roman Empire with the ten horns of the fourth Beast mentioned in the Book of Daniel—it is this which Freud is doing when he "lays bare" the secret significance of his patients' dreams, symptoms, errors, memories, and associations, and explains "what the symptoms signify, what instinctual impulses lurk behind them and are satisfied by them, and by what transitions the mysterious path has led from those impulses to these symptoms."

Why Can't a Woman
Be More Like a Man?*

Malcolm Macmillan

No aspect of Freud's work has aroused more objection than his treatment of female psychology. And understandably so, since the burden of his theory was that the self-evident superiority of male to female sex organs, once perceived by little girls, sends them into a lifetime's worth of devious and dependent behavior that can only retard the true (masculine) work of civilization. Freud apparently never budged from that position or worried about its suspicious congruence with the misogyny of his time. Instead, he labored to make a place, however minor, for womankind within his "universal" psychological laws by improvising girlish variants of the boy's Oedipus and castration complexes. Not even Freud himself was altogether proud of the result, but the embarrassment has long since become general and far more extreme. Although the Freudian movement succeeded in ostracizing such early heretics as the brave feminist Karen Horney, a tide of disbelief and outrage has by now washed away Freud's notions of penis envy, the vaginal orgasm, "normal" female masochism, and the moral and cultural weakness of women.

Nevertheless, there is good reason to pass in review what Freud had to say about female sexuality and identity. Our concern in this book is not so much with erroneous ideas as with the basis on which we have been asked to believe them. For seven decades or so, psychoanalysts reported with persuasive authority that the Freudian picture of

* From *Freud Evaluated: The Completed Arc* (1991; Cambridge: The MIT Press, 1997).

womanhood, however disagreeable, had been confirmed over and over by irrefutable "clinical findings." Now the same investigative procedure—the analysis of free associations and of the transference—is said to yield opposite conclusions. Working without empirical safeguards, psychoanalysts continue to "learn" from their patients whatever they are already inclined to believe; as the political winds shift, clinical results obligingly change as well. Thus when we are told that, on the question of female psychology, "psychoanalysis has advanced beyond Freud," we should understand the statement to mean that the analysts have been scurrying to catch up with the feminist revolution before it leaves them completely in the dust.

If we really want to free ourselves from Freud's errors about women, it won't suffice to give his concepts an ideological makeover— for example, by supplanting penis envy with womb envy or by putting the preoedipal mother where the oedipal father once stood. As Malcolm Macmillan insists in his exhaustive study *Freud Evaluated: The Completed Arc* (1997), the whole array of concepts being realigned— repression, infantile sexuality, the Oedipus complex, the stages of libidinal development—lacked any observational grounding in the first place. Such notions deserve not to be feminized but to be put definitively to rest.

The following excerpt from *Freud Evaluated* is well suited to this end. Macmillan begins by examining Freud's earliest foray into the female unconscious in *Three Essays on the Theory of Sexuality* (1905) and then skips ahead to five papers and a lecture from the 1920s. By the time Freud turned his theoretical attention to women, Macmillan shows, he was already committed to the dubious postulates that male sexuality is the only genuine kind and that psychological maleness and femaleness must be worked out afresh by each girl and boy after they have anxiously glimpsed one another's genitals. Freud's "discoveries" about women—for example, that in a girl's unconscious a baby is equivalent to a penis, or that female inferiority has been inscribed in racial memory from the days of the primal horde—were patches, themselves quite flimsy, stitched across the awkward gaps in his larger theory.

A past president of the Australian Psychological Society, Malcolm Macmillan has taught psychology at both Monash and Deakin Universities in Australia. His publications cover a wide variety of psychological topics, including brain localization and disability. Macmillan was one of the first observers to point out the contradictions in Freud's several accounts of his "seduction theory" (Macmillan, 1977), and his *Freud Evaluated,* first published in 1991, is the most thorough attempt yet made to assess the entire body of Freudian propositions from an independent point of view.

[In Freud's scheme of sexual development,] sharp distinctions were established at puberty between the masculine and the feminine characters. Before puberty there were differences in the development of inhibitions that took place earlier in girls than boys; in the expression of the component instincts, which tended to take the passive form in females; and in repression, which tended to be greater in females. Otherwise the differences were minimal. Indeed, the autoerotic activity was so similar between the sexes that Freud believed libido was "invariably and necessarily of a masculine nature" and that the sexuality of little girls was "wholly masculine." Puberty induced two quite different processes. Boys experienced a great accession of libido, but girls "a fresh wave of repression." The repression was precisely of the girl's clitoral, that is, masculine, sexuality. Stimulation of the clitoris now had to produce excitation of the vagina if the vagina was to supplant the clitoris as the predominant zone. Repression of the girl's masculine sexuality thus prepared the way for the full development of female sexuality. Because females had to change their leading erotogenic zone and males did not, they were more prone to neuroses, especially to hysteria.

Having explained how the genital zone had achieved primacy and how the new sexual aim had been adopted, Freud now turned to the process of explaining how the adult sexual object was found at puberty. He described the period of earliest infancy in which the sexual instinctual drive was linked to nourishment as one in which the mother's breast had been a sexual object. Autoerotism began with the loss of the breast and the subsequent redirection of the sexual impulse to the subject's own body. When autoerotism ceased at puberty, the direction taken by the sexual impulse was once again toward the breast: "There are thus good reasons why a child sucking at his mother's breast has become the prototype of every relation of love. The finding of an object is in fact a refinding of it." Throughout the whole time of the child's dependence on others, "even after sexual activity has become detached from the taking of nourishment," children learned to feel love for those who helped them and who satisfied their needs.

Freud believed this love to be modeled on the suckling's relation. The sexual character of the child's dependence on others was to be seen in the anxiety of children, "originally nothing other" than a feeling they had lost the person whom they loved: "In this respect a child, by turning his libido into anxiety when he cannot satisfy it, behaves like an adult. On the other hand an adult who has become neurotic owing to his libido being unsatisfied behaves in his anxiety like a child: he begins to be frightened when he is alone."

Why, then, did male and female adults not both choose the mothers? After all, both had had her breast as their first object. Adult object-choice was, Freud said, first of all guided by the exclusion of blood relatives from consideration. In the human child the postponement of sexual maturation meant that an incest barrier could be erected. Freud believed that pubertal fantasies, based as they were on infantile tendencies now strengthened by somatic pressure, showed the direction of the child's sexual impulse to be toward the parent of the opposite sex. When the fantasies were repudiated, a process of detachment from parental authority could take place and an object other than the parent be chosen. Failure of detachment occurred most often in girls, who, if they retained their fathers as objects, would be sexually anesthetic and cold toward their husbands. Because the psychoneurotic had repudiated sexuality generally, the activity of finding an object remained unconscious. A characteristic combination of an exaggerated need for affection with an equally exaggerated horror of sexuality developed as a consequence.

Freud claimed that psychoanalyses showed that in neurotic females this characteristic resulted from incestuous object-choices. But even when no such abnormal consequence ensued, he believed the incestuous choices of infancy had long-lasting effects: "There can be no doubt that every object-choice whatever is based, though less closely, on these prototypes. A man, especially, looks for someone who can represent his picture of his mother, as it has dominated his mind from his earliest childhood." Although Freud said that "other starting points" from infancy might affect adult object-choice, he did not specify them.

Guidance of the adult choice also had to prevent inversion. An adult of the opposite sex had to be chosen. Freud thought that the strongest factor was the attraction "opposing sexual characters exercise upon one another," the same factor responsible for sexual differentiation in the fantasies of puberty. He was unable to indicate the basis of this attraction, and supposed further that by itself it was insufficiently strong to determine an opposite-sex choice. Reinforcement by social prohibitions against inversion was necessary because "where inversion is not regarded as a crime it will be found that it answers fully to the sexual inclinations of no small number of people." Freud presumed that a further powerful contribution to the choice of female objects by men came from the man's recollection of the affection shown him in childhood by his mother and other women who cared for him. In women the development of impulses of rivalry toward other females was thought to "play a part," as well as the sexual repression at puberty, in discouraging them from choosing among their own sex. . . .

OBJECT CHOICE

One of the main deficiencies of Freud's account of object choice is that it does not explain how the female comes to choose an object of the opposite sex. The basis of the deficiency lies in the assumptions that the object of importance to the child of either sex is the mother's breast, that the breast is the first object, and that the suckling's relation with the mother is the prototype of all other prepubertal relations. On these assumptions the male child was provided with a female object from the beginning. At puberty he had only to erect the barrier against incest by taking "up into himself the moral precepts" expressly excluding the choice of his mother or someone in the circle of his immediate relatives.

Something more than this mechanism was required to ensure an opposite sex choice in the female, for were she simply to undergo the same development as the male, she would still be left with female objects. To overcome this problem Freud proposed that at puberty repression transformed the sexuality of the female from its masculine, infantile form into its feminine, adult form. Once the basic sexuality of the female had been so changed, it appeared to be simply a matter of the attraction of opposites coming into operation, a mechanism he described as "the strongest force working against a permanent inversion of the sexual object." Both steps in this process were made necessary by the assumption that the important object had been the mother's breast. But neither the first and crucial step, the replacement of masculine sexuality by feminine sexuality, nor the second, choosing a male adult, was explained adequately.

Because Freud assumed that the little girl's sexuality was masculine, he had also to explain how it changed into feminine sexuality. Changes at puberty that supposedly increased libido in the male were supposed to produce a fresh wave of repression in the female. Nothing else in the theory presupposed such an outcome, except perhaps the circularly based and equally ad hoc assumption that in females "the tendency to sexual repression seems in general to be greater." What this repression had to produce was the exchange of the excitability of the clitoris for that of the vagina. What Freud described was a selective inhibitory process that put an end to the capacity of the clitoris to respond to manipulation in the old way, but which somehow allowed it to become excited enough during the normal sexual act for clitoral excitability to be transferred to the vagina.

It was the *male's* sexual drive, aroused by the very repression of libido in the female, that actually created the new female response:

> The intensification of the brake upon sexuality brought about by pubertal repression in women serves as a stimulus to the libido *in men* and causes an increase of its activity. Along with this heightening of [male] libido there is also an increase of sexual over-valuation [by the male] which only emerges [. . .] in relation to a woman who holds herself back and who denies her sexuality. *When at last the sexual act is permitted and the clitoris itself becomes excited, it still retains a function: the task, namely, of transmitting the excitation to the adjacent female sexual parts* [emphasis added].

Consequently, although pubertal repression was supposed to inhibit clitoral excitability, it did so with very strange selectivity: the inhibition lasted only until heightened male sexuality incited the normal sexual act. The reexcitation of the previously restrained but now disinhibited clitoris then sparked off vaginal responsiveness rather than its own orgasm. No real explanation of the change in the sexuality of the female was being offered. Freud merely described what he needed to explain.

With respect to the choice of an adult male as the female object,

Freud's explanation broke down completely. First, even if repression accounted for the change in the leading erotogenic zone, that change together with the attraction of opposite sexual characters did not account for the repudiation of the mother. In any case, Freud described the repudiation only for the male. The female was described as repudiating the *father,* although the theory not only failed to provide her with such an object, her relation to the father as object was not even mentioned. Nor was male homosexual object choice touched on.

We must note that *Three Essays* at least contains and may even be built on a paradox: although it was the unconscious perverse tendencies of the psychoneurotic female that posed the original problem, Freud's theory was written almost completely from the point of view of male sexuality. By this I do not refer to the quite trivial point of the masculine linguistic forms with which his ideas are expressed, but to such things as the male model implicit in Freud's accounts of the suckling's relation to the mother, the mother's role in teaching the child how to love, the role of the male in awakening normal female sexual responsiveness, and the discharge of sexual substances in relieving sexual tension, to name just a few. The inability of the theory to portray female psychosexual development with any consistency, especially female object choice, stems partly from this male orientation. . . .

THE FEMALE AS SEXUALLY MASCULINE

For Freud the sharp distinction between male and female sexual characteristics was not established until puberty: until then clitoris and penis were both phallic in function, the vicissitudes of psychosexual development were the same, and the mother was the first sexual object for both sexes. Libido and sexuality were essentially masculine. It was within the constraints posed by this conception that Freud had to explain how the female child came to be possessed by the twin desires of sexual love for the father and murderous hostility toward the mother, or how she developed a feminine superego.

When he began his theorizing about the female superego, Freud pictured the little girl as choosing the father, forming a primary identification with the mother, and emerging from the oedipal situation in a way "precisely analogous" to that of the little boy. The analogy has several problems. First, the girl could not choose the father as a sexual object anaclitically because he satisfied no self-preservation drives. Second, resolution of the Oedipus complex required that the father be identified with by incorporation; as a consequence, the girl's superego would have had masculine characteristics, a patently absurd result. Third, it was implicit in this description that the girl's sexuality was feminine, not masculine. Freud had no basis for his claim that the outcome of the Oedipus complex in the girl was precisely analogous to that of the male.

Female Sexuality Within essentially the same period that saw the completion of *The Ego and the Id,* Freud began the first of five works (four papers and a lecture) that bore on the origins of female sexuality and over which he continued to worry during the next eight years. The works are as relevant to his attempt to complete the account of superego formation as they are to femininity as such.

Throughout the papers and the lecture, Freud insisted that the female child's sexuality was initially masculine. In the first paper, "The Infantile Genital Organization," he implied that he had previously underestimated genital primacy. The dominance of the genitals in the infantile genital organization was not far removed from that of the mature form, but it was a primacy of the *phallus* rather than of the genitals. Because only maleness existed, he had no doubt that the girl also went through the phallic phase.

In the second paper, "The Dissolution of the Oedipus Complex," he noted that the girl could not experience the fear of castration that destroyed the boy's Oedipus complex and established his superego. What essentially differentiated the girl from the boy was her acceptance of castration as "an accomplished fact." After becoming aware that a boy had a penis and she did not, she explained the deficiency by assuming that an earlier castration had robbed her of it. Without the fear of castration, "a powerful motive" dropped out for the formation of the female superego. Nevertheless it was set up.

In the third paper, "Some Psychical Consequences of the Anatomical Distinction between the Sexes," Freud described what turned the little girl away from the mother, and made her choose the father, as a passive "loosening" of the tie. But, for the analogy to hold properly, she had to feel hostility toward her mother. Although in the fourth paper, "Female Sexuality," Freud described the attachment as being broken because of active feelings of hostility on the girl's part, it took him some time to propose that the hatred was because the mother was responsible for the absence of a penis. Girls never forgave their mothers the lifelong disadvantage to which they had thus been put. Freud could then argue in the lecture "Femininity" that the source of the superego, as with the boy, was the castration complex.

The Choice of the Father How was the father chosen? Freud drew on two of his much earlier notions: the male as a provider of the penis and the symbolic equivalence of penis with baby. He brought them together by describing the little girl as attempting to compensate for the assumed loss of her penis by symbolically transforming her wish for that organ into a wish for a baby and turning to her father for its gratification. What brought her female sexuality into being, then, was the stealing of her masculinity, and what consolidated it was her attempt at restitution. . . .

Femininity The process by which Freud imagined the girl's Oedipus complex to be dissolved resulted in a superego that was less harsh and more forgiving than the boy's. Lacking castration anxiety, she had no real motive to surmount the Oedipus complex. She thus stayed in the oedipal situation for an indeterminate length of time, the complex was demolished only incompletely, and the resulting superego was less like that of the male on which it was modeled. In a word, she had acquired feminine characteristics. The female superego was less inexorable, less impersonal, and less independent of its emotional origins than the male's. Related traits—woman's lesser sense of justice, her greater unwillingness "to submit to the great exigencies of life," and her being more readily swayed by feelings of affection and hostility—were all, Freud thought, "amply accounted for" by the incompleteness of the oedipal situation.

Apart from peculiarities in the formation of the female superego, it seemed to Freud that feminine psychological characteristics were created in two other ways. Some appeared to be residuals from the pre-oedipal phase: repeated alternations between masculinity and femininity, the failure of the libido of females to incorporate an aggressive component, the frequency of sexual frigidity, peculiarities in the choice of husband, and typical attitudes toward him and his male children. Other characteristics seemed to derive directly from penis envy, although Freud was rather less certain about them. He thought they included narcissism, vanity, and shame, as well as jealousy and envy itself.

Freud briefly summarized these various results of the girl's remaining in the Oedipus situation for an indeterminate period and of her late and incomplete demolition of the complex: "In these circumstances the formation of the super-ego must suffer; it cannot attain the strength and independence which give it its cultural significance." I shall examine his claim of lesser cultural significance before concluding this discussion of the superego.

THE FEMALE AND CULTURAL DEVELOPMENT

In the remote prehistoric past, Freud proposed, some young members of the primal horde, in which people then lived, collectively killed the horde leader. The remorse that arose in the killers had two momentous and simultaneous consequences: a religion was established that centered around the worship of a totem animal ancestral figure representing the slain leader, and systems of taboos were set up forbidding the killing of the totem animal and denying sexual relations between the remaining members of the horde. The killing was the "great event with which civilization began," and Freud repeatedly emphasized its significance.

Because the leader of the horde was the father and his killers were his sons, civilization was solely a male creation. True, Freud did also assert that love, including woman's love, had to be recognized as one of the foundations of civilization, but it was pretty obvious to him that woman's contribution could not be of the same magnitude as that of the man. Woman's love was fundamentally passive and narcissistic and led her to acquiesce in the desire of the male to keep his sexual objects near him. What contribution even that made was before the males had taken the really decisive action of killing their father.

However, for Freud there was a much more fundamental basis for woman's limited contribution to civilization. He believed her to have less capacity than man to sublimate her instinctual drives, that is, to have a slighter ability to redirect her libido onto cultural ends. She could not contribute to the growth of civilization to the same extent as man. Her very limited sublimation also led her to make sexual demands on man that prevented him from deploying his libido for cultural purposes as fully as he might otherwise do. And, to the extent that he did not meet her sexual needs, she became hostile toward him, his civilizing mission, and its end product. Thus she doubly restrained and retarded the development of civilization.

Woman's deficiencies came about during the formation of the superego. When the Oedipus complex was overcome, identifications replaced object cathexes and Eros and Thanatos were defused. Because the female surmounted the oedipal situation only partially, the defusion also was only partial. Less sexual energy could therefore be liberated in her than in the male and less be made available to be sublimated. And if, as Freud also asserted, every identification was a sublimation, the incomplete identification meant that the female made less use of what was a smaller store of sublimated libido. Further, because less of the death instinct was freed, less of it was available to be taken up into the superego. Woman's superego was necessarily less harsh and less opposed to sexuality than man's. A final consequence of the partial defusion was that more of the remaining alloy of Eros with Thanatos was left behind in the female than in the male. To the extent that it was internally directed, her erotogenic masochism—what Freud saw as the entire basis for feminine masochism—had therefore to be stronger.

The female superego could not be other than as Freud described it, and woman's contribution to civilization could not be other than minor. So, after the killing of the primal father, when the superego formed, Freud could not allow that it was even through that agency that woman might have made one of her few contributions to civilization. Plaiting and weaving, which he grudgingly conceded that she "may have invented," sprang directly from genital deficiency; they were techniques based on an unconscious imitation of the way in which, at puberty, her matted pubic hair came to conceal her deficient genitals.

Civilization was, it must be repeated, a *male* creation—woman had no part in it. Similarly, the remorse, and later the guilt that came to sustain it, was substantially a *male* feeling. What moral standards woman had, what capacity she had to resist instinctual demands, she acquired from the male by "cross-inheritance." When, then, in the course of her own development, Freud pictured the little girl as creating yet another incomplete superego, he was also picturing her as reaffirming the masculine foundation of civilization, her own relatively trivial later contributions, and the paucity of her moral standards.

Fundamentally, it is because Freud considers her to be a male, although an incomplete one, that he ends by representing the female so abjectly. We see, however, that her supposed inadequacies are much more a result of his postulate that her infantile sexuality is masculine than because of any supposed anatomical deficiency. Even were he correct, however, we also see that the mechanisms of identification and sublimation he proposes would be unable to bring about any change in her. . . .

It seems to me obvious that Freud was not describing his female patients so much as putting forward the stereotyped view of women typically held by men of his time and social outlook. The "facts" he wanted to explain were certainly not clinical facts and were hardly facts at all. The secondary developmental transformation has a similar status. Given a "masculine" starting point, the changes were more or less demanded by the end point, and failure to confirm them was almost inevitable. Freud's account of the psychosexual development of the female is not so much wrong as totally unnecessary.

III

PSYCHIC INSPECTOR CLOUSEAU

"*The distinction between conscious and unconscious mental states is the sovereign means for believing what one likes.*"
—William James

OVERVIEW

In Part II we saw that Freudian psychoanalysis lacks the methodological controls that are needed if genuine progress in science and medicine is to occur. Working in semiprivacy from a set of dubious theoretical assumptions, receiving encouragement from suggestible and indoctrinated clients, and reporting his findings in an anecdotal mode that thwarts objective challenge, the therapist cannot be drawn up short by countervailing data. Even if he is wary of the sweeping causal inferences that Freud drew about early traumas and their pathogenic consequences, a Freudian is left saddled with an all too facile habit of symbolic translation and a body of unclear dogma from which no path back to observation can be traced. Far from providing grounds for revising or refuting psychological hypotheses, then, Freudian interpretation tends to promote them into specious certainties. Or, as Freud himself incautiously put it, "applications of analysis are always confirmations of it as well" (SE, 22: 146). Part III weighs the effects of such complacency on his handling of individual cases.

As Barbara Von Eckardt observes above, the successful outcome of a given case was Freud's ultimate warrant for the correctness of the interpretations that led to that outcome. Yet even applying his own indulgent criteria, with no allowance for placebo factors and no systematic follow-up to check for relapses, Freud was unable to document a single unambiguously efficacious treatment. Not only did the master psychologist not cure his most famous clients, he seems to have been only fleetingly interested in doing so. His goal was rather to reach *intellectual* closure by proving to the patient—and, later, to his admirers and detractors—the correctness of his etiological reconstructions.

When addressing the broad public, Freud continued for a long while to tout psychoanalysis as the only lasting cure for psychoneuroses— indeed, as a cure "second to none of the finest in the field of internal medicine" (SE, 16: 458; see also, for example, SE, 16: 261; 18: 250; 19: 202). But he was lying. As he wrote discreetly to Jung in 1906, "I have kept certain things that might be said concerning the limits of the therapy to myself" (Freud and Jung, 1974, page 12). Only much later, when his fame as a deep modern thinker appeared secure, did he begin dropping hints that he had "never been a therapeutic enthusiast" (SE, 21: 151) and that his remediative powers were minimal (for example, SE, 20: 27; 23: 220).

Psychoanalytic patients, Sándor Ferenczi recalled Freud as having said, were "a rabble," good for nothing but "to provide us with a livelihood and material to learn from" (Ferenczi, 1988, page 93). That secondhand report gibes with what Freud himself wrote to Edoardo Weiss in 1922: "Regretfully, only a few patients are worth the trouble we spend on them . . ." (Weiss, 1970, page 37). The reputed healer was eager to turn away the sick just as soon as he could afford to do so (around 1920). As he confided to Joseph Wortis in 1934, "I prefer a student ten times more than a neurotic" (Wortis, 1975, page 18). But in the course of Wortis's own abortive training analysis, Freud proved to be as blundering, capricious, and ill-tempered as during his ministrations to the neurotic rabble.

Until very recently, Freud's major case histories have been regarded as the empirical bedrock of the analytic discipline. That is the role they have played in training institutes, where the pedagogical vacuum left by the absence of any clear manual of clinical method has been largely filled by these intriguing yarns. Yet time, scholarly diligence, and the emergence of further documents and testimony have conjoined to peel away Freud's pretense that he was carefully reasoning his way through to hypotheses that were then confirmed by the patient's assent, revelatory behavior, or cure. In Chapters 12–15 we will note how the most famous of his case histories are characterized by waywardness of reasoning, a refusal to countenance crucial but inconvenient factors, and rhetorical sleight of hand.

■ ■ ■

In Freud's view, a psychoanalyst's greatest assurance of accuracy was supplied by the physical presence of the patient, whose responses to interpretations supposedly acted as a corrective to faulty inferences. (Never mind that both agreement and disagreement could be taken to signify that the therapist was right.) The interpreter who tried to dispense with that presence would be practicing "wild analysis," a cause for rebuke. Yet Freud himself could not resist precisely such speculation in the void, hazarding guesses about the "unconscious meaning," for their creators, of such works of art as *Oedipus Rex, Hamlet, The Brothers Karamazov*, Wilhelm Jensen's little-known *Gradiva*, and Michelangelo's famous statue of Moses. And in a viler spirit, he collaborated (with William Bullitt) on a posthumously published psychobiography of his bête noire, Woodrow Wilson, ascribing the provisions of the galling Treaty of Versailles not to national interests but to "little Tommy's" nursery conflicts, carried forward into adulthood. All of those analytic exercises can be loosely regarded as case studies, though hardly as case histories.

Although Freud's psychophilosophizing about history and art compels wonder for its range of reference, its rhetorical dexterity, and its sheer bravado, posterity has not been kind to any of the specific theses advanced in that mode. As with his live patients, Freud was given to reading his own "case" into his objects of study. His disciples noted with amusement, for example, that the primal father of *Totem and Taboo* (1912) looked suspiciously like Freud in a loincloth—and Freud did not deny it. Similarly, the Moses of *Moses and Monotheism* (1939) tells us less about biblical times than about Freud's self-image as an unjustly spurned visionary. Moreover, his empathy with great artists tended to be cut short by a peculiarly condescending and hostile reductionism.

Thus in "Dostoyevsky and Parricide" (1928), Freud offered a pathologizing and infantalizing account of Dostoyevsky's character and fiction alike (see Frank, 1976; Rice, 1993). Freud regarded the writer's seeming epilepsy—by today a firmly established fact—as merely a disguise for his real affliction, hysteria, rooted in an early primal scene and a permanently unresolved Oedipus complex. Everything of psychological value in the fiction could thus be assigned to a determinism operating beneath the writer's deluded and enthralled consciousness. Dostoyevsky turned out to be profound, on this reading, only insofar as he had inadvertently manifested the truth of Freud's own doctrine.

In Chapter 16 we will see the same tendency at work in the most admired of Freud's exercises in applied analysis, his little book of 1910 about Leonardo da Vinci. Much has been made of the biographical misinformation that, in this instance, superficially marred an otherwise astute inquiry. But just what, we must ask, did Freud get *right* about Leonardo that wasn't common knowledge? Even if all of his facts had been correct, Freud's Leonardo would still rank with Dora, Little Hans, and the Wolf Man as a victim—albeit a posthumous one—of his typical rush to judgment.

Delusion and Dream in Freud's "Dora"*

Allen Esterson

The first of Freud's major psychoanalytic cases to be written up was that of "Dora" (Ida Bauer), conducted for about eleven weeks in 1900 before the patient abruptly decided that her treatment was no longer worth pursuing. The complex facts of Bauer's immediately prior history are summarized in Allen Esterson's discussion below. Suffice it to add that we now know her to have been not eighteen (as Freud wrote) but seventeen when she began treatment and thirteen, not fourteen, at the time of the forced embrace that she "hysterically" regarded as disagreeable (see Mahony, 1996, pages 8–9, 13 note)—an age difference that can only exacerbate our discomfort at the doctor's prurient and taunting conduct toward her.

Up until 1962, when Erik H. Erikson dared to suggest that Freud had misunderstood and harassed Bauer (Erikson, 1962), the Freudian community stood solidly behind the Dora case, treating it as a model of insight into the workings of hysteria. More recently, other psychoanalysts have at last begun to back away in revulsion:

> The case of Dora has an array of negative distinctions. It is one of the great psychotherapeutic disasters; one of the most remarkable exhibitions of a clinician's published rejection of his patient; spectacular, though tragic, evidence of sexual abuse

* From *Seductive Mirage: An Exploration of the Work of Sigmund Freud* (Chicago: Open Court, 1993).

of a young girl, and her own analyst's published exoneration of that abuse; an eminent case of forced associations, forced remembering, and perhaps several forced dreams. . . . [T]he case, the published history, and the subsequent reception can be called an example of continued sexual abuse. Dora had been traumatized, and Freud retraumatized her. And for roughly half a century the psychoanalytic community remained either collusively silent about that abuse or, because of blind adoration, simply ignorant of it (Mahony, 1996, pages 148–149).

These are the words of a practicing analyst, responding sympatheti-cally to a chorus of feminist dissent from Freud's quintessentially patriar-chal narrative (see, for example, Cixous, 1975; Bernheimer and Kahane, 1985; Sprengnether, 1990; Lakoff and Coyne, 1993; Merck, 1993).

Oddly, however, even the angriest students of the Dora case tend to employ scarcely modified Freudian terms when offering their own anatomies of Bauer's psyche—as if only Freud's attitude and not his method were gravely flawed. Many of them, for example, take as proven Bauer's supposed homosexuality, though it rests on no more substan-tial basis than Freud's aprioristic Fliessian speculations at the time. And they gratuitously concede that Bauer did, after all, "learn the his-tory of her desire, which had left aches throughout her body, in verbal-izable meanings" (Mahony, 1996, page 145). On the contrary, so far as can be objectively ascertained, all of the "meanings" in the Dora case pertained only to Freud's imagination.

It is easy to hurl ideological barbs at the sexist Freud—just as easy as it used to be to worship him. More pedestrian but ultimately more rev-olutionary is the task of showing that, in this and other cases, Freud's translations of "verbalizable" somatic hieroglyphs lack any demon-strable basis. That is what Allen Esterson documents in the following pages. The Dora story *is* a locus classicus of sexually invasive dis-course, but it is also a uniquely candid record of how Freud passed his analytic hours—namely, not in listening to his patients but in brow-beating them to accept wild interpretations.

It was long supposed that Freud waited from 1901 until 1905 to publish the Dora case (SE, 7: 7–122) in order to protect Ida Bauer's anonymity. After all, that was what Freud himself proclaimed in 1925

(SE, 19: 248). But well-connected Viennese observers would have had no trouble identifying Bauer from Freud's account even in 1905. Moreover, immediately after writing up the case in January 1901, just after its termination, Freud tried unsuccessfully to get it published (Mahony, 1996, pages 139–142)—a clear act of spite against the desperate, borderline suicidal teenager whose alleged desires to suck her father's penis and to have lesbian sex with that father's mistress were now to be broadcast to the world. So hostile was Freud toward Bauer that when she tried to consult him about a painful neuralgia sixteen months later, he dismissed her as being "not in earnest" (SE, 7: 121). Yet with his customary absence of self-knowledge, Freud ascribed a "malignant vindictiveness" to poor Bauer herself (SE, 7: 105 note).

Before his recent retirement, Allen Esterson was Lecturer in Mathematics at Southwark College, London. His book *Seductive Mirage*, from which this chapter is taken, concisely and uncompromisingly expounds the liberties Freud habitually took with both facts and logic.

With the relinquishing of the infantile seduction theory, Freud believed he had discovered the existence of unconscious phantasies and that he was in possession of a technique for elucidating their contents. The first publication containing a detailed account of his therapeutic procedure was the "Dora" case history ("Fragment of an Analysis of a Case of Hysteria"), which he completed early in 1901 but published only in 1905. In the Prefatory Remarks he makes clear that his purpose in writing it is to present his views on the causes and structure of hysteria, to demonstrate that "hysterical symptoms are the expression of [the patient's] most secret and repressed wishes," and to show how dream interpretation "can become the means of filling in amnesias and elucidating symptoms." Regarding the practicalities of writing up the case history, he reports that he made no notes during sessions, that he recorded the wording of dreams immediately after the session in which they had been recounted, and that the paper was written from memory after the treatment was at an end.

Before looking at the actual analysis, there is one other point concerning the Prefatory Remarks which is of interest. In his opening comments

Freud states that in the paper he is proposing to substantiate the views he had put forward in 1895 and 1896 upon the pathogenesis of hysterical symptoms. In an obvious reference to the fact that in "The Aetiology of Hysteria" he had implied that he had available the clinical material that would substantiate his claims of infantile seductions, he writes that at the time it was "awkward" that he was obliged to publish the results of his enquiries without there being any possibility of other workers in the field testing and checking them. He continues: "But [. . .] now that I am beginning to bring forward some of the material upon which my conclusions were based [. . .] I shall not escape blame by this means. Only, whereas before I was accused of giving *no* information about my patients, now I shall be accused of giving information about my patients which ought not to be given. I can only hope that in both cases the critics will be the same, and that they will merely have shifted the pretext for their reproaches; if so, I can resign in advance any possibility of ever removing their objections."

It was, of course, a justifiable complaint that Freud had not produced the clinical material on which his conclusions in the 1896 papers were based in spite of his implying he would do so. By surmising that it would be the same people who would now accuse him of giving too much information about his patients, he ingeniously manages to sidestep a perfectly legitimate criticism, while at the same time putting himself into a position where he is able to insinuate that his critics are "narrow-minded" and acting out of "ill-will." In the case history itself he suggests that Dora utilised reproaches against other people as an unconscious device to avoid becoming aware of self-reproaches. In these opening remarks Freud appears to be using a rather similar device to draw attention away from a fact of which he must have been painfully aware, that in his last major communication on the subject of his present paper he had proclaimed a momentous discovery concerning which at the time of writing he had yet to admit publicly that he had blundered.

The paper proper opens with a résumé of the background to the case. Dora was eighteen at the time of her treatment, which terminated after about three months. Freud lists her somatic symptoms as dyspnoea (shortness of breath), a nervous cough, aphonia (loss of voice), and possibly migraines, along with depression and "hysterical unsociability." Together with her father, at whose behest she has reluctantly come to Freud, the people who feature most prominently in the account are Herr and Frau K., long-standing friends of the family. (Her mother plays only a peripheral role.) Dora is distressed because she believes that her father is having an affair with Frau K., and also because Herr K. has for some time been paying her unwelcome attention. Moreover, she senses that her father, in his own interests, has tacitly encouraged him, and she is distressed at her father's making such a use of her. She reports that on two occasions Herr K. has made sexual advances towards her. When she was fourteen he had used duplicity to contrive a meeting at his place of business where he had "suddenly clasped the girl to him and pressed a kiss upon her lips," at which she had "a violent feeling of disgust" and "tore herself free from the man." (Freud here remarks that "In this scene [. . .] the behaviour of this child of fourteen was already entirely and completely hysterical," for he would "without question consider a person hysterical in whom an occasion for sexual excitement elicited feelings that were preponderantly or exclusively unpleasurable.") The second occasion occurred when she was sixteen. She and her father were staying with Herr and Frau K. near a lake in the Alps, and Herr K. had made "a proposal" to her after a trip upon the lake. Dora had slapped his face and hurried away. Nevertheless, he continued to endeavour to spend his spare time in her presence and to ply her with flowers and expensive presents.

The analysis centres on the interpretations of Dora's somatic symptoms and of two dreams. Much of the account is concerned with Freud's attempt to convince his patient that she is unconsciously in love with Herr K. To this end he suggests that her repeated recriminations against her father for carrying on an affair with Frau K. point to the existence of similar recriminations against herself, and that they had the purpose of cloaking thoughts that she was anxious to keep from consciousness. Certain parallels indicated the content of these unconscious ideas. Her father had encouraged Herr K. to keep company with Dora, and had not wished to look too closely into Herr K.'s behaviour towards his daughter. In a similar way Dora had at first failed to recognise the true character of the friendship between her father and Frau K., and Freud suggests that this was in the interests of her relationship with Herr K. Her own governess had been in love with her father, and Dora had taken a great interest in Herr K.'s children. "What the governess had from time to time been to Dora, Dora had been to Herr K.'s children.[. . .] Her preoccupation with his children was evidently a cloak for something else that Dora was anxious to hide from herself and from other people."

When Freud informs her of his conclusion that this indicated she was unconsciously in love with Herr K., she does not assent to it. However, he has more arguments to bring to bear on her, culminating in the suggestion that the appearance and disappearance of her attacks of coughing and loss of voice were related to the presence or absence of the man she loved. He elicits that the average length of her attacks was "from three to six weeks, perhaps," and that Herr K.'s absences were for a similar period. "Her illness was therefore a demonstration of her love for K. [. . .] It was only necessary to suppose that [. . .] she had been ill when he was absent and well when he had come back. And this really seemed to have been so, at least during the first period of the attacks. Later on it no doubt became necessary to obscure the coincidence between her attacks of illness and the absence of the man she secretly loved, lest its regularity should betray her secret."

It is of interest to examine this passage in the light of information given elsewhere in the paper. Freud had earlier reported that the symptoms of persistent coughing and loss of voice had started when Dora was about twelve. This in itself is of no significance, since he argues that the unconscious utilises somatic symptoms for its own purposes. But he writes in regard to the coinciding of Dora's attacks and Herr K.'s absences that "this really seemed to have been so, at least during the first period of the attacks," and this does not bear serious examination. Are we really supposed to believe that Dora's unconscious love for Herr K. started when she was twelve, at the age of the first period of her attacks? Or that she could remember from that time (six years before) that the attacks coincided with Herr K.'s absences? Freud's words make it clear that in recent years there had been no coinciding, and the indecisive manner in which he makes the claim that at one time there had been raises the suspicion that this is a doubtful inference tendentiously adduced to lend support to his argument. . . .

Freud devotes the last paragraph relating to this interpretation to a discussion of the improvement in writing skill in the case of people who have lost the capacity to speak. He writes with regard to Dora that "in the first days of her attacks of aphonia 'writing had always come especially easy to her'" (no source is given for the quotation), and he concludes: "When the man she loved was away she gave up speaking; speech had lost its value since she could not speak to *him*. On the other hand, writing gained in importance, as being the only means of communication with him in his absence." But though Freud tells us that Herr K. used to write to Dora at length, there is no mention of any cards or letters being sent by her to him in return. The whole paragraph seems calculated to create an impression that it lends support to Freud's interpretation, but if one looks for the facts through the smoke screen of inferences, it is clear that it does nothing of the kind.

Freud emphasises that the basis of a somatic symptom is as a rule constitutional or organic and that unconscious thoughts utilise the "somatic compliance" of the symptom as a means of finding expression. It follows that a given symptom may be representative of more than one unconscious idea, and a little later he is able to discover a second "determinant" of Dora's cough. He was led to it by two things, one being the fact that her cough continued while she repeatedly complained about her father, suggesting that the symptom might have some meaning connected with him; the other being that the previous explanation had not fulfilled a requirement he was accustomed to making in such cases: "According to the rule which I have found confirmed over and over again by experience [. . .] a symptom signifies the representation—the realisation—of a phantasy with a sexual content, that is to say, it signifies a sexual situation."

Fortunately, "an opportunity very soon occurred for interpreting Dora's nervous cough in this way." From a statement by Dora that Frau K. only loved her father because he was "a man of means," Freud infers that behind this phrase its opposite lay concealed, namely that he was "a man without means," i.e., impotent. Following an admission that she knew her father was impotent, Dora acknowledges an awareness of nongenital ways of sexual gratification. She must, Freud writes, have in mind precisely those parts of the body which in her case were in a state of irritation—the throat and the oral cavity. This led to the "inevitable" conclusion "that with her spasmodic cough, which, as is usual, was referred for its exciting stimulus to a tickling in the throat, she pictured to herself a scene of sexual gratification *per os* [oral]" between her father and Frau K.

Not surprisingly, Dora "would not hear of going so far as this in recognising her own thoughts." However, "a very short time after she had tacitly accepted this explanation her cough vanished—which fitted in very well with my view." Having made his point, he adds: "But I do not wish to lay too much stress upon this development, since her cough had so often before disappeared spontaneously." Quite what Freud means by saying that Dora tacitly accepted his explanation is not clear. In all probability it signifies nothing more than that she had tired of disputing his colourful interpretations.

A little later Freud extends the meaning of the symptom. He adduces material from which he infers that Dora was putting herself in her mother's place, and he suggests that she was also putting herself in Frau K.'s place in the phantasy involving oral sex. She was therefore "identifying herself both with the woman her father had once loved and with the woman he loved now." It followed that her affection for her father was a much stronger one than she would have cared to admit, that in fact "she was in love with him." Freud writes at this point that he has "learnt to look upon unconscious love relations like this [. . .] as a revival of germs of feeling in infancy" and that he had "shown at length elsewhere at what an early age sexual attraction makes itself felt between parents and children." For years on end Dora had given no expression to "this passion for her father," but now she had revived it so as to suppress something else, namely, her love for Herr K. And with the recognition that "a part of her libido had once more turned towards her father," a further meaning of Dora's throat complaint could be derived: "it came to represent sexual intercourse with her father by means of Dora's identifying herself with Frau K."

Dora gives a negative response in each instance when Freud tells her she is unconsciously in love with Herr K. and with her father. However, he is "by no means disappointed" when an explanation of his is met with an emphatic negative, for such a denial "does no more than to register the existence of a repression and its severity." By interpreting associations brought forward by Dora as agreeing with the content of his assertion, he is able to obtain "confirmation from the unconscious" of his inferences. "No other kind of 'Yes' can be extracted from the unconscious: there is no such thing at all as an unconscious 'No.' " Clearly, Freud has few difficulties in obtaining confirmation (one way or another) of his interpretations from the responses of his patients.

At this point he brings forward fresh arguments (for example, that a friend of Dora's had noted that she had gone white on meeting Herr K. in the street) in support of his contention that Dora was in love with Herr K. Nevertheless, Freud writes, she persisted in her denials for some time longer, "until, towards the end of the analysis, the conclusive proof of its correctness came to light." As we shall see in due course, this "conclusive proof" turns out to be yet another interpretation, and the implication that

Dora at last accepted his contention is not borne out by Freud's account of her response: "Dora had listened to me without any of her usual contradictions. She seemed to be moved; she said goodbye to me very warmly, with the heartiest wishes for the New Year and—came no more."

Before completing this section Freud introduces us to a further complication concerning the multifarious contents of Dora's unconscious. Behind her reproaches towards her father relating to his affair with Frau K. was concealed not only her unconscious love for Herr K. but also "a feeling of jealousy which had that lady as its *object*." This leads to the inference that her conscious concern involving her father was "designed [. . .] also to conceal her love for Frau K." This can hardly have come as a surprise to Freud, for he had "never yet come through a single psychoanalysis of a man or a woman without having to take into account a very considerable current of homosexuality." In fact, he later concludes that Dora's "homosexual (gynaecophilic) love for Frau K. was the strongest unconscious current in her mental life." However, the premature termination of the treatment occurred before the analysis could throw light on this stratum of her unconscious.

THE FIRST DREAM

The rest of the analysis revolves around the interpretations of two dreams. The first of these is recorded as follows:

> A house was on fire. My father was standing beside my bed and woke me up. I dressed quickly. Mother wanted to stop and save her jewel case; but Father said: "I refuse to let myself and my two children be burnt for the sake of your jewel case." We hurried downstairs, and as soon as I was outside I woke up.

The analysis of this dream and its associations is too complex to deal with in detail here, and for the most part only the conclusions reached by Freud will be presented.

On the basis of the fact that Herr K. had recently given Dora a present of a jewel case and that the latter represented the female genitals, and assuming that repression had caused "every one of [the dream-elements] to be turned into its opposite," Freud is able to interpret the dream as meaning that Dora wished to give Herr K. a "return present." So she was "ready to give Herr K. what his wife withholds from him," and this was "the thought which has had to be repressed with so much energy." The dream also confirmed that she was summoning up her old love for her father in order to protect herself against her love for Herr K.

The dream indicated to Freud that Dora had wet her bed at an age later than is usual and that this was because she had masturbated in early childhood. (Freud writes that to the words of Dora's father in the dream, "I refuse to let my two children go to their destruction," should be added from the dream thoughts: "as a result of masturbation.") At one stage in the discussion Freud reports that they were "engaged upon a line of enquiry which led straight towards an admission that she had masturbated in childhood." That this is rather overstating the situation is clear from his words a short time later: "Dora denied flatly that she could remember any such thing." But he writes that a few days later she did something which he could only regard "as a further step towards the confession." As she talked she kept playing with a small reticule which she wore at her waist. Close observation of such acts had shown Freud that they "give expression to unconscious thoughts and impulses" and are therefore "manifestations of the unconscious." Dora's reticule "was nothing but a representation of the genitals, and her playing with it, her opening it and putting her finger in it, was an entirely unembarrassed yet unmistakable pantomimic announcement of what she would like to do with them—namely, to masturbate."

Freud now invokes an incident when Dora hurriedly concealed a letter she was reading as he came into the waiting room. He naturally asked her who it was from, but at first she refused to tell him. It turned out to be from her grandmother and of no relation to the treatment. However, Freud infers that Dora wanted to play "secrets" with him and to hint that she was on the point of allowing her secret to be torn from her by the doctor. She was afraid that the foundation of her illness might be discovered, that he might guess that she had masturbated. Adding this incident to the reproaches against her father for having made her ill (together with the self-reproach underlying them), her leucorrhoea, the playing with the reticule, and the bed-wetting after her sixth year, Freud concludes that the circumstantial evidence of her having masturbated in childhood was "complete and without a flaw."

Since in children "hysterical symptoms [. . .] form a substitute for masturbatory satisfaction," Freud is now able to relate Dora's supposed masturbation to her dyspnoea. Her "symptomatic acts and certain other signs" give him "good reasons" to believe that as a child she had overheard her father "breathing hard while [her parents] had intercourse." He had long maintained that "the dyspnoea and palpitations that occur in hysteria and anxiety neurosis are only detached fragments of the act of copulation." In Dora's case her "sympathetic excitement" on overhearing sexual intercourse taking place between her parents may very easily have caused her inclination to masturbation to be replaced by an inclination to anxiety. Then, when her father was away and she was wishing him back, "she must have reproduced in the form of an attack of asthma the impression she had received." Her train of thought could be conjectured to have been as follows: The first attack had come when she had over-exerted herself in climbing; her father was forbidden to climb mountains or to over-exert himself because he suffered from shortness of breath; then came the recollection of how much he had exerted himself with her mother that night and the question of whether it might not have done him harm; next came concern whether she might not have over-exerted herself in masturbating; and finally came the return of the dyspnoea in an intensified form as a symptom.

In addition to uncovering childhood material (infantile masturbation) supposedly alluded to in the dream, Freud is also able to draw out a further connection with Herr K. after Dora belatedly relates that on waking up from the dream she had smelt smoke. At first he suggests that this indicated it had a special relation to himself, because when Dora denied that something was hidden behind this or that he would often respond, "There can be no smoke without fire!" Dora objects to such a purely personal interpretation, pointing out that her father and Herr K. were smokers. Freud now argues that since the smell of smoke had only come up as an addendum to the dream, it must therefore have had to overcome a particularly strong effort on the part of the repression. Accordingly, it must relate to the thoughts which were the most obscurely presented and the most successfully repressed in the dream, that is, those concerned with the temptation to yield to Herr K. It could therefore "scarcely mean anything else than the longing for a kiss, which, with a smoker, would necessarily smell of smoke." This must hark back to the incident a few years earlier (at age fourteen) when Herr K. had given her a kiss, against whose "seductive influence" she had defended herself at the time by the feeling of disgust. Further, taking into account "indications which seemed to point to there having been a transference" onto himself, who was also a smoker, he concludes that "the idea had probably occurred to her one day during a session that she would like to have a kiss" from him. This would have been the "exciting cause" which led to the occurrence of the "warning dream" and to her intention of stopping the treatment.

THE SECOND DREAM

The other dream whose interpretation plays a major role in the analysis is considerably longer than the first. The following is an abridged version of it: Dora was walking in a strange town. She came to a house in which she found a letter from her mother which told her that her father was dead. She then went to the station and asked repeatedly "Where is the station?" She next went into a thick wood and met a man who offered to accompany her, but she refused his request. Finally she found herself at home and was told that her mother and the others were already at the cemetery.

By means of associations to events in Dora's life, Freud is able to translate her question in the dream about the station to mean, "Where is the box [woman]?" and also "Where is the key?" He interprets the latter question to be "the masculine counterpart to the question 'Where is the *box?*'" and concludes: "They are therefore questions referring to—the genitals." A little later he associates the wood in the dream with one near the lake where the incident with Herr K. occurred and also to a wood in a picture at an exhibition Dora had visited the previous day. In the background of this picture there were nymphs. Freud continues:

> At this point a certain suspicion of mine became a certainty. The use of "Bahnhof" [station] and "Friedhof" [cemetery] to represent the female genitals was striking enough in itself, but it also served to direct my awakened curiosity to the similarly formed "Vorhof" [vestibulum]—an anatomical term for a particular region of the female genitals. This might have been no more than mistaken ingenuity. But now, with the addition of "nymphs" visible in the background of a "thick wood," no fur-

ther doubts could be entertained. Here was a symbolic geography of sex! "Nymphae," as is known to physicians, though not to laymen (and even by the former the term is not very commonly used), is the name given to the labia minora, which lie in the background of the "thick wood" of the pubic hair. [. . .] If this interpretation were correct, therefore, there lay concealed behind the first situation in the dream a phantasy of defloration, the phantasy of a man seeking to force an entrance into the female genitals.

In the course of expounding his interpretation, Freud comments that "anyone who employed such technical names as 'vestibulum' and 'nymphae' must have derived his knowledge from [. . .] anatomical textbooks or from an encyclopaedia." But this statement only serves to underline the absurdity of the interpretation, since these associations occur in his own mind, and it is clear from the text that it was he, not Dora, who employed the technical terms.

Seemingly oblivious of this obvious flaw in his argument, Freud goes on to describe how he convinces himself that Dora must have at some time looked up the technical words in question in an encyclopaedia, though all Dora recollects is that she had once looked up the symptoms of appendicitis in an encyclopaedia because a cousin of hers had that illness. He now seizes on the fact that she herself had had a feverish disorder which was diagnosed as appendicitis. After demonstrating to his own satisfaction that these were hysterical symptoms, he utilises the fact that they apparently occurred nine months after the incident by the lake involving Herr K. to assert that they represented a phantasy of childbirth consequent upon that incident—further evidence that Dora was indeed in love with Herr K. At this point Freud reports, "And Dora disputed the fact no longer," though it is unclear whether this is because of the persuasiveness of his arguments or simply that she was rendered speechless by the onslaught of fantastic interpretations to which she had been subjected.

From the comments that follow, however, there is little doubt which of these was the case. Freud writes that at the end of the session he expressed his satisfaction at the result, to which "Dora replied in a depreciatory tone: 'Why, has anything so very remarkable come out?' " At this he tells us, "These words prepared me for the advent of fresh revelations."

They turn out to be nothing less than her announcement that she is terminating the treatment, for he continues: "She opened the [next] session with these words: 'Do you know that I am here for the last time today?' "

CONCLUSION OF THE TREATMENT

During this last session Dora recounts that a governess with the K.'s had given notice while she was staying with them by the lake. The girl had confided to Dora that Herr K. had made advances to her on an occasion when his wife was away and that she had yielded to them, but that after a time he had lost interest in her. At this point Freud informs us that here was a piece of material information coming to light to help solve problems of the analysis. He is able to tell Dora that he now knows her motive for the slap in the face with which she had answered Herr K.'s "proposal." It was not that she was offended at his suggestions; she was actuated by jealousy and revenge. More inferences are then brought forward to justify his contention that she "wanted to wait for him" and that she "took it that he was only waiting till [she was] grown up enough to be his wife." He concludes: "So it must have been a bitter piece of disillusionment for you when the effect of your charges against Herr K. was not that he renewed his proposals but that he replied instead with denials and slanders. [. . .] I know now [. . .] that you *did* fancy that Herr K.'s proposals were serious, and that he would not leave off until you had married him."

This, then, is the "conclusive proof" promised by Freud that Dora was unconsciously in love with Herr K. What the poor girl thought of all this one can only conjecture. We know only that "she came no more." It is clear that Herr K.'s unwanted attentions were largely responsible for the depression and suicidal ideas that led to her being induced to come for treatment in the first place, for her father told Freud that the incident by the lake was the reason for his daughter's mental state and that she kept pressing him to break off relations with Herr K. and his wife. Freud quotes him as saying that Dora "cannot be moved from her hatred of the K.s. She had her last attack after a conversation in which she had again pressed me to break with them." Given her distressed state, it would seem to be reprehensible that she should receive the kind of treatment to which Freud subjected her in his efforts to overcome her "resistance" to the notion that she was unconsciously in love with the man she in actuality detested. . . .

Equally apparent is Freud's preoccupation with the sexual. When he informs Dora that "jewel case" is to be interpreted as the female genitals, she responds, "I knew *you* would say that." Characteristically, he interprets this as confirmation of his suggestion, whereas to the reader it is clear that she is merely pointing to a self-evident fact, namely, that it is difficult to conceive of any material for which Freud would not find a sexual connotation. One is reminded that in this connection Jung came to regard him as a "tragic figure [. . .] a man in the grip of his daimon." He wrote that when Freud spoke of the importance of sexuality, "his tone became urgent, almost anxious. [. . .] A strange, deeply moved expression came over his face, the cause of which I was at a loss to understand." For Jung, "there was no mistaking the fact that Freud was emotionally involved in his sexual theory to an extraordinary degree."

Precisely the same impression is conveyed by certain passages in the Dora case history, and indeed the paper as a whole lends support to Jung's view. In the Postscript, Freud emphasises that a major reason for publishing it was that he was "anxious to show that sexuality [. . .] provides the motive power for every single symptom, and for every single manifestation of a symptom. The symptoms of the disease are nothing else than *the patient's sexual activity.* [. . .] I can only repeat over and over again—for I never find it otherwise—that sexuality is the key to the problem of the psychoneuroses and of the neuroses in general." It is singularly ironic that the man who claimed to have solved the problem of the origins of neuroses should himself have suffered from something akin to an obsession which centred around this very solution. . . .

In the light of the above, as Anthony Stadlen writes, Freud does not merely misdiagnose Dora's complaints, he fails to see that the primary problem is not any complaint of Dora's but her father's complaint *about* Dora. He is too preoccupied with his own preconceptions to recognise this, and therein lies his failure in the case of Dora.

13

A Little Child Shall Mislead Them*

Joseph Wolpe and Stanley Rachman

Not all of Freud's major case histories deal with patients he treated in person. The psychotic Dr. Schreber, for example (SE, 12: 3–79), was known to him only through published books. And in the still more celebrated case of "Little Hans" (SE, 10: 5–149), who grew up to become the operatic producer Herbert Graf, the "analysis" was conducted almost entirely by the five-year-old's father, Max Graf, one of Freud's most devoted early supporters and the husband of a former patient.

In January 1908, Herbert—let us bow to tradition and call him Hans—developed an acute and worsening fear of horses, thus affording both Graf senior and Freud himself a precious opportunity to study the phenomenon of childhood phobia. Freud saw Hans only once but was able to reassure him, on the basis of previous communications with the father, that he needn't worry; the dreaded horse was nothing but a stand-in for that father, who did *not,* Freud explained, actually intend to castrate him just because Hans unconsciously considered him a sexual rival. And thus comforted—the story goes—Hans immediately began to improve: "From the moment that Freud kindly interpreted these realities to his five-year-old patient, Hans's phobia began to recede and his anxiety to disappear" (Gay, 1988, page 259). What a therapeutic triumph, and what a "splendid illustration of defense mechanisms at work in the oedipal phase" (Gay, 1988, page 259)!

* From "Psychoanalytic Evidence: A Critique Based on Freud's Case of Little Hans," in *Critical Essays on Psychoanalysis*, ed. Stanley Rachman (New York: Macmillan, 1963): 198–220.

Freud was especially delighted with the case because in his analyses of adults, employing the tenuous inferential maneuvers that we examined in Part II, he could only "reconstruct" the tempest of childhood sexuality. Here, in contrast, the thing itself was being disclosed at point-blank range by a boy who seemed all but ready to confess that he wished to fornicate with his mother, murder his father, and do away with his little sister in the bargain. And just as Freud's theory anticipated, the symbolically determined horse phobia, a compromise formation par excellence, lost its power when the tabooed desires were brought into consciousness. Hans's cure was supposedly so thoroughgoing that when he renewed acquaintance with Freud at age nineteen and looked over the case history, "he felt he was reading about a complete stranger" (Gay, 1988, page 260). Could there be a stronger proof that psychoanalysis can tame the oedipal furies and put them altogether out of mind?

That is the myth of Little Hans. As Joseph Wolpe and Stanley Rachman show in the following pages, there was no correlation between Hans's symptom abatement and the interpretations he was given by Freud and his father. Nor was Hans's "acceptance" of those interpretations genuine; the adults kept putting words in his mouth, repeatedly demanding that he play Oedipus when he simply wanted to play. Above all, Freud and the elder Graf discounted the elemental fact that Hans had acquired his horse phobia when he was frightened by a horse. By replacing that fact with his own scholastic dogmatism, Freud turned the "Analysis of a Phobia in a Five-Year-Old Boy" into what may well be the most farcical case history on record anywhere.

Even so, there is a hint of future tragedy here. It relates not to Little Hans, whose phobia was apparently self-limiting and whose "treatment" appears to have done no harm, but to a foretaste of the leading questions that psychologists, social workers, and detectives would address to children in our own time, drawing from them "evidence" not of oedipal fantasizing but of sexual abuse at the hands of day-care workers, divorced spouses, and others (Ceci and Bruck, 1995). Freud's case history is a textbook model of how to extract desired misinformation from the young.

Wolpe and Rachman's article, first published in 1960, stands among the classics of Freud criticism. Its influence has been decisive for some workers in the field (see, for example, Scharnberg, 1993). The late Joseph Wolpe, a pioneer of behavior therapy, taught for many years at Temple University and later at Pepperdine University. Stanley Rachman taught in England for a number of years before becoming Professor of Psychology at the University of British Columbia.

In early January, 1908, the father wrote to Freud that Hans had developed "a nervous disorder." The symptoms he reported were a fear of going into the streets, depression in the evening, and a fear that a horse would bite him in the street. Hans's father suggested that "the ground was prepared by sexual over-excitation due to his mother's tenderness" and that the fear of the horse "seems somehow to be connected with his having been frightened by a large penis." The first signs appeared on January 7, when Hans was being taken to the park by his nursemaid as usual. He started crying and said he wanted to "coax" (caress) with his mother. At home "he was asked why he had refused to go any further and had cried, but he would not say." The following day, after hesitation and crying, he went out with his mother. Returning home, Hans said ("after much internal struggling"), *"I was afraid a horse would bite me"* [original emphasis]. As on the previous day, Hans showed fear in the evening and asked to be "coaxed." He is also reported as saying, "I know I shall have to go for a walk again tomorrow," and "The horse'll come into the room." On the same day he was asked by his mother if he put his hand to his widdler. He replied in the affirmative. The following day his mother warned him to refrain from doing this.

At this point in the narrative, Freud provided an interpretation of Hans's behavior and consequently arranged with the boy's father "that he should tell the boy that all this nonsense about horses was a piece of nonsense and nothing more. The truth was, his father was to say, that he was very fond of his mother and wanted to be taken into her bed. The reason he was afraid of horses now was that he had taken so much interest in their widdlers." Freud also suggested giving Hans some sexual enlightenment and telling him that females "had no widdler at all."

"After Hans had been enlightened there followed a fairly quiet period." After an attack of influenza which kept him in bed for two weeks, the phobia got worse. He then had his tonsils out and was indoors for a further week. The phobia became "very much worse."

During March, 1908, after his physical illnesses had been cured, Hans apparently had many talks with his father about the phobia. On March 1, his father again told Hans that horses do not bite. Hans replied that white horses bite and related that while at Gmunden he had heard and seen Lizzi (a playmate) being warned by her father to avoid a white horse lest it bite. The father said to Lizzi, *"Don't put your finger to the white horse"* [original emphasis]. Hans's father's reply to this account given by his son was, "I say, it strikes me it isn't a horse you mean, but a widdler, that one mustn't put one's hand to." Hans answered, "But a widdler doesn't bite." The father: "Perhaps it does, though." Hans then "went on eagerly to try to prove to me that it was a white horse." The following day, in answer to a remark of his father's, Hans said that his phobia was "so bad because I still put my hand to my widdler every night." Freud remarks here that "Doctor and patient, father and son, were therefore at one in ascribing the chief share in the pathogenesis of Hans's present condition to his habit of onanism." He implies that this unanimity is significant, quite disregarding the father's indoctrination of Hans the previous day.

On March 13, the father told Hans that his fear would disappear if he stopped putting his hand to his widdler. Hans replied, "But I don't put my hand to my widdler any more." Father: "But you still want to." Hans agreed, "Yes, I do." His father suggested that he should sleep in a sack to prevent him from wanting to touch his widdler. Hans accepted this view and on the following day was much less afraid of horses.

Two days later the father again told Hans that girls and women have no widdlers. "Mummy has none, Anna has none, and so on." Hans asked how they managed to widdle and was told, "They don't have widdlers like yours. Haven't you noticed already when Hanna was being given her bath?" On March 17 Hans reported a phantasy in which he saw his mother naked. On the basis of this phantasy and the conversation related above, Freud concluded that Hans had not accepted the enlightenment given by his father. Freud says, "He regretted that it should be so, and stuck to his former view in phantasy. He may also perhaps have had his reasons for refusing to believe his father at first." Discussing this matter subsequently, Freud says that the "enlightenment" given a short time before to the effect that women really do not possess a widdler was bound to have a shattering effect upon his self-confidence and to have aroused his castration complex. For this reason he resisted the information, and for this reason it had no therapeutic effect.

For reasons of space we shall recount the subsequent events in very brief form. On a visit to the zoo Hans expressed fear of the giraffe, the elephant, and all large animals. Hans's father said to him, "Do you know why you're afraid of big animals? Big animals have big widdlers and you're really afraid of big widdlers." This was denied by the boy.

The next event of prominence was a dream (or phantasy) reported by Hans. "In the night there was a big giraffe in the room and a crumpled one; and the big one called out because I took the crumpled one away from it. Then it stopped calling out; and then I sat down on the top of the crumpled one."

After talking to the boy the father reported to Freud that this dream was "a matrimonial scene transposed into giraffe life. He was seized in the night with a longing for his mother, for her caresses, for her genital organ, and came into the room for that reason. The whole thing is a continuation of his fear of horses." The father infers that the dream is related to Hans's habit of occasionally getting into his parents' bed in the face of his father's disapproval. Freud's addition to "the father's penetrating observation" is that sitting down on the crumpled giraffe means taking possession of his mother. Confirmation of this dream interpretation is claimed by reference to an incident which occurred the next day. The father wrote that on leaving the house with Hans he said to his wife, "Goodbye, big giraffe." "Why giraffe?" asked Hans. "Mummy's the big giraffe," replied the father. "Oh, yes," said Hans, "and [baby sister] Hanna's the crumpled giraffe, isn't she?" The father's account continues, "In the train I explained the giraffe phantasy to him, upon which he said 'Yes, that's right,' and when I said to him that I was the big giraffe and that its long neck reminded him of a widdler, he said, 'Mummy has a neck like a giraffe too. I saw when she was washing her white neck.' "

On March 30, the boy had a short consultation with Freud, who reports that despite all the enlightenment given to Hans, the fear of horses continued undiminished. Hans explained that he was especially bothered "by what horses wear in front of their eyes and the black round their mouths." This latter detail Freud interpreted as meaning a moustache. "I asked him whether he meant a moustache," and then "disclosed to him that he was afraid of his father precisely because he was so fond of his mother." Freud pointed out that this was a groundless fear. On April 2, the father was able to report "the first real improvement." The next day Hans, in answer to his father's inquiry, explained that he came into his father's bed when he was frightened. In the next few days further details of Hans's fear were elaborated. He told his father that he was most scared of horses with "a thing on their mouths," that he was scared lest the horses fall, and that he was most scared of horse-drawn buses.

Hans: "I'm most afraid too when a bus comes along."
Father: "Why? Because it's so big?"
Hans: "No. Because once a horse in a bus fell."
Father: "When?"

Hans then recounted such an incident. This was later confirmed by his mother.

Father: "What did you think when the horse fell down?"
Hans: "Now it will always be like this. All horses in buses'll fall down."
Father: "In all buses?"
Hans: "Yes. And in furniture vans too. Not often in furniture vans."
Father: "You had your nonsense already at that time?"
Hans: "*No* [emphasis added]. I only got it then. When the horse in the bus fell down, it gave me such a fright really: That was when I got the nonsense."

The father adds that "all of this was confirmed by my wife, as well as the fact that *the anxiety broke immediately afterwards*" [emphasis added].

Hans's father continued probing for a meaning of the black thing around the horses' mouths. Hans said it looked like a muzzle, but his father had never seen such a horse, "although Hans asseverates that such horses do exist." He continues, "I suspect that some part of the horse's bridle really reminded him of a moustache and that after I alluded to this the fear disappeared.". . .

Further details about the horse that fell were also elicited from Hans. He said there were actually two horses pulling the bus and that they were both black and "very big and fat." Hans's father again asked about the boy's thoughts when the horse fell.

Father: "When the horse fell down, did you think of your daddy?"
Hans: "Perhaps. Yes. It's possible."

For several days after these talks about horses Hans's interests, as indicated by the father's reports, "centered upon lumf (feces) and widdle, but we cannot tell why." Freud comments that at this point "the analysis began to be obscure and uncertain."

On April 11 Hans related this phantasy. "I was in the bath and then the plumber came and unscrewed it. Then he took a big borer and stuck it into my stomach." Hans's father translated this phantasy as follows: "I was in bed with Mamma. Then Pappa came and drove me away. With his big penis he pushed me out of my place by Mamma."

The remainder of the case history material, until Hans's recovery from the phobia early in May, is concerned with the lumf theme and Hans's feelings towards his parents and sister. It can be stated immediately that as corroboration for Freud's theories all of this remaining material is unsatisfactory. For the most part it consists of the father expounding theories to a boy who occasionally agrees and occasionally disagrees. . . .

Before proceeding to Freud's interpretation of the case, let us examine the value of the evidence presented. First, there is the matter of selection of the material. The greatest attention is naturally paid to material related to psychoanalytic theory, and there is a tendency to ignore other facts. The father and mother, we are told by Freud, "were both among my closest adherents." Hans himself was constantly encouraged, directly and indirectly, to relate material of relevance to the psychoanalytic doctrine.

Second, we must assess the value to be placed on the testimony of the father and of Hans. The father's account of Hans's behavior is in several instances suspect. For example, he twice presents his own interpretations of Hans's remarks as observed facts. This is the father's report of a conversation with Hans about the birth of his sister Hanna.

Father: "What did Hanna look like?"
  Hans (hypocritically): "All white and lovely. So pretty."

On another occasion, despite several clear statements by Hans of his affection for his sister (and also the voicing of complaints about her screaming), the father said to Hans, "If you'd rather she weren't alive, you can't be fond of her at all." Hans (assenting): "Hm . . . well." The comment in parenthesis in each of these two extracts is presented as observed fact. Or again, when Hans observes that Hanna's widdler is "so lovely," the father states that this is a "disingenuous" reply and that "in reality her widdler seemed to him funny." Distortions of this kind are common in the father's reports.

Hans's testimony is for many reasons unreliable. Apart from the numerous lies he told in the last few weeks of his phobia, Hans gave many inconsistent and occasionally conflicting reports. Most important of all, much of what purports to be Hans's views and feelings is simply the father speaking. Freud himself admits this but attempts to gloss over it. He says, "It is true that during the analysis Hans had to be told many things which he could not say himself, that he had to be presented with thoughts which he had so far shown no signs of possessing and that his attention had to be turned in the direction from which his father was expecting something to come. This detracts from the evidential value of the analysis but the procedure is the same in every case. For a psychoanalysis is not an impartial scientific investigation but a therapeutic measure." To sum this matter up, Hans's testimony not only is subject to "mere suggestion" but contains much material that is not his testimony at all! . . .

Freud's interpretation of Hans's phobia is that the boy's oedipal conflicts formed the basis of the illness, which "burst out" when he underwent "a time of privation and the intensified sexual excitement." Freud says, "These were tendencies in Hans which had already been suppressed and which, so far as we can tell, had never been able to find uninhibited expression: hostile and jealous feelings against his father, and sadistic impulses (premonitions, as it were, of copulation) towards his mother. These early suppressions may perhaps have gone to form the predisposition for his subsequent illness. These aggressive propensities of Hans's found no outlet, and as soon as there came a time of privation and of intensified sexual excitement, they tried to break their way out with reinforced strength. It was then that the battle which we call his 'phobia' burst out."

This is the familiar oedipal theory, according to which Hans wished to replace his father, "whom he could not help hating as a rival," and then to complete the act by "taking possession of his mother." Freud refers for confirmation to the following. "Another symptomatic act, happening as though by accident, involved a confession that he had wished his father dead; for, just at the moment that his father was talking of his death-wish Hans let a horse that he was playing with fall down—knocked it over, in fact." Freud claims that "Hans was really a little Oedipus who wanted to have his father 'out of the way' to get rid of him, so that be might be alone with his handsome mother and sleep with her." The predisposition to illness provided by the oedipal conflicts is supposed to have formed the basis for "the transformation of his libidinal longing into anxiety.". . .

Hans, we are told, "transposed from his father onto the horses." At his sole interview with Hans, Freud told him "that he was afraid of his father because he himself nourished jealous and hostile wishes against him." Freud says of this, "In telling him this, I had partly interpreted his fear of horses for him: the horse must be his father—whom he had good internal reasons for fearing." Freud claims that Hans's fear of the black things on the horses' mouths and the things in front of their eyes was based on moustaches and eye-glasses and had been "directly transposed from his father onto the horses." The horses "had been shown to represent his father.". . .

It is our contention that Freud's view of this case is not supported by the data, either in its particulars or as a whole. The major points that he regards as demonstrated are these: (1) Hans had a sexual desire for his mother, (2) he hated and feared his father and wished to kill him, (3) his sexual excitement and desire for his mother were transformed into anxiety, (4) his fear of horses was symbolic of his fear of his father, (5) the purpose of the illness was to keep near his mother, and finally (6) his phobia disappeared because he resolved his Oedipus complex.

Let us examine each of these points.

1. That Hans derived satisfaction from his mother and enjoyed her presence we will not even attempt to dispute. But nowhere is there any evidence of his wish to copulate with her. Yet Freud says that "if matters had lain entirely in my hands [. . .] I should have confirmed his instinctive premonitions, by telling him of the existence of the vagina and of copulation." The "instinctive premonitions" are referred to as though a matter of fact, though no evidence of their existence is given. . . . Even if it is assumed that stimulation provided by his mother was especially desired, the two other features of an Oedipus complex (a wish to possess the mother and replace the father) are not demonstrated by the facts of the case.

2. Never having expressed either fear or hatred of his father, Hans was told by Freud that he possessed these emotions. On subsequent occasions Hans denied the existence of these feelings when questioned by his father. Eventually, he said "Yes" to a statement of this kind by his

father. This simple affirmative obtained after considerable pressure on the part of the father and Freud is accepted as the true state of affairs, and all Hans's denials are ignored. The "symptomatic act" of knocking over the toy horse is taken as further evidence of Hans's aggression towards his father. There are three assumptions underlying this "interpreted fact"—first, that the horse represents Hans's father; second, that the knocking over of the horse is not accidental; and third, that this act indicates a wish for the removal of whatever the horse symbolized.

Hans consistently denied the relationship between the horse and his father. He was, he said, afraid of horses. The mysterious black around the horses' mouths and the things on their eyes were later discovered by the father to be horses' muzzles and blinkers. This discovery undermines the suggestion (made by Freud) that they were transposed moustaches and eye-glasses. There is no other evidence that the horses represented Hans's father. . . . As there is nothing to sustain the first two assumptions made by Freud in interpreting this "symptomatic act," the third assumption (that this act indicated a wish for his father's death) is untenable. . . .

3. Freud's third claim is that Hans's sexual excitement and desire for his mother were transformed into anxiety. This claim is based on the assertion that "theoretical considerations require that what is today the object of a phobia must at one time in the past have been the source of a high degree of pleasure." Certainly such a transformation is not displayed by the facts presented. As stated above, there is no evidence that Hans sexually desired his mother. There is also no evidence of any change in his attitude to her before the onset of the phobia. Even though there is some evidence that horses were to some extent previously a source of pleasure, in general the view that phobic objects must have been the source of former pleasures is amply contradicted by experimental evidence. . . .

4. The assertion that Hans's horse phobia symbolized a fear of his father has already been criticized. The assumed relationship between the father and the horse is unsupported and appears to have arisen as a result of the father's strange failure to believe that by the "black around their mouths" Hans meant the horses' muzzles.

5. The fifth claim is that the purpose of Hans's phobia was to keep him near his mother. Aside from the questionable view that neurotic

disturbances occur for a purpose, this interpretation fails to account for the fact that Hans experienced anxiety even when he was out walking *with his mother*.

6. Finally, we are told that the phobia disappeared as a result of Hans's resolution of his oedipal conflicts. . . . The claim that this assumed complex was resolved is based on a single conversation between Hans and his father—a blatant example of what Freud himself refers to as Hans having to "be told many things he could not say himself, that he had to be presented with thoughts which he had so far shown no signs of possessing, and that his attention had to be turned in the direction that his father was expecting something to come."

There is also no satisfactory evidence that the "insights" that were incessantly brought to the boy's attention had any therapeutic value. Reference to the facts of the case shows only occasional coincidences between interpretations and changes in the child's phobic reactions. For example, "a quiet period" followed the father's statement that the fear of horses was a "piece of nonsense" and that Hans really wanted to be taken into his mother's bed. But soon afterwards, when Hans became ill, the phobia was worse than ever. Later, having had many talks without effect, the father notes that on March 13 Hans, after agreeing that he still *wanted* to play with his widdler, was "much less afraid of horses." On March 15, however, he was frightened of horses, after the information that females have no widdlers (though he had previously been told the opposite by his mother). Freud asserts that Hans resisted this piece of enlightenment because it aroused castration fears, and therefore no therapeutic success was to be observed. The "first real improvement" of April 2 is attributed to the "moustache enlightenment" of March 30 (later proved erroneous), the boy having been told that he was "afraid of his father precisely because he was so fond of his mother." On April 7, though Hans was constantly improving, Freud commented that the situation was "decidedly obscure" and that "the analysis was making little progress." Such sparse and tenuous data do not begin to justify the attribution of Hans's recovery to the bringing to consciousness of various unacceptable, unconscious, repressed wishes. . . .

In general, Freud infers relationships in a scientifically inadmissible manner: if the enlightenments or interpretations given to Hans are followed by behavioural improvements, then they are automatically accepted as valid. If they are not followed by improvement, we are told that the patient has not accepted them, and not that they are invalid. . . .

. . . We have combed Freud's account for evidence that would be acceptable in the court of science, and have found none. Yet Freud fully believed that he had obtained in Little Hans a direct confirmation of his theories, for he speaks towards the end of "the infantile complexes that were revealed behind Hans's phobia." It seems clear that although he wanted to be scientific, Freud was surprisingly naive regarding the requirements of scientific evidence. Infantile complexes were not *revealed* (demonstrated) behind Hans's phobia: they were merely hypothesized.

It is remarkable that countless psychoanalysts have paid homage to the case of Little Hans without being offended by its glaring inadequacies. We shall not here attempt to explain this, except to point to one probable major influence—a tacit belief among analysts that Freud possessed a kind of unerring insight that absolved him from the obligation to obey rules applicable to ordinary men. . . . It may of course be argued that some of the conclusions drawn from Little Hans are no longer held and that there is now other evidence for some of the conclusions; but there is no evidence that in general, psychoanalytic conclusions are based on any better logic than that used by Freud in respect of Little Hans. Certainly no analyst has ever pointed to the failings of this account or disowned its reasoning, and it has continued to be regarded as one of the foundation stones on which psychoanalytic theory was built.

Exemplary Botches*

Frank J. Sulloway

Twelve years after the appearance of his groundbreaking *Freud, Biologist of the Mind* (see pages 54–68 above), Frank J. Sulloway published the influential article from which this chapter is excerpted. His book had demonstrated the "cryptobiological" origins of Freud's thought without, however, fully confronting the extent to which those origins compromised the empirical standing of psychoanalysis (see Crews, 1986, pages 88–111). But by 1991 Sulloway had resolved any remaining doubts. "Cryptic or not," he now declared, "bad biology ultimately spawned bad psychology. Freud erected his psychoanalytic edifice on a kind of intellectual quicksand, a circumstance that consequently doomed many of his most important theoretical conclusions from the outset" (Sulloway, 1991, page 245).

Sulloway now wished to explore the effects of "bad psychology" on two related aspects of Freud's work: his practical handling of cases and the building of his personal legend and institutional power. In both realms, Sulloway argued, the appearance of medical/scientific success could be maintained only by continual and systematic distortion of the record. Thus while Freud was misrepresenting his past, creating a myth of solitary and heroic discovery, he was also teaching his followers to replace the empirical attitude with blind loyalty, censorship, and ruthlessness toward dissent. And instead of producing an objective

* From "Reassessing Freud's Case Histories: The Social Construction of Psychoanalysis," *Isis,* 82 (June 1991): 245–275.

account of his therapeutic results and spelling out a clinical method that outsiders could test for cogency, he chose to personify psychoanalysis through seductive anecdotes about his work in a handful of dramatic instances.

We are already acquainted with two of the cases Sulloway discusses below, those of Dora (Chapter 12) and Little Hans (Chapter 13), and in Chapter 15 we will take a second look at the Wolf Man narrative from the standpoint of its rhetorical tactics. The case of the "female homosexual" can be found in SE, 18: 146–172. The Schreber case (SE, 12: 3–79) has been variously assessed by Niederland, 1959; Schatzman, 1973; Busse, 1991; and Lothane, 1992. A revealing study of the Rat Man case (SE, 10: 153–318) is Mahony, 1986. The work cited in the closing sentence of Sulloway's chapter is Eysenck, 1985.

Freud published only six detailed case histories after he broke with Breuer and developed the "talking cure" into psychoanalysis proper. Examined critically, these six case histories are by no means compelling empirical demonstrations of the correctness of his psychoanalytic views. Indeed, some of the cases present such dubious evidence in favor of psychoanalytic theory that one may seriously wonder why Freud even bothered to publish them. As Seymour Fisher and Roger P. Greenberg have commented in connection with their own review of the case histories, "It is curious and striking that Freud chose to demonstrate the utility of psychoanalysis through descriptions of largely unsuccessful cases."

BRIEF TREATMENTS

Two of the cases were incomplete and the therapy ineffective. Freud's first case history dealt with an eighteen-year-old hysterical patient named Dora. Treatment lasted only three months, when the patient, fed up with Freud's badgering manner and insensitive insinuations, fled therapy. Freud's much later case of a female homosexual also terminated after a short time and involved no therapeutic improvement or even real treatment. A third case was not actually treated by Freud. He was five-year-old Little Hans, who was seen by Freud only once, the "analysis" having been conducted by the boy's father, a devout Freudian. Moreover, Little Hans, whose statements were repeatedly reinterpreted by his father and Freud to suit psychoanalytic theory, appears to have understood the straight-forward traumatic source of his horse phobia, which followed his witnessing a carriage accident, better than either of his two would-be therapists. Using considerable common sense, Little Hans tried his best to resist Freud's oedipal "reconstructions" and interpretations; but his father and Freud, working in concert, gradually wore him down in an effort to get the case history to come out in a psychoanalytically correct fashion. Freud's other three cases reveal even more severe shortcomings.

SCHREBER AND HIS FATHER

The case of Daniel Paul Schreber involved a psychotic German magistrate whom Freud never met but whom he analyzed from Schreber's published memoir of 1903 about his illness. The extensive shortcomings of Freud's analysis have been revealed by the diligent research of several scholars. Two aspects of the case have invited significant reevaluation by these scholars: Schreber's relationship with his father and Schreber's supposed homosexuality.

Schreber's father, Moritz, was an orthopedic physician who had written numerous works on the upbringing and education of children. Freud, who had already reached his theory of paranoia before encountering Schreber's memoir, made no effort to read the father's published works. Yet there are seeming links between the son's delusions (that his chest was being suffocated, that his head was being compressed, and that his hair was being pulled) and various mechanical devices that the father recommended to insure proper posture in children. For example, Moritz Schreber advocated the use of a "straightener" to prevent children from leaning forward while reading or writing. This instrument consisted of a horizontal bar that attached to a desk in front of the child and that pressed on the chest at the level of the clavicle and shoulders. Another of his devices was a "head holder" which discouraged a drooping head by causing the child's hair to be pulled whenever the head was lowered. Whether Daniel Paul Schreber was ever subjected to any of these devices is not known, but William Niederland and Morton Schatzman have both made a case that Schreber's symptoms, interpreted by Freud as stemming from repressed homosexuality, were linked to his father's methods of upbringing.

The father's role in his son's psychosis is still far from clear. Niederland and especially Schatzman may have gone too far in arguing that the father was a tyrant who actually drove his son insane. Han Israëls claims that Moritz Schreber was a loving father who was adored by his wife and children and whose views on child rearing and correct posture were hardly unusual for the times. If Moritz Schreber was strict about posture and maintained high social ideals for his children, he also advocated "a cheerful, talkative, laughing, singing, playful conduct towards the child" and stressed how important it was to praise the child. He particularly warned that "the child should not be made into a slave of another's will." Niederland and Schatzman both omitted this evidence.

Whereas Niederland and Schatzman effectively distorted the record about Moritz Schreber as a father, Freud went even further by omitting considerable concrete evidence about the father's personality and educational beliefs. Had this omission been based on ignorance, it would be understandable. But, in fact, Freud had evidence that contradicted his assertions about the father. In a remarkable letter to Sándor Ferenczi, written while Freud was working on the case, he referred to the father as a "despot in his household." He had apparently obtained this information from Dr. Arnold Georg Stegmann, a psychoanalytic follower who was acquainted not only with the various psychiatrists who had treated Daniel Paul Schreber but also with relatives of the patient. Astonishingly, Freud suppressed this information in his published case history and instead referred to Moritz Schreber as "an excellent father."

Why Freud suppressed information about the father becomes clear from Zvi Lothane's reappraisal of the evidence that Schreber was a homosexual. Freud was anxious to show that paranoia originated in repressed homosexuality, which in Schreber's instance was supposedly a repressed homosexual attachment to the father. Before his illness, Schreber had displayed only heterosexual inclinations. Just before one of his hospitalizations, however, and while still half asleep, Schreber had suddenly experienced the "highly peculiar" and alien thought that it "really must be rather pleasant to be a woman succumbing to intercourse." His subsequent illness involved his delusion that his psychiatrist and God were slowly changing him into a woman, a process against which he struggled for many years before finally becoming reconciled to God's plan. (That divine plan required Schreber's feminization so that the world might eventually be redeemed.) Naturally, Freud interpreted these delusions as evidence of Schreber's unconscious homosexuality. But Lothane has concluded from a careful analysis of Schreber's *Memoir* that Freud "manipulated the events described by Schreber and changed them to suit his bias." These distortions involved imputing homosexual desires to Schreber under the most dubious of circumstances and ignoring the rage that Schreber felt toward his psychiatrist for abandoning him as a patient by having him transferred to an asylum for incurable patients. (Schreber had been treated and cured by the same psychiatrist a decade earlier.) After his illness had stabilized into a number of harmless delusions, Schreber struggled for many years to obtain his release from this asylum. Using brilliant legal means in his own defense, he finally won his case in a German court, despite the protests of the obdurate asylum director.

In any event, Freud evidently concluded that portraying Moritz Schreber as a despotic and persecutory father might only weaken his case for the homosexual and hence inverted oedipal nature of Schreber's illness. "Such a [superior] father as this," Freud argued in his case history, "was by no means unsuitable for transfiguration into a God in the affectionate memory of the son." Indeed, it was "the fact that his father-complex was in the main positively toned" and "unclouded" that finally allowed Schreber, in Freud's view, to reconcile himself to his homosexual fantasies and thereby to achieve a partial mental recovery. So the "despot in his household" was reconstructed by Freud as the "excellent father" of the published case history.

THE RAT MAN AS SHOWPIECE

Even the most complete and seemingly successful case histories of people actually treated by Freud are flawed by shaky "constructions" and lack of adequate follow-ups. His case histories of the Rat Man and the Wolf Man particularly illustrate this assertion. Freud was led to publish the first of these two case histories because he was feeling pressured to show the world that psychoanalysis could achieve successful therapeutic results. Since the Rat Man had previously consulted Julius von Wagner-Jauregg, Freud's eminent psychiatric colleague at the University of Vienna, the case was a particularly critical test of Freud's therapeutic abilities. Before October 1908, when he communicated this case history at the First International Psychoanalytic Congress in Salzburg, Freud had yet to publish the results of a successful psychoanalysis. Astonishing as it may seem, it is unclear whether he had conducted any successful analyses since Dora fled his office in 1900. "I have no case that is complete and can be viewed as a whole," Freud informed Carl Jung in a letter of 19 April 1908, just a week before the Salzburg Congress. Freud also considered presenting details from the case history of Little Hans, whose treatment he was supervising at the time. But when Little Hans refused to be cured on schedule, the Rat Man became, apparently by default, Freud's first public communication of a psychoanalytic cure.

The Rat Man, whose real name was Ernst Lanzer, first came to Freud in October 1907 complaining of obsessive fears and compulsive impulses. Lanzer's principal fear was that something terrible was going to happen to two of the people whom he cared about the most—his father and a lady friend, whom he eventually married. This fear had grown out of a vivid verbal account he had recently heard from a fellow army officer concerning a horrible Chinese torture. The torture involved strapping a large pot to the buttocks of the naked victim, who is chained and unable to move. Inside the pot, just before it is strapped on, the torturer places a large hungry rat. The rat is then terrorized by a red-hot poker introduced into the bottom of the pot through a small hole. In its fright, the rat retreats, tears at the buttocks of the victim, and finally, in desperation, attempts to bore into the victim's anus. Both the rat (through suffocation) and the victim (from hemorrhaging) eventually expire from this ghoulish torture.

Freud was able to understand the nature of Lanzer's obsession with rats by interpreting a number of his patients' associations to the German word *Ratten* (rats). Lanzer had revealed in analysis that his father had been a gambler, once losing money over a game of cards that he could not repay. Hence his father was a *Spielratte,* or "gambling rat." According to Freud, Lanzer also associated "rats" directly with money through the word *Raten* (installments). The connection of the rat association with Lanzer's lady friend was hidden behind the screen-association *heiraten* (to marry). But the most crucial link in Freud's analysis was his patient's eventual identification of rats with children and, through children, with an episode in his own childhood when he had *bitten* someone and was punished by his father for this misbehavior. According to Freud's analysis, Lanzer unconsciously identified *himself* with rats. Since Freud, in a previous publication, had claimed that children sometimes imagine intercourse as occurring *per anum,* the meaning of Lanzer's rat obsession became clear. Lanzer was unconsciously fantasizing that he—a rat and a biter—was having anal intercourse with his father and with his lady friend. This appalling thought, kept from Lanzer's consciousness by repression, had become the source of his obsessive symptoms. Its ultimate psychological motive was Lanzer's aggression toward his father, who Freud believed, through further psychoanalytic reconstruction, had interrupted his son's early sexual life and threatened him with castration. According to Freud, his communication of this oedipal reconstruction "led to the complete restoration of the patient's personality, and to the removal of his inhibition."

A number of significant discrepancies between the published case history and Freud's process notes, which were discovered among his papers after his death, have been pointed out by Patrick Mahony. According to Mahony, who is himself an analyst and sympathetic to the general goals of psychoanalysis, Freud's published case history is "muddled" and "inconsistent" on various matters of fact and also exhibits "glaring" omissions of information. In particular, there is an overemphasis on the father to the exclusion of the mother. Mahony also points out that Freud misrepresented the length of his patient's treatment. The process notes show that Freud treated his patient for a little more than three months on a regular daily basis. The treatment was irregular for the next three months and sporadic, at best, after that. (There is no actual record of any treatment after the first six months.) Yet Freud claimed that he had treated his patient "for more than eleven months," a claim that Mahony shows is quite impossible and thus represents a "deliberate" distortion.

In the published case history, Freud engaged in another misrepresentation of chronology in recounting one of his key reconstructions. On 27 December 1907, Lanzer reported certain information to Freud. This information included Lanzer's habit of opening the door to his flat between midnight and 1:00 A.M., apparently so that his father's ghost could enter. Lanzer would then stare at his penis, sometimes using a mirror. In the published case history, Freud builds on this information:

> Starting from these indications and from other data of a similar
> kind, I ventured to put forth a construction to the effect that

when he was a child of under six he had been guilty of some sexual misdemeanor connected with masturbation and had been soundly castigated for it by his father. This punishment, according to my hypothesis, had, it was true, put an end to his masturbating, but on the other hand it had left behind it an ineradicable grudge against his father and had established him for all time in his role of an interferer with the patient's sexual life.

Obviously, Freud thought that it made more empirical sense for him to propose his reconstruction *after* hearing about the ghost story, and so that is how he presented it in the case history, even though he had actually proposed this reconstruction a month earlier. "Through alteration of temporal sequence," Mahony concludes from this particular distortion, "Freud's construction given to the Rat Man becomes in turn a fictionalized reconstruction shown to the reader."

Such fictionalized reconstructions are especially common at key points in Freud's argument, and they influence, in subtle but significant ways, his reporting of what the Rat Man actually said to him. Freud was concerned, for example, to show that the Rat Man's sexuality was liberated by the death of his father. He reports in the case history that the Rat Man was overcome by "compulsive" masturbation when he was 21, *"shortly after his father's death"* [Freud's emphasis]. The process notes tell a somewhat different story. "He [Lanzer] began it [masturbation] when he was about 21—after his father's death, as I got him to confirm—because he had heard of it and felt a certain curiosity." The patient apparently mentioned nothing about a "compulsion" to masturbate. Moreover, the whole connection between the Rat Man's masturbation and his father's death was largely engineered by Freud rather than volunteered by the patient through his "free associations." To make the reconstruction even more convincing, Freud omitted the word "about" from the original phrase "about 21" and inserted the word "shortly" into the phrase "after his father's death." In actual fact, the father had died two years earlier, when Lanzer was 19.

Freud's Rat Man case history is also characterized by exaggerated assertions regarding its therapeutic outcome. His claim to have cured his patient and to have brought about "the complete restoration of the patient's personality" is highly implausible on several grounds. To begin with, Lanzer had broken off his analysis with Freud after a relatively brief period and well before his transference had been fully resolved. Just after Freud had completed the written version of the case history in October 1909, he confessed to Jung that his patient was still having ongoing problems. "He is facing life with courage and ability," Freud reported. "The point that still gives him trouble (father-complex and transference) has shown up clearly in my conversations with this intelligent and grateful man." Given that Lanzer's neurosis supposedly centered on his father-complex, it is extremely difficult to imagine how Freud could have considered his patient "cured" after such a brief analysis ending in a still unresolved transference. At best, Freud might have expected to achieve a symptomatic relief of this patient's rat obsession, which is apparently what did happen. But he could hardly have expected a complete dissipation of the broad spectrum of obsessions and compulsions that had engrossed his patient's psychic life since childhood. As Mahony sums up, "Freud mixed momentous insights with exaggerated claims," some of which "were made in his zeal to protect and promote a new discipline." The Rat Man—cured or not—was clearly intended to be a showpiece for Freud's nascent psychoanalytic movement. That this case history became one (and for the loyal has remained one) is evidenced by Peter Gay's conclusion that it "brilliantly served to buttress Freud's theories, notably those postulating the childhood roots of neurosis. . . . Freud was not masochist enough to publish only failures." Since the patient died in World War I, there is no follow-up information on the case allowing us to assess the longer-term consequences of Freud's brief therapy.

CONVERSATIONS WITH THE WOLF MAN

One major patient of Freud's who did live long enough to provide a clear indication of the long-term consequences of his psychoanalysis was the Wolf Man. Freud treated the Wolf Man for four years, from 1910 to 1914, and he also conducted a brief second analysis five years later to remove a remnant of "transference" that had remained unresolved during the first treatment. In subsequent years the Wolf Man, whose real name was Sergei Pankeev, was reanalyzed twice by Ruth Mack Brunswick. After World War II a number of different psychoanalysts treated him until his death in 1978. The Wolf Man was therefore in and out of analysis repeatedly for more than sixty years. Unlike the Rat Man, he had the opportunity to tell about it.

Freud's reconstruction of the traumatic event that supposedly caused the Wolf Man's obsessional neurosis typifies the problematic nature of the psychoanalytic enterprise. According to Freud, the patient witnessed his parents having intercourse when he was one and a half, which prematurely awakened his libido and induced a passive homosexual attitude toward men. Freud reconstructed this traumatic event on the basis of a dream that the patient had had at the age of four:

> I dreamt that it was night and that I was lying in my bed. . . . Suddenly, the window opened of its own accord, and I was terrified to see that some white wolves were sitting on the big walnut tree in front of the window. . . . In great terror, evidently of being eaten up by the wolves, I screamed and woke up.

Freud's analysis of this dream led him to conclude that the white wolves represented the parents' white underwear and that the castration fears of the dreamer stemmed from his having witnessed "coitus *a tergo,* three times repeated," which enabled the Wolf Man to see that his mother lacked a phallus. After a four-year analysis and a shorter reanalysis following a brief relapse, Freud discharged the patient as cured. James Strachey has called this "the most elaborate and no doubt the most important of all Freud's case histories." It is also generally regarded by psychoanalysts as a considerable therapeutic success.

Owing to the indefatigable efforts of an Austrian journalist, Karin Obholzer, who located the Wolf Man in Vienna in the early 1970s, we now have access to the Wolf Man's own impressions of his analysis with Freud. From Obholzer's conversations, we learn that the Wolf Man himself considered Freud's interpretation of his famous dream to be "terribly farfetched" and that he also felt betrayed by Freud, who had promised him that he would one day actually remember the traumatic event that had made him ill. "The whole thing is improbable," the Wolf Man also pointed out, "because in Russia, children sleep in their nanny's bedroom, not in their parents'." The Wolf Man has also reported that the "wolves" in his famous dream were not wolves at all, but rather a special breed of wolflike dogs—a curious and unexplained discrepancy.

We also learn from Obholzer's interviews that the Wolf Man was by no means cured, either by Freud or by subsequent analysts. He remained a compulsively brooding personality with endless self-doubts; and he himself strongly disputed the analytic myth of his "cure." "That was the theory," he told Obholzer, "that Freud had cured me 100 percent. . . . And that's why [Muriel] Gardiner recommended that I write memoirs. To show the world how Freud cured a seriously ill person. . . . It's all false." As the Wolf Man, who by then was close to ninety, plaintively concluded of his psychoanalysis, "In reality, the whole thing looks like a catastrophe. I am in the same state as when I first came to Freud, and Freud is no more." Furthermore, subsequent analysts refused to leave the Wolf Man alone; they insisted on giving him free psychoanalysis as a means of keeping historical tabs on him, contradicted one another's advice and opinions, and undermined the independence of his judgment. "Psychoanalysts are a problem," the Wolf Man confided to Obholzer, "no doubt about it."

Finally, we learn from Obholzer's account that Kurt Eissler, through the Sigmund Freud Archives, was sending the Wolf Man money regularly to help him pay off a certain lady friend and former sexual partner who was bleeding him dry. When the Wolf Man expressed his wish to emigrate to America so as to escape this costly and unpleasant situation, his request was repeatedly discouraged, apparently because the psychoanalytic movement preferred to support him financially in Vienna, where he was living in anonymity, rather than risk his discovery in America as Freud's most famous but still highly neurotic patient. (Just imagine him "telling all" to a newscaster on one of television's major investigative reporting shows!) Eissler and other analysts also made strenuous efforts to dissuade the Wolf Man from talking with Obholzer, who succeeded in her efforts only because of her extraordinary perseverance and her promise not to publish her conversations with her ever-fearful informant until after his death. These conversations were, so to speak, the Wolf Man's dying protest against the false promises and disappointments of psychoanalysis. "Instead of doing me some good," he exclaimed to Obholzer, "psychoanalysts did me harm," adding plaintively, "I am telling you this confidentially." In short, one must wonder whether this famous case history was, as claimed, a therapeutic success and hence a demonstration of Freud's brilliant analytic powers. Stripped of the convenient censorship and the dubious reconstructions made possible by the patient's anonymity, the case history appears instead to have been a tacitly recognized embarrassment whose true nature needed to be hidden by the arm-twisting and the financial resources of the Sigmund Freud Archives.

Of course, that the Wolf Man, Anna O., and various other famous psychoanalytic patients were not cured is not technically a refutation of Freud's clinical theories and claims. These cases can be admitted as failures, or as only partial successes, and Freud's theories still be correct. But research since the 1930s has repeatedly shown that psychoanalytic patients fare no better than patients who participate in over a hundred other different forms of psychotherapy. Freud maintained that, on the contrary, psychoanalysis was the only form of psychotherapy that could produce true and permanent cures—all other therapeutic successes being due to suggestion. As Hans Eysenck has argued, the failure of psychoanalysis to achieve promised *superior* cure rates should be taken as strong evidence of its theoretical failure.

The Primal Scene of Persuasion*

Stanley Fish

The dubieties of the Wolf Man case (SE, 17: 3–122), which is briefly summarized by Frank J. Sulloway on pages 182–185 above, are by now quite familiar, and the number of informed readers who still accept Freud's account with childlike faith (for example, Richard Wollheim— see Freud, 1993) has become vanishingly small. More ample discussions than Sulloway's, all tending to support his conclusion that Freud neither understood nor cured his most famous patient, have been offered by Karin Obholzer (1982), Patrick Mahony (1984, 1995), James L. Rice (1993), and Allen Esterson (1993).

Here we will not belabor the emerging consensus but will focus instead on Freud's means of persuasion—a topic whose interest to scholars has grown proportionately with the loss of literal faith in his narratives. In recent years, a number of literary critics such as Robert Wilcocks (1994), Alexander Welsh (1994), and John Farrell (1996) have been tracing just how brilliantly Freud manipulated his readers' sympathies at every juncture. A model for all such exercises was set by the 1986 essay excerpted below, which begins from the obvious flimsiness of Freud's detective work in the Wolf Man case and asks how the crafty Freud was able to make it look so attractive.

Although Stanley Fish's argument, like Freud's own, hinges on the question of anality, he is not out to corroborate Freud's theory of libidi-

---

* From "Withholding the Missing Portion: Power, Meaning and Persuasion in Freud's 'The Wolf-Man,'" [London] Times Literary Supplement, August 29, 1986: 935–938.

nal stages. Rather, he perceives a generalized "withholdingness" (however explained) to be both Freud's master rhetorical strategy and the leading theme imputed to the Wolf Man's unconscious. As Fish shows, Freud turns the seemingly objective saga of the Wolf Man's "cure" into an analogue of his own task of enlisting the reader's assent. Like Pankeev himself in Freud's hands, we consumers of the case history are left begging for an explanatory "missing portion" that is eventually issued to us when we are in no fit state to test its cogency. Only by becoming conscious students of Freud's rhetoric, Fish implies, can we free ourselves altogether from its spell.

Stanley Fish is a Professor of both Law and Literature at Duke University as well as Director of the Duke University Press. He has written a number of influential books, including the one in which a version of the following essay appears (Fish, 1989). His most recent book is *Professional Correctness: Literary Studies and Political Change* (1995).

"I dreamt that it was night and that I was lying in my bed. . . . Suddenly the window opened of its own accord, and I was terrified to see that some white wolves were sitting on the big walnut tree in front of the window." Thus begins Freud's account of the most famous dream in the literature of psychoanalysis, the centerpiece of his most famous case. Freud tells us that although the patient recalled the dream at a "very early stage in the analysis," its "interpretation was a task that dragged on over several years" without notable success. The breakthrough, as it is reported, came in an instant and apparently without preparation. "One day the patient began to continue with the interpretation of the dream. He thought that the part of the dream which said . . . 'suddenly the window opened of its own accord' was not completely explained." Immediately and without explanation, the explanation came forth: "it must mean: 'my eyes suddenly opened.' I was asleep . . . and suddenly woke up, and as I woke up I saw something: the tree with the wolves." It is important to note that the patient does not say, "Now I remember" but rather, "It *must* mean." His is not an act of recollection but of construction. The question I would ask— and it is a question that will take us far—is what is the content of "must"? What compels him to this particular interpretation among all those he might have hit upon? To this Freud's answer is "nothing," at least nothing external to the patient's own efforts. For a long time, he tells us, his young charge "remained . . . entrenched behind an attitude of obliging apathy"; he refused, that is, to "take an independent share in the work." Clearly Freud is here not only characterizing his patient; he is also providing us with a scenario of the analysis in which both his and the patient's roles are carefully specified: the analyst waits patiently for the patient to begin to work on his own and suddenly "one day" his patience is rewarded, when the patient declares, "it must mean [. . .]."

There is, however, another scenario embedded in this same paragraph, and it is considerably less benign: the full sentence in which one finds the phrase "independent share in the work" reads as follows: "It required a long education to persuade and induce him to take an independent share in the work." The sentence is obviously divided against itself, one half proclaiming an independence which in the other half is compromised when it is identified as the product of persuasion and force. That independence is further compromised when Freud reveals the method by which it has been "induced." At the moment when he saw that the patient's attachment to him had become strong enough to counterbalance his resistance, he announced that "the treatment must be brought to an end at a particular fixed date, no matter how far it had advanced." As it is delivered, the announcement would seem to indicate that Freud doesn't care whether or not "advancement" will occur, but in fact it is a device for assuring advancement, and for assuring it in a form he will approve. What Freud *says* is "do as you like, it makes no difference to me." What he *means* is, "if you do not do as I like and do it at the time I specify, you will lose the satisfaction of pleasing me to whom I know you to be attached by the strongest of bonds because I forged them."

The coercion could not be more obvious, and Freud does not shrink from naming it as an exercise of "inexorable pressure"; yet in the very same sentence he contrives to detach the pressure from the result it produces: "Under the inexorable pressure of the fixed limit [the patient's] resistance gave way, and now in a disproportionately short time, the analysis produced all the material which made it possible to clear up his inhibitions and remove his symptoms." Here the analysis is presented as if it were independent of the constraints that father it, and at the end of the sentence the clearing up of inhibitions and the removal of symptoms appear as effects without a cause, natural phenomena that simply emerge in the course of their own time, the time, presumably, when the patient suddenly, and of his own accord, exclaims, "it *must* mean. . . ."

It is a remarkable sequence, and one that is repeated in a variety of ways in the paragraphs that follow. Always the pattern is the same: the claim of independence—for the analysis, for the patient's share, for the "materials"—is made in the context of an account that powerfully subverts it, and then it is made again. The question that arises is one of motive. Why is Freud doing this? Is it a matter, simply, of a desire for personal power? The text suggests that he would reply in the negative and say that he was only defending the honor of psychoanalysis against what John Wisdom has identified as the oldest charge against it, the charge that it "acts by suggestion," that what the analyst claims to uncover (in the archaeological sense of which Freud was so fond) he actually creates by verbal and rhetorical means.

Freud is vehement in his rejection of this accusation, declaring at one point that "it is unjust to attribute the results of analysis to the physician's imagination" and confessing at another that he finds it "impossible" even to argue with those who regard the findings of psychoanalysis as "artefacts." These and similar statements would seem to suggest that his motives are not personal, but institutional; he speaks not for himself, but on behalf of the integrity of a discipline. But the discipline is one of which he is quite literally the father, and his defense of its integrity involves him in the same contradiction that marks his relationship with the patient and the reader: no sooner has he insisted on the independence of psychoanalysis as a science than he feels compelled to specify, and to specify authoritatively, what the nature of that science is; and once he does that he is in the untenable position of insisting on the autonomy of something of which he is unable to let go. . . .

. . . Although Freud will repeatedly urge us in the following pages to take up our "independent share" in the work, that independence has long since been taken from us. The judgment he will soon solicit is a judgment he already controls. . . .

I am aware that this is not the usual description of Freud's labors, which have recently been characterized by Peter Brooks in *Reading for the Plot* (1984) as "heroic," a characterization first offered by Freud in 1938 as he cast a final retrospective look at his most famous case. In Brooks's reading the Wolf Man is a "radically modernist" text, a "structure of indeterminacy" and "undecidability" which "perilously destabilizes belief in . . .

exhaustive accounts whose authority derives from the force of closure." Freud's heroism, according to Brooks, consists precisely in resisting closure, in forgoing the satisfaction of crafting a "coherent, finished, enclosed, and authoritative narrative."

This is an attractive thesis, but it has absolutely nothing to do with the text we have been reading. . . . Freud's own characterization of his narrative insists precisely on those qualities Brooks would deny to it: completeness, exhaustiveness, authority, and above all, closure. The requirement that he expects his presentation to meet is forthrightly stated in a footnote as he begins to interpret the wolf dream: "it is always a strict law of dream-interpretation that an explanation must be found for every detail." This is the vocabulary not of any "post-modernist narrative" or "structure of indeterminacy" but of a more traditional and familiar genre—one of which we know Freud to have been very fond—the classic story of detection; a genre in which an absolutely omniscient author distributes clues to a master meaning of which he is fully cognizant and toward which the reader moves uncertainly, but always under the direction of a guide who builds the structure of the narrative and the structure of understanding at the same time.

The reader comes to his tasks with a double disability: not only must he look to Freud for the material on which his intelligence is to work; he must also be supplied with a way of making that material intelligible. And of course it will be Freud who supplies him, and who by supplying him will immeasurably increase the control he already exercises. Not only will he monitor the flow of information and point to the object that is to be understood, he will stipulate the form in which the act of understanding will be allowed to occur.

That is the business of Chapter Three, "The Seduction and Its Immediate Consequences." The seduction in question is (or appears to be) the seduction of the Wolf Man by his sister. The occasion is a succession of dreams "concerned with aggressive actions on the boy's part against his sister or against the governess." For a while, Freud reports, a firm interpretation of these dreams seemed unavailable; but then "the explanation came at a single blow, when the patient suddenly called to mind the fact that when he was still very small . . . his sister had seduced him into sexual practices." What happens next is a bit of sleight of hand: first of all, the patient's recollection is not the explanation, which therefore does not come at a single blow (at least not at the single blow to which the reader's attention is directed). Rather, the explanation emerges as the result of interpretative work done by Freud, but never seen by us; the "single blow," in other words, occurs off-stage and what we are presented with is its result, offered as if it were self-evident and self-generating. These dreams, Freud says, "were meant to efface the memory of an event which later on seemed offensive to the patient's masculine self-esteem, and they reached this end by putting an imaginary and desirable converse in the place of the historical truth." That is to say, the patient's masculine self-esteem was threatened by the fact that his sister, not he, was the aggressive seducer, and this threat is defended against in the dream material by reversing their respective positions.

One critic has objected to this as one of Freud's "apparently arbitrary inversions," but it is far from arbitrary, for it is in effect a precise and concise direction to both the patient and the reader, providing them with a method for dealing with the material they will soon meet, and telling them in advance what will result when that method is applied: "if you want to know what something—a dream, a piece of neurotic behavior—means, simply reverse its apparent significance, and what you will find is an attempt to preserve masculine self-esteem against the threat of passivity and femininity." The real seduction in this chapter (which is accomplished at this moment and in a single blow) is the seduction not of the patient by his sister, but of both the patient and the reader by Freud. . . .

Moreover, in performing this act-of-seduction, Freud at once redoubles and reverses the behavior he explains: if the patient defends against his passivity by "weaving an imaginative composition" in which he is the aggressor, Freud defends against his own aggression by weaving an imaginative composition in which he is passive; and if it is the case, as Freud will later argue, that the patient is ambivalent and conflicted—at a level below consciousness he wants to be both passive and aggressive—it is no less the case with Freud, who wants to be the father of everything that happens in the analysis and at the same time wants the analysis to unfold of its own accord.

One is tempted then to say that the story Freud tells is doubled by the story of the telling, or that his performance mirrors or enacts the content of the analysis. But in fact it is the other way around: the content of the analysis mirrors or enacts the drama of the performance, a drama that is already playing itself out long before it has anything outside itself to be "about." . . . The real story of the case is the story of persuasion, and we

will be able to read it only when we tear our eyes away from the supposedly deeper story of the boy who had a dream.

Both stories receive their fullest telling in Chapter Four, which begins
as this paper begins: "I dreamt that it was night and I was lying in my
bed." Here finally is the centerpiece of the case, withheld from the reader
for three chapters, and now represented as the chief object of interpretation. But of course, it appears as an already interpreted object, even before
the first word has been said about it, since we know in advance that whatever configuration emerges need only be reversed for its "true" meaning to
be revealed; and, lest we forget what we have been taught, Freud rein-
forces the lesson with a pointed speculation. "We must naturally expect,"
he says, "to find that the dream material reproduces the unknown material of some previous scene in some distorted form, perhaps even distorted into its opposite." He then reports, as if it were uninfluenced by his
expectations, the moment when the patient takes up his "independent
share in the work." When in my dream the window suddenly opened of
its own accord, "It must mean 'my eyes suddenly opened.'" Indeed it
must, given the interpretative directions he has received, and it is hardly
surprising to hear Freud's response: "No objection could be made to this."
To be sure, there could be no objection to a meaning he has virtually
commanded, and in what follows, the pretense that the work is independent is abandoned. "The point," he says, "could be developed further,"
and he immediately proceeds to develop it, not bothering even to indicate
whether the development issues from him or from his patient:

> What then if the other factor emphasized by the dreamer were
> also distorted by means of a transposition or reversal? In that
> case instead of immobility (the wolves sat there motionless) . . .
> the meaning would have to be: the most violent emotion. . . .
> He suddenly woke up, and saw in front of him a scene of vio-
> lent movement at which he looked with strained attention.

There remains only the final step of determining what the scene of violent motion precisely was, but before taking that step Freud pauses in a
way that heightens its drama. "I have now reached the point," he says, "at
which I must abandon the support I have hitherto had from the course of
the analysis. I am afraid it will also be the point at which the reader's
belief will abandon me."

Presumably it is because of gestures like this one that Brooks is moved to characterize Freud's text as open and nonauthoritative; but I trust that *my* reader will immediately see this as the gesture of someone who is so confident of his authority that he can increase it by (apparently) questioning it. We can hardly take seriously the fear that he will be abandoned by the reader's belief, since that belief—our belief—rather than being independent of his will, is by now the child of his will, accepting as evidence only what he certifies. Abandon him? To abandon him at this point would be to abandon the constraints and desires that make us, as readers, what we are. By raising the possibility Freud only tightens the bonds by which we are attached to him, and makes us all the more eager to receive the key revelation at his hands. I give it to you now:

> What sprang into activity that night out of the chaos of the dreamer's unconscious memory traces was the picture of copulation between his parents, copulation in circumstances which were not entirely usual and were especially available for observation.

The credibility of this revelation is not a function of its probability—we have had many demonstrations of how improbable it is that any such event ever took place—but of its explanatory power. It satisfies the need Freud has created in us to understand, and by understanding to become his partner in the construction of the story. As at so many places in the text, what Freud presents here for our judgment is quite literally irresistible: for resistance would require an independence we have already surrendered. In return for that independence we are given the opportunity to nod in agreement—to say, "It *must* mean"—as Freud, newly constructed primal scene in hand, solves every puzzle the case had seemed to offer. In rapid order he accounts for the patient's fear of wolves, his fantasies of beating and being beaten, his simultaneous identification with and rejection of his father, his marked castration anxiety:

> His anxiety was a repudiation of the wish for sexual satisfaction from his father. . . . The form taken by the anxiety, the fear of "being eaten by the wolf," was only the . . . transposition of the wish to be copulated with by his father. . . . His last sexual aim, the passive attitude towards his father, succumbed

to repression, and fear of his father appeared in its place in the shape of the wolf phobia. And the driving force of this repression? . . . it can only have been his narcissistic genital libido, which . . . was fighting against a satisfaction whose attainment seemed to involve the renunciation of that organ.

What we have here is a picture of someone who alternates between passive and aggressive behavior, now assuming the dominant position of the male aggressor, now submitting in feminine fashion to forces that overwhelm him. This, we are told, is the secret content of the patient's behavior, expressed indirectly in his symptoms and phantasies and brought triumphantly by Freud to the light of day. But if it is a secret, the drama of its disclosing serves to deflect our attention from a secret deeper still, the secret that has (paradoxically) been on display since the opening paragraphs. Once more Freud contrives to keep that secret by publishing it, by discovering at the heart of the *patient's* phantasy the very conflicts that he himself has been acting out in his relationships with the patient, the analysis, the reader, and his critics. In all of these relationships he is driven by the obsessions he uncovers, by the continual need to control, to convince, and to seduce, in endless vacillation with the equally powerful need to disclaim any trace of influence, and to present himself as the passive conduit of forces that exist independently of him. . . .

The mechanism he employs is the announcement that he has omitted a detail from the reconstruction of the primal scene. "Lastly," Freud tells us, the boy "interrupted his parents' intercourse in a manner which will be discussed later." By calling attention to this missing portion, Freud produces a desire for its restoration, a desire he then periodically inflames by reminding us of the deficiency in our understanding and promising to supply it. "I have hinted," he says in Chapter Five, "that my description of the primal scene has remained incomplete because I have reserved for a later moment my account of the way in which the child interrupted his parents' intercourse. I must now add that this method of interruption is the same in every case." Again he leaves us without the crucial piece of information, and by suggesting that it is even more valuable than we had thought— it is a key not only to this case but to all cases—he intensifies our need for it. Moreover, in a manner entirely characteristic, he then shifts that need onto the patient, who is described in the following chapter as "longing for someone who should give him the last pieces of information that were still missing upon the riddle of sexual intercourse." The displacement is transparent: it is of course we who are longing for a piece of information to be given us by a father with whom we will then join. Once again the drama of Freud's rhetorical mastery is at once foregrounded and concealed when it appears, only thinly disguised, as an event in his patient's history.

This technique of open concealment reaches a virtuoso level of performance when, in a gesture of excessive candor, Freud reveals that there is a subject he has "intentionally . . . left to one side." He then introduces as a *new* topic of discussion a term that names the very behavior he has been engaging in all the while, anal eroticism. Of course, as he presents it, it is an aspect only of the patient's behavior, easily discernible, says Freud, in his inability to evacuate spontaneously without the aid of enemas, his habit of "making a mess in his bed" whenever he was forced to share a bedroom with a despised governess, his great fear of dysentery, his fierce piety which alternated with phantasies of Christ defecating, and above all his attitude towards money, with which he was sometimes exceedingly liberal and at other times miserly in the extreme.

All of this Freud relates to the management of "excretory pleasure," which he says plays "an extraordinarily important part . . . in building up sexual life and mental activity." Of course he offers this as an observation about *others,* evidence (if it is evidence at all) only of his perspicuity. "At last," he tells us, "I recognized the importance of the intestinal trouble for my purposes"; but as we shall see, he says this without any recognition whatsoever of what his real purposes are.

Freud's announced purpose is to find a way of overcoming the patient's resistance. For a long time, the analysis was blocked by the Wolf-Man's doubt. He remained skeptical of the efficacy of psychoanalysis, and it seemed that there "was no way of convincing him" until

> I promised the patient a complete recovery of his intestinal activity, and by means of this promise made his incredulity manifest. I then had the satisfaction of seeing his doubt dwindle away, as in the course of the work his bowel began, like a hysterically affected organ, to "join in the conversation," and in a few weeks' time recovered its normal function.

One might describe this remarkable passage as an allegory of persuasion were it not so transparently literal. One persuades, in this account, by emptying the other of his "preexisting convictions." The patient's doubts, or to speak more affirmatively, his beliefs, are quite literally eliminated; the fragmentary portions that comprise his convictions pass out through his bowel and he is left an empty vessel, ready to be filled up with whatever new convictions the rhetorician brings forward. . . . The bowel that is said to "join in the conversation" is in fact the medium of the analyst's ventriloquism: it speaks, but the words are his. So is the satisfaction, as Freud explicitly acknowledges ("I then had the satisfaction"); the managing of "excretory pleasure," the mainspring of the patient's psychic life, is taken over by the analyst, who gives up nothing while forcing the other to give up everything. And even as Freud reveals and revels in his strategy, he conceals it, telling the story of persuasion to a reader who is himself that story's object, and who, no less than the patient, is falling totally under the control of the teller.

All of these stories come together at the moment when the missing portion is finally put into place. "I have already hinted," says Freud (in fact he has already already hinted), "that one portion of the primal scene has been kept back." In the original German the sentence is continued in a relative clause whose literal translation is "which I am now able to offer as a supplement." James Strachey makes the clause into an independent unit and renders it "I am now in a position to produce this missing portion." It would seem that this is one of those departures from the text for which the translator has been so often taken to task. But in fact Strachey is here being more literal than Freud himself; rather than departing from the text, he eliminates its coyness and brings us closer to the nature of the act the prose performs, an act to which Strachey alerts us by the insistent physicality of the words "position" and "produce."

Just what that position and production are becomes dazzlingly clear when the secret is finally out in the open: "The child . . . interrupted his parents' intercourse by passing a stool." We commit no fallacy of imitative form by pointing out what hardly needs pointing out, that Freud enacts precisely what he reports; the position he is in is the squatting position of defecation and it is he who, at a crucial juncture and to dramatic effect, passes a stool that he has long held back. What is even more remarkable is that immediately after engaging in this behavior, Freud produces (almost as another piece of stool) an analysis of it. In anal-erotic behavior, he tells us, a person sacrifices or makes a gift of "a portion of his own body which he is ready to part with, but only for the sake of someone he loves." . . . What the anal erotic seeks is to capture and absorb the other by the stimulation and gratifying of desire; what he seeks, in short, is power, and he gains it at the moment when his excretions become the focus and even the content of the other's attention.

However accurate this is as an account of anal eroticism, it is a perfect account of the act of persuasion, which is, I would argue, the primal act for which the anal erotic is only a metaphor. It is persuasion that Freud has been practicing in this case on a massive scale, and the "instinct for mastery" of which persuasion is the expression finds its fulfillment here when the reader accepts from Freud that piece of deferred information which completes the structure of his own understanding. Once that acceptance has been made, the reader belongs to Freud as much as any lover belongs to the beloved. By giving up a portion of himself Freud is not diminished but enlarged, since what he gets back is the surrender of the reader's will, which now becomes an extension of his own.

The reader on his part receives a moment of pleasure—the pleasure of seeing the pieces of the puzzle finally fitting together; but Freud reserves to himself the much greater pleasure of total mastery. It is a pleasure that is intensely erotic, full of the "sexual excitement" that is said to mark the *patient's* passing of a stool; it is a pleasure that is anal, phallic, and even oral, affording the multiple satisfactions of domination, penetration, and engulfment. It is, in a word, the pleasure of persuasion.

In what remains of his performance Freud savors that pleasure and adds to it by placing it in apparent jeopardy. . . . First he imagines what Jung and Adler would say if they were presented with the materials he has now marshaled. He imagines them as "bad" readers, readers who are unconvinced, and he rehearses their likely objections. No doubt they would regard the primal scene as the invention of a neurotic who was seeking to rationalize his "flight from the world" and who was "driven to embark on this long backward course either because he had come up against some task . . . which he was too lazy to perform, or because he had every reason to be aware of his own inferiority and thought he could best protect himself . . . by elaborating such contrivances as these." What Freud is staging here is a moment of scrupulosity, very much like some earlier moments when he presses interpretative suggestions on a resistant patient and then points to the patient's resistance as a proof of the independence of the analysis. Here it is we who are (once more) in the position of the patient, as Freud urges on us an interpretative direction and waits for us to reject it "of our own accord"; but of course at this late stage, any rejection we might perform would be dictated not by an independent judgment but by a judgment Freud has in large measure shaped. Even so, he is unwilling to run the risk (really no risk at all) that we might respond in some errant way, and accordingly he responds for us:

> All this would be very nice, if only the unlucky wretch had not had a dream when he was no more than four years old, which signaled the beginning of his neurosis . . . and the interpretation of which necessitates the assumption of this primal scene. All the alleviations which the theories of Jung and Adler seek to afford us come to grief, alas, upon such paltry but unimpeachable facts as these.

Everything happens so fast in this sequence that we may not notice that the "unimpeachable fact" which anchors it is the *assumption* of the primal scene. In most arguments assumptions are what must be proved, but in this argument the assumption is offered as proof, and what supports it is not any independent fact but the polemical fact that without the assumption the story Freud has so laboriously constructed falls apart. In effect Freud says to us, "look, we've worked incredibly hard to put something together; are we now going to entertain doubts about the very assumption that enabled us to succeed?" The necessity Freud invokes here is a narrative necessity. The primal scene is important because it allows the story of its own discovery to unfold. In that story—the story, basically, of the analysis—the wolf dream comes first and initiates a search for its origin; that search then leads to the "uncovering" of the primal scene, and although it is the last thing to be put in place, it immediately becomes the anchor and the explanation of everything that precedes it. What Freud is relying on here is not something newly or additionally persuasive but the fact that persuasion has occurred, and, it having occurred, that we will be unwilling and indeed unable to undo it. . . .

One might say then that at the conclusion of the case history the primal scene emerges triumphant as both the end of the story and its self-authenticating origin; but what is really triumphant is not this particular scene, which after all might well have assumed a quite different shape if the analysis had taken the slightest of turns, but the discursive power of which and by which it has been constructed. The true content of the primal scene is the story of its making. At bottom the primal scene is the scene of persuasion.

16

Culture Vulture*

David E. Stannard

Freud's case studies—that is, his psychoanalytic investigations of artists, writers, and historical figures whom he had no opportunity to analyze in person—bear a natural kinship with his no less famous case histories. That the line between the two categories is blurred can be shown by the fact that Freud's treatise on the psychotic Dr. Schreber (SE, 12: 3–79) is traditionally counted as a case history, even though Freud and Schreber never met. Supposedly, Freud used his real-life cases to infer the concepts and laws that are merely illustrated in the case studies. By now, however, we have seen that apriorism characterized his method on all occasions whatsoever.

Freud's pioneering exercise in psychobiography, *Leonardo da Vinci and a Memory of His Childhood* (1910; SE, 11: 63–137), puts on display his confidence that, with almost no evidence to work with, he can nevertheless find the key to genius within his established diagnostic repertoire. Leonardo, he grants, stood "among the greatest of the human race"—a master painter and, as a scientific investigator, a "by no means unworthy rival of Bacon and Copernicus" (SE, 11: 63, 65). But in Freud's discourse, such praise is always the prelude to a "diagnostic" comeuppance. As his armchair analysis of Leonardo progresses, the Renaissance titan shrinks to a standard exhibit of the man who must have been rendered homosexual in boyhood through deprivation

* From *Shrinking History: On Freud and the Failure of Psychohistory* (New York: Oxford University Press, 1980).

of maternal love. In the following chapter from his book *Shrinking History*, David E. Stannard shows Freud's argument to be a tissue of misunderstandings and forced readings that would lack substance even if the dubious Freudian approach to homosexuality were warranted.

In a passage that does not appear below, Stannard mentions that the alleged circumstances of Leonardo's upbringing were suggested to Freud not by psychoanalytic sleuthing but by a popular historical novel, Dmitri Merejkowski's *The Romance of Leonardo da Vinci*. Freud's seeming detective work in reconstructing Leonardo's childhood was really a matter of working backwards to arrive at secondhand, now discredited conclusions. With historical figures as with live patients, he sought—and always found—symbols and symptoms that "proved" whatever he had previously decided to be the case.

For other critiques of Freud's book on Leonardo, see Schapiro, 1955–56, 1956; a more sympathetic view is given by Collins, 1997.

David E. Stannard is Professor of American Studies at the University of Hawaii. His most recent book is *American Holocaust: The Conquest of the New World* (1992).

Freud's *Leonardo da Vinci and a Memory of His Childhood,* published in 1910, was the first true example of psychohistorical analysis. A genuine tour de force, it remains, along with Erik H. Erikson's work, among the finest indicators of the potentials—and the limits—of psychohistory. Within its brief compass this work contains some of the brightest examples of what makes the best psychohistory so stimulating: insight, learning, sensitivity, and, most of all, imagination. It also contains some of the clearest illustrations of the pitfalls of works of this sort: it is dazzlingly dismissive of the most elementary canons of evidence, logic, and, most of all, imaginative restraint. There is much to be learned from it.

Freud begins his study with a brief apology for his intended invasion of the privacy of such a great personage as Leonardo, then launches immediately into a search for those most intriguing and possibly revelatory attributes of the great man. Leonardo was known to have possessed what Freud calls a "feminine delicacy of feeling" (exhibited, for instance, in his vegetarianism and his habit of buying caged birds in the market, only to set them free), but was also capable of seemingly contradictory behavior such as studying and sketching the faces of condemned and soon-to-be executed criminals and designing "the cruelest offensive weapons" of war. Leonardo often seemed inactive and indifferent to competition and controversy; he had a habit of leaving work unfinished; he worked very slowly. The list goes on, but initially what interests Freud most is the fact that Leonardo seemed to combine in his adult life a "frigidity," a "cool repudiation of sexuality," and a "stunted" sexual life (evident not only in his behavior but also in his art) with an "insatiable and indefatigable thirst for knowledge."

This last combination of traits is not surprising to Freud. It is, he says, a result of sublimation. "When the period of infantile sexual researches has been terminated by a wave of energetic sexual repression," he asserts, "the instinct for research has three distinct possible vicissitudes open to it owing to its early connection with sexual interests." These are: 1) an inhibition of curiosity; 2) a return of the curiosity in the form of "compulsive brooding," wherein "investigation becomes a sexual activity, often the exclusive one [. . .] but the interminable character of the child's researches is also repeated in the fact that this brooding never ends and that the intellectual feeling, so much desired, of having found a solution recedes more and more into the distance"; or 3) "in virtue of a special disposition" in some people the investigative impulse provides an outlet for repressed sexuality (the process of sublimation) and "the instinct can operate freely in the service of intellectual interest [. . .] [while] it avoids any concern with sexual themes."

Leonardo, Freud suggests, seems "a model instance of our third type." But here we encounter difficulty. To substantiate this hypothesis we would "need some picture of his mental development in the first years of his childhood." And there is almost no such information extant. Indeed, Freud admits, all we know of Leonardo's childhood is that he was born in 1452, the illegitimate child of Ser Piero da Vinci, a notary, and "a certain Caterina, probably a peasant girl." Beyond this, the only record of his youth is a 1457 tax register in which the five-year-old Leonardo is mentioned as a member of Ser Piero's household.

At this point Freud turns to the life of Leonardo from another direction. He quotes a curious passage that appears as an interruption in one of his scientific notes on the flight of birds:

> It seems that I was always destined to be so deeply concerned
> with vultures; for I recall as one of my very earliest memories,

that while I was in my cradle a vulture came down to me, and opened my mouth with its tail, and struck me many times with its tail against my lips.

So important does Freud find this sentence that he announces his intent to use it, by means of "the techniques of psycho-analysis," to "fill the gap in Leonardo's life story by analyzing his childhood fantasy." The analysis that follows is nothing short of imaginative wizardry.

The tail of the vulture, beating against Leonardo's infant lips, is translated into a "substitutive expression" for a penis. The scene is thus illustrative of fellatio, of a "passive" homosexual experience. But there is another side to the fantasy, Freud notes, since the desire to suck on a penis "may be traced to an origin of the most innocent kind": "merely a reminiscence of sucking—or being suckled—at his mother's breast."

But why is the bird a vulture? At this point Freud's great breadth of learning takes over: in ancient Egyptian hieroglyphics "the mother is represented by a picture of a vulture." Further, the name of a vulturelike Egyptian female deity was pronounced *mut*—a sound very similar to *Mutter* (mother). In addition, other classical writings indicate that "the vulture was regarded as a symbol of motherhood because only female vultures were believed to exist"—females who conceive "in mid-flight" when they "open their vaginas and are impregnated by the wind," a notion used by certain Fathers of the Church "as a proof drawn from natural history" against those who doubted the virgin birth and a notion with which, Freud writes, "it can hardly be doubted" Leonardo was aware. The importance of the vulture fantasy to Leonardo, then, can be seen in his recognition "that he also had been such a vulture-child—he had had a mother, but no father, [. . .] [and] in this way he was able to identify himself with the child Christ, the comforter and savior not of this one woman alone."

Having so ingeniously solved the puzzle of Leonardo's vulture fantasy, Freud returns to the problem of the lack of information available on Leonardo's childhood beyond the date of his birth and his parentage and the lonely fact that he appears as a member of his father's household at age five. Freud writes that since "the replacement of his mother by the vulture indicates that the child was aware of his father's absence and found himself alone with his mother," the vulture fantasy serves as a replacement for the missing historical data, as it "seems to tell us" that Leonardo spent "the first critical years of his life not by the side of his father and stepmother, but with his poor, forsaken, real mother, so that he had time to feel the absence of his father."

Freud thenceforth accepts this surmise as "this fact about his childhood" and determines that Leonardo's having "spent the first years of his life alone with his mother will have been of decisive influence in the formation of his inner life." How decisive? So decisive that Leonardo, "more than other children," would have encountered the problem of the missing father. The fact that he would "brood on this riddle with special intensity," indeed that he was "tormented as he was by the great question of where babies come from and what the father has to do with their origin," thus explains (it was "an inevitable effect of this state of affairs," Freud says) why Leonardo "at a tender age became a researcher."

Content now with his reconstruction of Leonardo's outer and inner lives during his infancy and early childhood, Freud next turns to the problem of connecting these analytically unearthed childhood experiences with Leonardo's adult behavior and predispositions. He begins again with the vulture: how is it possible, Freud asks, that this maternal image is furnished with a symbol of maleness—a tail which "cannot possibly signify anything other than a male genital, a penis"? For an answer Freud draws on his then-developing theory of infantile sexuality.

The young male child, Freud believed, always assumes that everyone (including his mother) has a penis. Even when confronted with evidence to the contrary, the child assumes that the female once had a penis, but that it was cut off. Since all this thinking derives initially from the child's great interest in his own genitals, he then becomes threatened by the possibility "that the organ which is so dear to him will be taken away from him if he shows his interest in it too plainly, [. . .] [and] henceforth he will tremble for his masculinity, but at the same time he will despise the unhappy creatures on whom the cruel punishment has, as he supposes, already fallen." A further bit of insight regarding the vulture fantasy now becomes clear to Freud: at the time when Leonardo directed his "fond curiosity" to his mother he still believed her to have a penis. This insight becomes "more evidence of Leonardo's early sexual researches, which in our opinion had a decisive effect on the whole of his later life."

But decisive in what way? It is decisive, Freud observes, in that it allows us to begin seeking "a causal connection between Leonardo's relation with his mother in childhood and his later manifest, if ideal [sublimated], homosexuality."

The pursuit of this "causal connection" starts with Freud's clinical observations that homosexuals have in early life "a very intense erotic attachment to a female person, as a rule their mother." This attachment, though subsequently forgotten, is "evoked or encouraged by too much tenderness on the part of the mother herself, and further reinforced by the small part played by the father during their childhood." (This situation, of course, precisely describes Leonardo's childhood, at least as reconstructed in Freud's analysis of the vulture fantasy.) The erotic attachment to the mother, Freud notes, is eventually repressed by the young male, but only because "he puts himself in her place, identifies himself with her." Such attachments may be avoided by "the presence of a strong father, [which] would ensure that the son made the correct decision in his choice of object, namely someone of the opposite sex." In some lives, however, this is not to be the case—and instead the process that leads to self-identification with the mother results in adult homosexuality: "for the boys whom he now loves as he grows up are after all only substitutive figures and revivals of himself in childhood—boys whom he loves in the way in which his mother loved *him* when he was a child."

This analysis of infantile sexuality is critical to the unfolding picture of Leonardo because it provides the theoretical link between the nature of Leonardo's childhood experiences and the "historical probability" that beneath the "cool sexual rejection" that seemed to characterize much of his adult life, there lay the fact that Leonardo was "one who was emotionally homosexual." True, evidence to support this contention is rather thin. Indeed, it is singular and questionable: at age twenty-four Leonardo was anonymously accused, with three others, of homosexuality; the accusation was investigated and the charges were dismissed. That is all. But for Freud it is just the beginning. He then couples with this historical datum the additional information that Leonardo often took as pupils handsome young men toward whom he showed kindness and consideration. (Lest one miss the implications of this fact, Freud goes out of his way to note that in so showing kindness and consideration to his pupils Leonardo was caring for them "just as his own mother might have tended him.") Further, Leonardo's diary contains, among its many entries, notes of small financial expenditures on his pupils. This appears to be innocent enough, but not for the psychoanalyst: "the fact that he left these pieces of evidence" of kindness "calls for explanation."

Freud points out that among Leonardo's papers is also a different note of financial expenditure—one for the funeral of a woman identified only as Caterina, the same name, it must be remembered, as his mother's. Indeed, Freud says (although there is no evidence to substantiate the assertion) that this Caterina *was* Leonardo's mother. When set side by side with the entries regarding expenditures on his pupils, this note for funeral expenditures tells a dramatic and hitherto unknown story: although constrained and inhibited from conscious expression, Leonardo's repressed feelings of erotic attraction for his mother and his pupils take on the character of an "obsessional neurosis" made evident by his "compulsion to note in laborious detail the sums he spent on them." The artist's hidden life now becomes apparent as this wealth of accumulated evidence allows us to see Leonardo's unconscious mind betraying what his conscious mind never could: "It was through this erotic relation with my mother that I became a homosexual."

Finally Freud comes to the relevancy of his analysis for understanding Leonardo's powers of artistic expression. We soon find that this reconstructed sexual biography is responsible for the greatness of Leonardo's *Mona Lisa* and other paintings and that "the key to all his achievements and misfortunes lay hidden in the childhood phantasy of the vulture."

Returning once again to the vulture/mother fantasy, Freud notes that it "is compounded from the memory of being suckled and being kissed by his mother." In fact, "this may be translated," Freud writes, thus: "My mother pressed innumerable passionate kisses on my mouth."

With that translation in mind, Freud turns to one of the outstanding characteristics of Leonardo's later paintings: "the remarkable smile, at once fascinating and puzzling, which he conjured up on the lips of his female subjects." It seems that, in encountering on the face of his model for the *Mona Lisa* this "smile of bliss and rapture," something was awakened in Leonardo "which had for long lain dormant in his mind— probably an old memory." It was, of course, the memory of his mother and the smile that had once encircled her mouth. Although by this time "he had long been under the dominance of an inhibition which forbade him ever again to desire such caresses from the lips of women," he could and did thenceforth endeavor "to reproduce the smile with his brush, giving it to all his pictures."

Such subsequent pictures include, most notably for Freud, the famous *Anna Metterza,* which depicts the child Jesus, his mother Mary, and her mother Saint Anne. The faces of both women, Freud notes, contain smiles similar to that on the *Mona Lisa,* though the "uncanny and mysterious character" of the original is now replaced by "inward feeling and quiet blissfulness." In addition, there is something at least equally striking: Saint Anne is depicted as possessed of an unfaded beauty, making her appear generationally coterminous with her daughter Mary. The conclusion is inescapable. This painting, says Freud, contains nothing less than "the synthesis of the history of his [Leonardo's] childhood." Freud had shown, earlier, through his analysis of the vulture fantasy, how Leonardo identified himself with the Christ child. Now he shows how this identification is represented in Leonardo's art, which gives the Christ child two mothers, just as Leonardo himself had two mothers—Caterina and his "kind stepmother, Donna Albiera." Leonardo endows each of the mothers with the maternal smile of his own childhood memory, the memory that had returned to him when he had reencountered the smile on the model for his *Mona Lisa.* From this point on the paintings of Leonardo often seem marked by this enigmatic smile, and thus "with the help of the oldest of all his erotic impulses he enjoyed the triumph of once more conquering the inhibition in his art." . . .

It is difficult to know exactly where to begin in evaluating this work. Even a historically untrained person with little knowledge of Leonardo's life, unless extraordinarily gullible and naïvely convinced of the magical powers of psychoanalysis, would have *some* questions to ask concerning the logical and evidentiary leaps and bounds Freud makes. But let us begin with what Freud considered the pivotal event in his analysis—the vulture fantasy. There was no vulture fantasy. The only time in his extant writings that Leonardo even mentions a vulture is under the heading "Gluttony" in that section of *The Notebooks* that is entitled "A Bestiary." The reference reads, in its entirety: "The vulture is so given up to gluttony that it would go a thousand miles in order to feed on carrion, and this is why it follows armies." Now this statement, I think it fair to say, does not lend much support to Freud's thesis that Leonardo unconsciously associated the image of the vulture with his beloved mother, thus recognized "that he also had been such a vulture-child," and by extension was led "to identify himself with the child Christ." On the contrary, the entry suggests that Leonardo had a rather different image of the vulture than the virgin mother of the Church Fathers—the image of which Freud had asserted, "it can hardly be doubted" Leonardo was aware.

But what about that recollection of an early memory? It does exist, written on the back of a page that contains various notations on the flight of birds . . . ; but the creature in question is a kite, a small hawk-like bird. It was a kite, not a vulture, that Leonardo recalled opening his mouth and striking his lips with its tail. The kite, of all the birds he wrote about, seems to have been of most interest to Leonardo, but the only time he imbues it with qualities that might be of interest to the psychobiographer is in the same "bestiary" section of *The Notebooks* in which he also mentions the vulture. The reference is under the heading "Envy" and is cold comfort to would-be supporters of Freud's thesis. "Of the kite," it says, "one reads that when it sees that its children in the nest are too fat it pecks their sides out of envy and keeps them without food." . . . To put it simply: Freud built most of his analysis in the manner of an inverted pyramid, the whole structure balancing on the keystone of a single questionable fact and its interpretation; once that fact is shown to be wrong, and removed as support, the entire edifice begins to crumble. . . .

To begin with, the entire body of contingent hypotheses that Freud joined to the vulture fantasy (hypotheses that themselves, in his hands, soon became "facts") now lose relevance. Since there was no vulture in the avian fantasy . . . , we no longer have any reason to believe that Leonardo was aware of or concerned (consciously or unconsciously) by his father's alleged absence during his childhood—the analysis of the specific vulture symbolism having been the sole initiating source of this idea. Further, since Freud relied entirely on his analysis of the vulture fantasy to "fill the gap" in Leonardo's childhood history, we now no longer have any reason to believe that Leonardo in fact did spend those years alone with his mother. Indeed, evidence unearthed subsequently to Freud's work now indicates quite strongly that the contrary was the case, that Leonardo was a welcomed member of his father's household from the time of his birth. . . .

We now know that there is no evidence to support the idea that Leonardo's early childhood was as Freud surmised—that is, that it paralleled that of the unspecified "small number" of homosexuals of Freud's clinical experience. In fact, the evidence we do have supports the very opposite conclusion. But even if Freud had been correct in his historical reconstruction, the most large-scale and sophisticated modern studies of the genesis of homosexuality provide no support for either the alleged importance of castration anxiety or for the importance of the Freudian warm mother/distant father hypothesis. In sum: Freud's reconstruction of Leonardo's early childhood must be discarded as historically worthless and clinically not much better.

Leonardo was *acquitted* of the allegation of homosexuality, and there is no other historically acceptable evidence of homosexuality. Even if there were support for this contention, it would not help Freud's case, which is based on Leonardo's presumed sublimation of his sexual impulses. In sum: the question of Leonardo's active homosexuality must be discarded as historically worthless, and in any case irrelevant to Freud's own argument. . . .

Leonardo did record an expenditure for the funeral of a woman named Caterina. There is no reason, however, to believe that this Caterina was his mother, while there *is* reason to believe she was his house servant of the same name, the same apparent house servant named Caterina who appears in Leonardo's financial accounts twice earlier as the recipient of "ten soldi" payments. . . . Freud's assumption that this Caterina was Leonardo's mother must be discarded as historically unestablished and most probably quite wrong. Further, if, as seems probable, this Caterina was not Leonardo's mother, then the expenditures on her funeral become irrelevant to Freud's argument.

It is true that there is no evidence that suggests an active adult sex life for Leonardo, though negative evidence of this sort must be treated with a good deal of caution. There is also no evidence to indicate that Leonardo washed behind his ears, masturbated, or came in out of the rain, but lack of evidence cannot be taken as proof that he did not do these things. That the problem here is a common one among historians does not make it less serious. In sum: the possibility that Leonardo may have been sexually inactive may be taken as of some very low level biographical interest if a significant number of historically credible and related facts make such a conjecture relevant. In Freud's work, at least, such facts do not exist. Thus, this matter too must be discarded. . . .

Thus far, then, after discarding those of Freud's notions that are flatly incorrect, unsupportable, and/or irrelevant, we are left with the following:

Leonardo left no record of sexual activity of any sort; he kept a record of small expenditures, some of which concerned his pupils; he was also very curious about things. That is all.

We turn now to the truly exciting part of Freud's biography, in which he links his analysis of Leonardo's life with the character of his art. The main foci here are two: 1) the "smile of bliss and rapture" on the face of the *Mona Lisa* (believed by many to have been the wife of the Florentine Francesco del Giocondo) and subsequently a similar smile on the faces of Saint Anne and Mary in the *Anna Metterza,* as well as on such later figures as John the Baptist and Leda; and 2) the generationally coterminous appearance, in the *Anna Metterza,* of Anne and Mary, despite the fact that they were mother and daughter. Of course, by this time Freud's thesis, based on the assumption that Leonardo was unconsciously motivated by specific early childhood experiences, makes no sense at all. Still, it is instructive to look independently at this concluding section of the argument.

It is crucial to Freud that the famed "Leonardesque" smile first appears on the *Mona Lisa* and only later in other of his works. For it was the woman depicted in that painting, he says, who reawakened in Leonardo the "old memory" of his mother's smile which had "long lain dormant in his mind." . . . But there exists a preliminary cartoon of the *Anna Metterza* that predates by several years the *Mona Lisa.* And in that cartoon the faces of Saint Anne and Mary possess the very same smiles as in the later full painting, the same painting that Freud incorrectly assumed *followed* the inspiration induced by Mona Lisa. In short, mere chronology is sufficient to show Freud's thesis to be incorrect. . . .

Perhaps, however, the most interesting insights to be gained from Freud's *Leonardo* concern not Leonardo but Freud himself. For unlike the story of Leonardo's life, about Freud we know quite a bit. And much of what we know shows that a good deal of what Freud claimed to find characteristic of Leonardo was characteristic of himself: an insatiable curiosity; a great love for his mother; a strong desire for privacy; extreme sexual repression; a very early withdrawal from all sexual activity; an acknowledged "piece of unruly homosexual feeling" and a "pronounced mental bisexuality"; a hesitancy about publishing completed works and a habit of declaring that none of his creations were complete; a rejection of "both dogmatic and personal religion"; and finally, a triumph of creativity "at the very summit of his life," to use Freud's own words in describing

Leonardo—Freud was in his early fifties when he wrote the Leonardo study, almost precisely the same age at which Leonardo painted the *Mona Lisa*.

This is just the sort of thing that makes for fine moments of armchair musing and psychologizing—and at best perhaps the forming a genuine hypothesis or two—but not much else. The same is true of Freud's *Leonardo*.

IV

WE FEW

"Who is really sufficiently analyzed?"

—Freud to Ernest Jones, 1927

OVERVIEW

Having studied Freud's early mistakes and impostures, his faulty logic, and his unreliable case histories, we can say with confidence that psychoanalysis did not make its way in the world either by curing sick patients or by demonstrating its scientific cogency. But how did it succeed, then? As Nathan G. Hale, Jr. (1971, 1995), Ernest Gellner (1996), and John Farrell (1996), among others, have shown, psychoanalysis flowed into deep currents of our century's thought and mood, at least within those societies that were primed to spurn religion-based traditionalism and thus to replace priests and preachers with mind doctors. And clearly, psychoanalysis afforded powerful satisfactions to its initiates, who came to see themselves as an avant-garde with a visionary mission. Freudian therapy may or may not yield cures, but it assuredly revolutionizes the worldview of many patients. They emerge not only with a sense of enhanced self-understanding but also with confidence that they can now decipher the workings of repression in others—particularly in those who remain stymied by unconscious resistance to psychoanalysis itself. That sense of militant exclusiveness is what we will examine from several angles in these concluding chapters.

In order to grasp why Freudianism generates such passionate certitude, we need to examine the therapist-patient compact and its implementation over the course of many months and years. As we will see in Chapter 17, psychoanalysis has no peer among therapies for its ability to disarm the patient's critical judgment, to heighten his dependency on an authority figure, and eventually to welcome him into a grateful sense of membership in an elite community. And though nearly sixty years have passed now since the death of Freud, something of his personal temper—his mordant distrust of appearances, his belief in buried psychic demons, his zeal for finding portent in every detail—still gets imparted to the typical psychoanalytic client who makes it all the way to "termination."

Indeed, if we want to assess the costs as well as the rewards of Freudian exclusiveness, we will find our most telling examples in Freud's own conduct and that of his immediate disciples, who felt the full impact of his jealous and imperious character. Chapters 18 and 19 show that his profoundly negative, indeed quasi-paranoid, view of outsiders and backsliders and his need to dominate his followers endowed the next generation of analysts with a combination of subservience, fear of disapproval, and eagerness to carry out their leader's wishes. As a result, they became unquestioning propagandists for whatever doctrine or slander Freud deemed useful for the advancement of his cause. "Did you ever see such a gang?" marveled Freud himself (page 252 below). Eventually, however, not even Freud could keep his disciples' hostility focused on the targets he designated; they had each other to fear and betray as well.

Propaganda, it must be added, was by no means an incidental feature in the Freudian success story. Chapters 18 and 19 both make reference to Freud's "Committee," a secret inner circle formed in 1912 at the urging of Sándor Ferenczi and Ernest Jones when the looming defection of Jung threatened to plunge the psychoanalytic movement into chaos (see Grosskurth, 1991). The other initial members, besides Freud himself, were Karl Abraham, Hanns Sachs, and Otto Rank, soon to become a schismatic in his own right—as was Ferenczi at the end of his career. The Committee, however, managed to remain in operation until 1926, devoting itself, in conspiratorial stealth and with Freud's enthusiastic approval, to celebrating his genius, upholding his latest contortions of theory, and annihilating heretics through malicious gossip, exclusion from official journals, and the planting of demeaning critiques in those same journals. The very existence of the Committee remained undisclosed until 1944.

Within these chapters, readers will note three thematic strands: analytic therapy as a form of recruitment and control, Freud's sense of isolation and his need for enemies, and the machinations of the early Freudian movement. Those themes merge, often farcically, when we see Freud's "sons" vying for his sole blessing by denigrating one another as incompletely analyzed. But our final chapter looks at a sobering episode in which the conjuction between therapeutic manipulation, Freud's personality, and movement politics proved tragic in the extreme.

In that instance, the case of Freud's American disciple Horace Frink, the founder of psychoanalysis can be seen acting with the Nietzschean moral license to which he felt entitled by virtue of his superiority to the deluded mass of humanity. Yet significantly, Freud's ruinous advice to Frink was proffered with the institutional interests of psychoanalysis, not with personal gain, uppermost in mind. The individual Frink and his wife and children were nothing to Freud, the movement everything. That Frink, despite all that he endured at Freud's instigation, continued to regard his callous leader as a "great man" is the saddest irony of the story—and our final bit of evidence that Freud's charisma could survive every failed scheme and every injury inflicted on those who revered him.

Free Fall*

Ernest Gellner

Early in his psychoanalytic career, Freud concluded that he had been too sanguine when he expected the full cooperation of patients in acceding to his hypotheses and "reconstructions." Psychoanalysis, it seemed, couldn't accomplish its work so straightforwardly. Instead, the patient would develop an emotional entanglement with the therapist based on a "transference" of long-unresolved feelings toward a parent, and would accept or resist the proffered interpretations on that precarious and shifting basis.

Thus, for example, Freud assumed that Emma Eckstein's reluctance to accept his psychogenic account of her nasal bleeding (pages 54–55 above) must have been rooted in her transference onto him, not in her exercise of inductive logic about the likely connection between surgical butchery and hemorrhages from the damaged site. It was by eventually getting Eckstein to believe in the reality and primacy of that transference that Freud managed to turn her into his first disciple, an anointed psychoanalyst who could teach other women, as he had taught her, that their stomach aches and menstrual problems were owing to repressed shame over childhood masturbation. And once again, when "Dora" walked out on him, he blamed the tempests of transference on her side—he had come to mean too much to her!—rather than his own tactless conduct or the absurdity of his lurid speculations.

* From *The Psychoanalytic Movement: The Cunning of Unreason* (1985, 1993; Evanston: Northwestern University Press, 1996).

Soon thereafter, Freud began making a theoretical virtue of necessity, placing the "analysis of the transference" at the heart of the therapeutic task. In his own words, "The transference is made conscious to the patient by the analyst, and it is resolved by convincing him that in his transference-attitude he is *re-experiencing* emotional relations which had their origins in his earliest object-attachments during the repressed period of his childhood" (SE, 20: 43; emphasis as found). Even today, most analysts regard transference as the least challengeable and most operationally potent of all Freudian concepts, the one that literally characterizes what goes on in the minute-by-minute struggle of the analytic hour.

However, as Ernest Gellner explains in the following excerpt from his book on the strange triumph of the psychoanalytic movement, this is a considerable mystification—one that serves to camouflage the analyst's suggestive influence while shifting the blame for any therapeutic unsuccess entirely onto the patient. Psychoanalysis, for Gellner, is essentially the transmission of a faith by means of a drawn-out process whereby the initiate is first stripped of prior certainties and rendered abject, then slowly rehabilitated as worthy according to criteria that are intrinsic to the belief system. It is precisely a shared belief in transference that makes such a process feasible. Transference, Gellner maintains, is a fiction of "pastness" (the projection onto the analyst of feelings harbored since childhood) that serves to legitimate an indoctrination existing entirely in the here and now.

Gellner casts an especially searching light on the only other "permanent" psychoanalytic concept, which figures prominently in our Chapters 6 through 8: free association. Adolf Grünbaum, Rosemarie Sand, and Sebastiano Timpanaro, we have seen, all dispute Freud's claim that a patient's subtly guided and winnowed "free" associations can point reliably to the causes that produced a given symptom, dream, or slip. Gellner agrees but takes the critique a crucial step further. What, he asks, is the effect of requiring one party but not the other to let her guard down, risk unseemly revelations, and generate renewed "evidence" of unresolved conflicts that will necessitate more therapy? Transference and free association (in German, *freier Einfall*) together constitute the medium through which the "free fall" into credulous dependency can occur.

Before his death in 1995, Ernest Gellner was Professor of Philosophy and Sociology at the London School of Economics and, later, Professor of Social Anthropology at Cambridge University. He published a number of influential books, including *Conditions of Liberty: Civil Society and Its Rivals* (1994) and *Anthropology and Politics: Revolutions in the Sacred Grove* (1995).

A would-be patient approaches an analyst, or is referred to him by a doctor. His inwardly and outwardly avowed motives may be various. He may be suffering from an ailment which, it is suspected, has a psychosomatic component. He may be suffering from no relevant physical ailment, but feel unhappy about aspects of his personal or professional life, and be persistently unsuccessful in his dealings with colleagues or family, and hope that these may be helped by a course of analysis. Or he may hope that analysis will help him in his professional work—notably if he is a doctor or social worker or social scientist. He may even live in a social milieu within which psychoanalysis has virtually become the norm. He may feel that he needs it to cope with the strains of his life. Any combination of these or similar motives may lead him to enter analysis: or rather, any combination of these or similar motives may be invoked, with or without sincerity, with or without conviction or doubt, as he is about to enter on this course of action.

Now take a last look at our patient as he is, so to speak, in the outer or public, ordinary world. He has an ailment or problem, specific or diffuse, acute or tolerable; he knows that a theory, technique, and agency exist which claim that they may be able to help him. There is a certain cost, in time, money, and commitment; and there is a certain risk, for what in this world is not fallible? So, in the light of his assessment of the risk, the intensity of the need, and the means at his disposal and their value for him, he decides whether or not to enter on this course of action. (Or so he says, but all he says will in due course be treated as suspect, as inconclusive, as susceptible to interpretation and inversion.)

In other words, he still acts in accordance with the established conventions of the outer world: or rather, his conduct can still be interpreted by those conventions. Those conventions assume that theories are fallible, and techniques based on these theories are likewise fallible (either because the theory is false or because the application may be faulty); and a therapy is therefore a risk, in which cost, probability of success, and need of cure are weighted against each other, as rationally as possible in the light of available evidence. (But another set of conventions for interpreting his subjective intentions and ideas is available, and the therapy consists of submitting at least *pro tem* to those other conventions; and someone other than himself will be authorized to decide which conventions are to apply. Someone else will control this switch.) . . .

The objective language—the opportunity—cost assessment, and all that goes with it—he leaves in the anteroom with his coat, hat and umbrella, not necessarily at the first visit, but not too long after. That he should do so is recognized as an integral part of the treatment. As he goes "into analysis," he enters a different world. . . . The basic assumption of analysis is that virtually everything that is really decisive in his life and psyche takes place in the Unconscious; that he has no immediate access to it at all; and that his hope of gaining some access to it in due course depends on the analysis and its successful pursuit—and this cannot be a quick and brief process.

The motives he had invoked consciously for coming at all are out in the waiting-room, with his hat and coat. They are suspended, in a state of complete *sursis;* that is of the very essence of analysis. What he has also left behind in the anteroom is that tentative, experimental, cost-benefit evaluating attitude: the only reality that really matters is within himself, and knowing it, knowing himself, is a good which is totally incommensurate with all others; in fact, it is a precondition of truly enjoying any other good. It is far beyond all calculation of opportunity-cost: rather, its accomplishment is the absolute precondition of all other rational calculations. He is in the presence of liberation from a merely superficial dream. When he had been assessing his own motives and evaluation of treatment prior to its commencement, he had still been at the mercy of his own powerful and very cunning Unconscious.

One can perhaps best describe all this as a kind of "free-fall" condition. All foundations have been removed from underneath the analysand's feet, *by the very terms of reference of the therapy which he has freely consented to undergo.* The terms of reference of that therapy are—the unmasking of all the deceptions which the all-cunning, nearly all-powerful Unconscious has imposed on him. . . . The concept of the Unconscious is a means of devaluing all previous certainties, above all his assessment of himself. It is not so much a hypothesis as a suspension of all other hypotheses. . . .

The Unconscious may lurk—it almost certainly does lurk—*precisely* there, in his own views of the motives, symptoms, expectations which have brought the patient to the therapist, in his anticipated criteria of cure, in his aspiration for a post-therapeutic condition. Just these things must be explored, "worked through," suspended, treated with suspicion, probably revalued, perhaps wholly inverted. Does he think the therapy is no good? Is he failing to get good value out of the analysis? Does he find the proffered interpretations far-fetched? Why, just that must be worked through [. . .]

The obligation to "work through" his own reactions and his attitude to the analyst supports the persistent impression that psychoanalysis is largely *about itself,* that, in Karl Kraus's celebrated words, it is itself the illness which it claims to cure. The analysand "works through" his attitude to analyst and analysis. . . . The consequence, however, is that the patient is and must be deprived, if he is cooperating with the therapy, of retaining some stance from which he could attempt a critical evaluation of it. The internal terms of reference preclude it; the external ones are superficial and devalued by the very concept of the Unconscious. If he does not cooperate, plainly he can't blame the therapy for failing to work; but if he does cooperate it is even plainer, for it is built into its theory and practice that he can't blame the therapy either. . . .

We have seen that the entry into the psychoanalytic world passes through a kind of "conceptual valve," permitting entry but blocking an exit. (Any self-respecting belief-system must be well equipped with these.) The tentative, uncommitted man-in-the-anteroom must, in order to try out this technique, assume certain doctrines about the Unconscious which, when adopted, then no longer logically allow him to return to his coat and hat and doubt in the anteroom. But the pulleys and levers of the trapdoor, which ensure that the passage is one way only, are made of frail materials: they are only logical, conceptual. An intelligent and forceful man, when he notices the creaking machinery, the pulleys moving and the doors shutting, could and would kick them down without difficulty and return to his normal coat and hat. Some of course do so. But many do not.

Transference is the key. Only transference can prevent the entrant from breaking through the ingenious, but utterly flimsy, logical contraptions of the valve. To put all this another way, psychoanalysis is powerfully addictive, and "transference" is the name, though not in any serious sense the explanation, of this phenomenon (though Freud was rather easily satisfied when it came to its explanation). Without transference, the entire system simply could not work. . . .

Why or how does transference work? The simple and correct answer to this question is that no one knows. Freud thought he knew, and that the answer was simple:

> All the libido, as well as everything opposing it, is made to converge solely on the relation with the doctor. In this process the symptoms are inevitably divested of libido. In the place of his patient's true illness there appears the artificially constructed transference illness. [. . .] Since a fresh repression is avoided, the alienation between ego and libido is brought to an end and the subject's mental unity is restored. When the libido is released once more from its temporary object in the person of the doctor, it cannot return to its earlier objects, but is at the disposal of the ego.

If you are satisfied with this kind of explanation, you'll be satisfied with anything. This level of sophistication and fastidiousness in explanation-seeking is alas entirely characteristic. At this level of generality, Freud was easily satisfied. . . .

While, until the appropriate research is done, it is impossible to answer with any confidence the question concerning why transference occurs, it is in the meantime well worthwhile to explore some plausible candidate explanations. . . .

1. The patient's duty is to "free-associate" in the presence and hearing of the therapist, withholding nothing. "Withholding" is the prime sin. In normal life, we spend all our time presenting a reasonably coherent and favourable, well-selected image of ourselves to others. The imperative of free association is in effect an obligation to do the very opposite: to refrain from both order and selectiveness. Though in one way it may be a great relief to abandon the strenuous efforts to maintain the normal façade, to let go the sphincters of the mind; on the other hand it cannot but inspire shame and guilt to present a mass of material, inevitably disreputable and undignified both logically and morally. The normal presentation of self *must* be selective: it isn't just the improper

parts that are hidden, but so is, perhaps primarily, that total chaos which pervades our stream of consciousness. To free-associate genuinely in the presence of another is like undressing on a day on which one is wearing badly soiled underwear: or like receiving someone in a bed-sitter which one hasn't tidied up for weeks. . . .

The manifest, official, or internal view of free association is that it eventually bypasses by stealth the defence mechanisms of the Unconscious, and thus in the end penetrates its secrets and leads to liberation from its compulsions, to an apprehension of previously hidden reality. . . . But the real, operational function of free association probably is that it furthers transference by first placing the patient in a situation of unselective nakedness vis-à-vis the therapist (thus heavily underscoring the special, dramatically life-discontinuous status of the whole situation), and then making him feel at the mercy of the willingness of the listener to condone these indulgences in both logical and moral abandon.

2. Closely connected with the shame of logical and moral abandon are the joy and pleasure to be found in it. Is it not nice to escape from the unending task of presenting a façade, into a state of suspension, *sursis,* a bolt-hole in which pretences are at long last, and at least for a relaxing interval, cast aside? We are most of us given to feeling that *tout comprendre c'est tout pardonner:* here at last there is a chance to give all the information and in due course receive, one hopes, total comprehension and total forgiveness, absolution.

3. Simple hope of cure, in the case of those impelled to enter analysis by some genuine anguish; the hope fed by the background authority of science and medicine endorsing the authority of the analyst, and protected from disenchantment by the analyst's silence, allowing all optimistic expectations and therapeutic powers to be projected onto him, while protecting him from uttering disappointing assertions.

4. The judo technique. Certain Japanese techniques of physical self-defence seem to hinge in part on not resisting the opponent's thrusts but, on the contrary, skilfully evading or "going with" them, thereby enlisting the opponent's own energy and force for one's own end, to his detriment. In ordinary encounters between two egos, the two individuals concerned make explicit and implicit claims on their own behalf, and try to torpedo those of the other, in the kind of verbal duel which constitutes conversation. In the analytic situation, the therapist

neither contests nor, of course, endorses the claims, poses, and challenges of the patient. The latter, habituated to opposition in ordinary life, has put a certain amount of psychic force behind each claim—and finds himself falling forward and bewildered when his habitual expectation of opposition fails to be fulfilled. Eventually brought quite off-balance by all this, he must lean on something, somebody—and who else, who but the therapist? . . .

5. Delayed pattern completion. . . . The analyst's silence does indeed constitute or engender not so much sensory as conceptual deprivation. The patient is not allowed to erect and maintain patterns of his own (that would not be free association), and he is initially denied any patterns by his prestigious therapist. . . . Eventually . . . the analyst does slowly begin to offer some partial "interpretations," patterns. The patient is now positively ravenous for them, but they only come slowly in very measured and often further and carefully delayed doses. His need for them, the gratitude he cannot but feel for what he gets, the anxiety for more, his dependence on a carefully controlled supply—are all these factors not likely to engender powerful "transference"?

6. Revaluation of the patient's environment and identity. . . . One or the other participant suggests interpretation and, eventually, acceptance is conditional on joint agreement. Each has a kind of *liberum veto* on interpretations, though the weaker partner, the analysand, needs a lot of tenacity if he is to stick to any ideas stigmatized as "resistance." This eventual consensuality is joined to another implicit rule of the game, namely, that the interpretations must in a reasonable proportion of cases contradict, invert, what the patient had initially supposed and feared. After all, unless the Unconscious has some surprises to offer, what point would there be in establishing a private line to it, and paying through the nose for it? . . .

But remember, the patient had started with a picture that made him feel uneasy and inadequate, if not worse. He lives in a competitive world and feels inadequate in it. The analytic *sursis* suspends his low rating in the public world, gives him top rating in a private one, and finally restores him to the public world at a higher point. . . . Must he not be grateful, will he not be dependent on the source and condition of such a welcome metamorphosis?

7. The price and value of attention. . . . The pleasure of receiving attention is enormous, but the thirst for role-resumption is at the same time

overwhelming. Could there be a greater pleasure than having both attention *and* a role? Only the therapist can grant this second boon—having already so generously, copiously, uniquely and professionally, *ex officio,* granted the first—by finally endorsing an "interpretation," i.e., a role, and giving it that stamp of acceptance by the Other, without which it altogether lacks the feel of reality. . . . Can one have anything other than overwhelmingly strong feelings about someone who has this tremendous power, who has so great a benefit in his gift, but is for the time being legitimately withholding it? . . .

8. A foolproof relation. The analytic relation may not be the only intense relation in a person's life (though it probably is the most intense one), but it differs from the others in one supremely important way: the loyalty and the qualities of the "cathected" person cannot be put to the test. An ordinary relationship which becomes important is very soon put to searching tests, which is of course why intense relationships tend to be turbulent and unstable: the beloved is asked for advice, more time, support in disputes, a loan, exclusiveness, and heaven knows what else. He or she may grant these requests and thereby show the required love and devotion, but, objectively or subjectively, a point will inevitably be reached when the lover proves *false,* by failing to deliver the required tokens of love. Not so the analyst. He is institutionally, professionally protected from such testing by the recognized rules of the therapeutic situation. . . .

9. The patient . . . must relax and abandon himself to free association, otherwise the required penetration of the unconscious defences will never ever occur. At the same time, however, it is well known that analyses "go well" or (more often perhaps) "go badly," and it is somehow up to the analysand to help make it go well. Under these contradictory rules, it can always be ensured and insinuated, tacitly conveyed, that it is *his* fault. Perhaps he is not trying hard enough? Or equally, and with even greater cogency, is it not failing because he is *trying,* exercising his will, when he should be surrendering himself? . . .

The double bind situation of any patient may also make its significant contribution to the transference. It is not easy to feel neutral about someone who has us in his power. Political prisoners love their interrogators, recruits love their drill sergeants. The analyst has all conceptual exits covered: and even total surrender does not ensure success. . . .

When so much is at stake, yet one doesn't know what one can do to influence the outcome (or rather, the instructions about what one can do are both contradictory and elusive), would one not develop strong feelings about the one agent who seems to have the power to make it go right, who alone has the power to declare it to have gone right, and who according to the theory has access, denied to oneself, to that realm within which it is all decided?

Psychoanalysis simultaneously swamps the patient with more attention than he has ever known before, thus enormously raising his sense of his own status; and at the very same time, wholly deprives him of any role, by ordering him to associate "freely," i.e., to refrain from presenting *any* coherent façade. He is given the expectation, however, that a role will eventually be restored to him—but only if for the time being he cooperates in temporarily shedding any and every role. The exquisite pleasure of being (at long last) listened to by someone, and the eager hope of acquiring a role (and a better one to boot) in due course, keep him shackled inside the system. The attention saturation, coupled with total role-deprivation, and the slow, very slow role-granting, is probably the main key to the understanding of transference.

18

Paranoia Methodized*

John Farrell

In Chapter 17 we saw how an individual client of psychoanalysis, entering into a therapeutic contract with a limited practical goal in mind, can be stripped of independent judgment and gradually made into a believer in the Freudian way of knowledge. The merit of that account by Ernest Gellner derives in part from its generality: since an intellectual seduction is virtually guaranteed by the unbalanced terms of exchange between patient and analyst, the identity of the analyst in question scarcely matters. Historically, however, it mattered a great deal that psychoanalysis took its initial bearings from Sigmund Freud, a man who infected his followers with his own intense suspicion of surface appearances and professed motives. As John Farrell shows in the book from which we excerpt this chapter, *Freud's Paranoid Quest: Psychoanalysis and Modern Suspicion* (1996), Freud's closest affinity lay not with the world's great scientists but with its intellectual paranoids, such as Rousseau and Nietzsche, whose reflexive hostility to the ignorant and petty mob blossomed into a whole philosophy that could be exercised with feverish and sometimes euphoric conviction.

To see Freud in the light of paranoia is not to turn the diagnostic tables on him, as if he could be regarded as Exhibit A of his own theory about mental disorder. Nor is it to limit the significance of the psychoanalytic movement to the scope of his personality. As Farrell empha-

* From *Freud's Paranoid Quest: Psychoanalysis and Modern Suspicion* (New York: New York University Press, 1996).

sizes, paranoia covers a broad psychological spectrum whose "normal" end is simply a habit of distrustful and reductive thinking. Although Freud did have trouble maintaining consistent boundaries between his own ideas and those of his rivals and patients, he also exercised a cultural sophistication, self-observant detachment, and ironic wit that lay beyond the capacity of any psychotic. What we find in Freud is not psychosis but the paranoid attitude or slant, an interpretive disposition that he was able to propagate with extraordinary persuasiveness.

In a passage just preceding our selection, Farrell lists and briefly discusses seven characteristics of paranoid thinking as they have been isolated by David Swanson et al. (1970). In condensed form, they are:

1. *Projection.* Paranoids project their self-critical tendencies outward onto others, seeing them as aggressive and threatening.
2. *Hostility.* The paranoid sees the world around him as fundamentally hostile, and his conviction that this is so makes him sensitive to every slight or trace of animus directed his way. Naturally, his attitude ensures that others will cooperate with his delusions by responding negatively to his rigid, defensive behavior.
3. *Suspicion.* The paranoid is hyperalert, fully mobilized at all times to defend himself against threat. He loses his appreciation of the normal social context by scanning it constantly for hints of malice, transforming his environment into a manifold of signs. Thus, the subject matter of his interest has to do with hidden motives, underlying purposes, special meanings, and the like.
4. *Centrality.* The paranoid senses that all eyes are focused upon him. He frequently makes errors of reference, supposing that remarks innocently directed elsewhere are actually about him.
5. *Delusions.* The delusions of paranoids tend to have a stable, systematic character. They may contain a grain of truth and often considerable plausibility.
6. *Loss of autonomy.* The paranoid is obsessed with controlling his own actions and reactions, and he fears the interference of others. The sense of being controlled by forces outside oneself is a major tendency of paranoid delusion.
7. *Grandiosity.* The paranoid tends to exaggerate the sense of his own power and worth. Many observers take this as a form of compensation for a more fundamental sense of inferiority.

This list forms the reference point for Farrell's opening paragraph below.

John Farrell is Associate Professor of Literature at Claremont McKenna College. He is now at work on a broader study of the paranoid tendency in Western thought.

As we now take up the subject of Freud's intellectual stance and personality as they are revealed in his theory, in his attitude toward his colleagues, his opponents, and the world at large, we shall see that each of these symptoms of paranoia, with the possible exception of delusion, is abundantly evident. It may seem surprising, to begin with, that the founder of psychoanalysis should be thought guilty of the cardinal sin of *projection,* for did he not extend suspicion even to his own thoughts and motives? Partisans of psychoanalysis will tell us that this was his greatest achievement. But is it not rather the case that this suspicion, and the profound hostility that underlies it, was the very substance of Freud's great projection? The fact that Freudian suspicion respects no limit, the fact that it is total, betrays . . . that it is a product of compulsive rhetoric and personal imperative rather than observation. . . . For the psychoanalytic mind, nothing is what it seems. Every human act must be reduced within the code of suspicion.

Employing the theory of narcissism, with its properly "uncanny" power, Freud keeps in play the freedom of the mind to master the world around it while acknowledging nothing beyond its own reflection. Whereas the narcissistic consciousness of religion or metaphysics sees itself positively reflected in the world that it "projects," the Freudian recognizes the reflection of his wishes with mistrust. For both, nevertheless, the play of such wishes is coextensive with the psychological domain itself, which means that the psychoanalyst can master this domain without having to surrender attention to anything that is foreign to his own sense of order and desire. All he has to do is to reverse the significance of each symptom of mental life, unmasking each pretense of idealism and bringing to light its subterranean connections with Eros and aggression. The interpretive force of suspicion cannot be resisted. . . . It never fails to discover in the behavior of others the charm of self-delusion, the mistaking of desire for reality, and the temptation to credit the honesty of conscious motives. . . .

The totalizing power of suspicion is a formidable weapon in the hands of a rhetorician like Freud, who has the skill to evoke in his readers an immediate sense of self-recognition. He asks that we reinterpret our actions in an ironic and suspicious light, but in return we experience a thrill of comprehension. We derive a sense of mastery even in recognizing the nature of our unfreedom. It is no slight to Freud's rhetorical gifts, furthermore, to recognize that suspicion is the most contagious of all attitudes next to simple fear, and that paranoia is the one communicable mental disease. . . . Psychoanalytic practitioners themselves undergo therapy before taking up the work of analysis, so that their first confirming experiences of the treatment have to do with their own symptoms, anxieties, and problems. For these reasons, it is by no means evident that the people who make this form of therapy a daily pursuit are more likely to evaluate the theory in an objective light than the general public.

The fact that Freudian suspicion has the simplifying appeal of a projection helps to illuminate one of the central psychoanalytic myths—the myth that an intellectual commitment to psychoanalysis demands a libidinal sacrifice. One of Freud's assumptions is that the psychoanalyst differs from the paranoid in being able to rechannel his narcissistic libido into scientific investigation, or to achieve simple renunciations, whereas the paranoid, unable to cope with his repressed desire, regresses to a primitive, narcissistic state. Paranoids "love their delusions as they love themselves. That is the secret," Freud once wrote, the implication being that, for such natures, self-love comes before the attachment to reality. This is where the scientist is superior, in his renunciation: thus Freud's strange boast to Sándor Ferenczi, "I have succeeded where the paranoiac fails." . . .

But history has not borne out Freud's view that embracing psychoanalysis requires psychoerotic, or "narcissistic," renunciation. Even though psychoanalytic doctrine exacts a drastic form of intellectual repression, it nevertheless seems to make some kind of satisfying psychological return. For, contrary to psychoanalytic dogma, the movement has commanded an attraction for the popular mind, a depth of commitment among its adherents, and a level of acceptance among intellectuals all of which exceed what is justified by the scientific validation of the theory. Taken in broad strokes it seems to be, for many people, a compelling, almost irresistible body of doctrine. Those who believe it vastly out-number those who understand it. It is the allure, the charisma of psycho-analysis that needs to be explained, not the imaginary resistance it evokes. And there seems no better way to explain this allure than to recognize its profound appeal to the mind's sense of what should be.

Freud's theory offers, then, after all of his disclaimers, the same plea-sure and attraction he imputed to the religious and philosophical systems he mocked; psychoanalysis and metaphysics cannot be distinguished upon psychological grounds. But it would be negligent of the character of psychoanalysis to portray its sole appeal as that of philosophical gener-ality. Psychoanalysis can legitimately claim to have brought its gaze to the level of everyday life. And here we see the full, paranoid development of the *interpretive system of suspicion. . . .* In the most trivial signs it finds the deepest significance. Nothing can be too small, or too large, for its attention: dreams, jokes, works of art, neuroses and psychoses, totemism and religion, group psychology, civilization itself—Freud reinterpreted the entire range of human experience. Inheriting a culture that had stripped the world of significance, he discovered a new kind of signifi-cance in every aspect of life that had ever once had a meaning. This is what gives psychoanalysis what Ernest Gellner called its "world-filling exhaustiveness." . . .

In a rare moment when Freud was attempting to restrain his tendency toward mistrust, he confessed that "the psychoanalytic habit of drawing important conclusions from small signs is [. . .] difficult to overcome." To comprehend the depth of Freud's habit-forming science of suspicion, and with it the microscopic focus of its scrutiny, it is enough simply to recall the subjects treated in the first ten chapters of *The Psychopathology of Everyday Life*: The Forgetting of Proper Names, The Forgetting of Foreign Words, The Forgetting of Names and Sets of Words, Childhood Memo-ries and Screen Memories, Slips of the Tongue, Misreadings and Slips of the Pen, The Forgetting of Impressions and Intentions, Bungled Actions, Symptomatic and Chance Actions, and Errors. Freud taught us in these chapters to discover the aggressive, self-serving motives that were so boldly and conspicuously displayed in the heroic origins of human cul-ture, now still at work in every stray and covert motion of the intellect. Inadvertency, ignorance, failure in this view are never insignificant but, rather, signs for the adept. It is a strip tease of the unconscious: "Every change in the clothing usually worn, every small sign of carelessness—

such as an unfastened button—every trace of exposure, is intended to express something which the wearer of the clothes does not want to say straight out and for which he is for the most part unaware." . . .

Paranoia hardly seems an aberration in this context, and Freud, as usual, does not deny the resemblance between his own operations and those of the paranoid. Rather, he gives generous credit to paranoid insight:

> A striking and generally observed feature of the behaviour of paranoics [sic] is that they attach the greatest significance to the minor details of other people's behaviour which we ordinarily neglect, interpret them and make them the basis of far-reaching conclusions. [. . .] The category of what is accidental and requires no motivation, in which the normal person includes a part of his own psychical performances and parapraxes, is thus rejected by the paranoic as far as the psychical manifestations of other people are concerned. Everything he observes in other people is full of significance, everything can be interpreted. . . .

The paranoid applies to others the suspicion that he, in his grandiose delusion, so thoroughly deserves. And Freud knows that all of us actually deserve this suspicion, for none of us are truly different from the paranoid. And once Freud has given us this insight—possessed in a worthless form by the paranoid, in scientific form by himself—we are ready to recognize the common egocentrism of humanity and to share the paranoid's suspicion in all of its exquisitely detailed and systematic elaboration. . . .

With such an attitude toward individual human beings, how threatening must humankind appear to Freud in the mass. In his ingenious case histories, like the analysis of "Dora" or of the "Wolf Man," he exercised the interpretive instruments of psychoanalysis to decode complexes of symbols and motives that could never have been uncovered, or imagined, by the patients themselves. These narratives compel by strangeness and complexity. The unconscious imitates the movements of a tragic fate, turning every evasion of the will to its own use, with results both pitiful and fearful. But when it moves from the oedipal genre, the analysis of individual minds and fates, to the life of social institutions and the emotional sources upon which they depend, the Freudian narrative becomes a simple morality play. Here the paranoid's *hostility toward the workings of society* is fully developed and justified. Every appearance of good must be exposed as unconscious hypocrisy, every commitment to public interests and to social institutions must be recognized for what it is—a disguise for narcissistic gratification or a painful instinctual concession. . . .

Here is Freud, for instance, on the psychological origins of social justice:

> What appears later on in society in the shape of *Gemeingeist, esprit de corps,* "group spirit," etc., does not belie its derivation from what was originally envy. No one must want to put himself forward, every one must be the same and have the same. Social justice means that we deny ourselves many things so that others may have to do without them as well, or, what is the same thing, may not be able to ask for them. This demand for equality is the root of social conscience and the sense of duty. It reveals itself unexpectedly in the syphilitic's dread of infecting other people, which psycho-analysis has taught us to understand. The dread exhibited by these poor wretches corresponds to their violent struggles against the unconscious wish to spread their infection on to other people; for why should they alone be infected and cut off from so much? why not other people as well? And the same germ is to be found in the apt story of the judgement of Solomon. If one woman's child is dead, the other shall not have a live one either. The bereaved woman is recognized by this wish.
>
> Thus social feeling is based upon the reversal of what was first a hostile feeling into a positively-toned tie in the nature of an identification.

It is in passages like this that Freud's programmatic intentions become clear. Only on the level of the individual can the true motives of human behavior be understood. Adherence to the social is a disguise: the good for human beings lies in private satisfaction alone. Social commitments depend upon paradoxical transformations of selfishness into harmony, greed into generosity, society being held together by illusions of justice and solidarity that benefit the strong and gratify the resentment of the weak. The portrait of the syphilitic tormented by an unconscious spite that can make its way into consciousness only as a painful form of altruism, this is suspicion taken to a level of daring that must be considered marvelous. . . .

There is only one fact that keeps psychoanalytic suspicion from reaching the elevation of paranoid psychosis—the fact that the psychoanalyst, unlike the full-blown paranoid, does not entirely exempt himself from the domain of suspicion. His suspicion does not rest on private grounds: it ascends to the level of the universal. The psychoanalyst is thus, in a sense, even more suspicious than the paranoid, less restricted in the form of his projection, so that it returns upon himself. He recognizes his own narcissistic character, his own false idealism and ambitious motives, as well as those of others. He sees himself as being dominated and driven by an other, an unconscious, which he recognizes as his true self, making the polite, idealistic character of his social persona admittedly a disguise. Yet, by the peculiar logic of suspicion, the analyst turns these recognitions into an advantage for his theory and another source of its grandiose appeal. He portrays human consciousness as an ironized form of heroism, or narcissism, yet the very acceptance of the irony implicit in the Freudian concept of narcissism is itself a test of strength. . . .

Here we must enter the consideration of Freud's own personality. Long before he brought psychoanalysis into existence, Freud struggled with his need for heroic admiration. From the period of his engagement to Martha Bernays, he was looking forward to the attention of his biographers, who would write the story of "The Development of the Hero." The young Freud found it difficult to cope with the recognition that he might not be a genius, and could be heartened to have his friend Breuer recognize his inner resolve: "He told me he had discovered that hidden under the surface of timidity there lay in me an extremely daring and fearless human being. I had always thought so, but never dared tell anyone." Arriving at his theory of the unconscious, Freud was jubilant to pronounce himself the "conquistador." Through all of the struggles with his errant followers, his need to prove his heroic nature only increased; thus he wrote to Ferenczi toward the end of the World War, "I am still the giant." As much as any paranoid, Freud identified himself, in his nature and in his intellectual form of daring, with the most exalted figures of history: the biblical Joseph, Moses, Oedipus, Alexander the Great, Hannibal, William the Conqueror, Columbus, Leonardo, Copernicus, Kepler, Cromwell, Danton, Napoleon, Garibaldi, Darwin, Bismarck, and, inadvertently, even Zeus. This was the company in which he habitually posed.

Yet beneath all of Freud's self-aggrandizement there was a powerful and gnawing sense of inferiority and of thwarted ambition, a sense of being resisted and disliked. During his studies with Charcot in Paris, he oscillated between grandeur and desperation. "I consider it a great misfortune," he wrote to his fiancée, "that nature has not granted me that indefinite something which attracts people. I believe it is this lack which has deprived me of a rosy existence. It has taken me so long to win my friends. I have had to struggle so long for my precious girl, and every time I meet someone I realize that an impulse, which defies analysis, leads that person to underestimate me. This may be a question of expression or temperament, or some other secret of nature, but whatever it may be it affects one deeply." Freud repeated the sentiment twenty years later to Carl Jung: "You are better fitted for propaganda," he wrote to his collaborator, "for I have always felt that there is something about my personality, my ideas and manner of speaking, that people find strange and repellent, whereas all hearts are open to you."

Freud's defensive stance had a powerful effect upon psychoanalysis as an institution, giving rise to a peculiar, hermetic form of social organization. Its unusual exclusivity and cultishness reflected Freud's hostile and suspicious attitude toward the world at large. . . . The psychoanalytic association was a throwback to the esoteric form of the ancient philosophical academies. Almost from the beginning of psychoanalysis, its founders had recourse to a canon of dogma with the primacy of the libido at its center. Adherence to this dogma separated initiates from the opposing professional community.

The exceptionalist and schismatic character of the movement made it susceptible to schisms within its own ranks and led to the fortification of an ever more rigid and defensive orthodoxy. In 1912, after the defection of Jung, Freud's "anointed [. . .] successor and crown prince," had shattered the morale of the movement, Freud's English disciple Ernest Jones proposed a secret committee to be established around the person of the master in order to ease the burdens of leadership. Freud was so much taken with the scheme that he suspected it to be a forgotten idea of his own.

"The Committee" was to be held together with bonds of special loyalty. Each of its members promised to share research and responsibility with the leader; each promised as well not to depart from the central teachings of psychoanalysis without discussing his doubts with the others. . . . "Like the Paladins of Charlemagne," Jones wrote Freud, its members would "guard the kingdom and policy of their master." Freud celebrated the first meeting of The Committee by giving each of the members a Greek intaglio from his collection, which they then had mounted on rings in imitation of the intaglio of Jupiter worn by their leader. . . . Freud's immediate concern was that "First of all: This committee would have to be *strictly secret* in its existence and in its actions." . . . The grandiosity of Freud, Jones, and the others may seem comical and quixotic, but there is no evidence that they saw it in that way.

The founders of psychoanalysis made Freud's theory the basis of an exclusive intellectual and professional commitment with special rituals of initiation; they also employed psychoanalytic theory to explain the world's supposed reluctance to give psychoanalysis an immediate hero's welcome. This reluctance was largely imaginary. In fact, Freud "projected," in the most uncomplicated sense of the term, his own hostility onto the surrounding intellectual community, imagining that it was peculiarly enraged by his findings. It is an obvious example of paranoid *centrality*. In the mythology of psychoanalysis, the imaginary hostility of the medical establishment was explained through the doctrine of resistance, which held that the repression of libido in the majority of human beings made the theory of libido itself a source of anxiety and thus a cause of resentment. . . . The doctrine of resistance seemed to have been designed as much for polemical as for analytic purposes. Psychoanalysis came to stand for the unconscious itself: the more its imperatives were repressed, the more powerful it seemed to become. . . . Freud had successfully imported into science the style of the avant-garde, which feeds upon the appearance of rejection, outrage, and the breach of bourgeois manners. His "movement" represents the most potent and long-lasting of all the self-advertising cultural provocations of the early twentieth century. . . .

It must be admitted, though, that whatever benefits the heroic myth of the founder may have provided to the psychoanalytic movement, the renunciations that he exacted even from his adherents proved to be exorbitantly great. For Freud's truly paranoid obsession with his autonomy and originality as an investigator proved to be a constantly divisive element. All signs among his followers of reluctance to agree with Freud had to be explained by means of the suspicious logic of the unconscious, revealing father complexes, narcissistic resistance, or oedipal hostility, depending upon the stage Freud's theory had reached. Of one of his adherents, Freud remarked, "I cannot stand the parricidal look in his eyes." Disagreement with Freud became a form of psychopathology, and members of the movement were adept at exposing the secret springs of all such transgressions. The practice of self-interested diagnoses continues among analysts to this day.

No wonder, then, that so many of the most gifted early psychoanalysts found themselves unable to continue under these humiliating terms. Freud had to be the master. It was an imperative of his personality, as he was well aware, and he did not often choose to resist it. In *The Psychopathology of Everyday Life,* written before the earliest beginnings of organized psychoanalysis, he reveals that "there is scarcely any group of ideas to which I feel so antagonistic as that of being someone's protégé [. . .] the role of the favourite child is one which is very little suited indeed to my character. I have always felt an unusually strong urge 'to be the strong man myself.' " . . . He had to be the primal father, yet he wondered why his disciples often could not accept his title. As he complained to Abraham, "All my life I have been looking for friends who would not exploit and then betray me."

Freud often derided his collaborators, but he did not want to meet his like among them. In a letter of congratulation to the Viennese writer Arthur Schnitzler, whose form of psychological intelligence had often been compared with his own, Freud speculated that the reason they had never met, though living in the same city, was that Freud was afraid to encounter his Doppelgänger. It was a telling example in the genre of the psychoanalytic compliment: Freud flattered Schnitzler in a self-congratulatory way by asserting the likeness between them, while assuming that this likeness would naturally produce a rivalry. The delusion of the double, it is interesting to note, is a concomitant of paranoia from which Freud on one occasion actually suffered in hallucinatory form.

It is one of the greatest ironies of the psychoanalytic phenomenon that Freud should have based his defense of the cultural value of science upon its ability to overcome the "over-estimation of thoughts," yet his most egregious failing was his difficulty establishing the boundary between thought and reality. His absurd exaggeration of hysteria as the cause of physical symptoms, and, indeed, his complete distrust of his patients' understanding of their own experience continues to have clinical consequences to this day. Yet the founder of psychoanalysis was himself by no means free of the tendency to let his obsessively charged preoccupations alter his view of the world around him. He was the victim, for instance, of morbid superstitions and was particularly plagued by significant numbers. The scientist who believed that it was impossible to pick a number at random without there being some subliminal motive for the choice nevertheless could not keep himself from believing that the numbers that appeared around him portended some special significance related to his fears of imminent death.

But it was not in numbers, those "persistent persecutors," that Freud found the most threatening reflections of his own intellectual activity; it was in the developments from his theoretical vocabulary made by his own colleagues, developments that frequently looked to the suspicious master like hostile urges in the direction of originality. The need to maintain control over the body of thought known as psychoanalysis presented Freud with the greatest difficulty. His entire career was beset with controversies about plagiarism and originality. There was a constant anxiety about what was his and what was not. And although Freud claimed that others' ideas were of no use to him unless they came at a time when he was ready for them, he proved enormously susceptible to their influence and even noted his own tendency to "cryptamnesia," by which he "unconsciously" contrived to forget his intellectual debts. He even came to believe that thoughts can be transferred from one mind to another not only unconsciously but by telepathy! . . .

It was in dealing with the heretics of psychoanalysis that Freud showed the depths of his contempt for others' disagreements, often falling back upon his most self-vaunting rhetoric. In his *History of the Psycho-Analytic Movement*, written to excommunicate Adler and Jung, two arch-dissidents, Freud mocks both of his former collaborators for having succumbed to unconscious resistance, to fear of libido. Shrinking back from the discipline of psychoanalysis, they had lapsed into the false comforts of idealism and system-building. Freud's grandiose and persecuted polemic ends on the following note:

> Men are strong so long as they represent a strong idea; they become powerless when they oppose it. Psycho-analysis will survive this loss and gain new adherents in place of these. In conclusion, I can only express a wish that fortune may grant an agreeable upward journey to all those who have found their stay in the underworld of psycho-analysis too uncomfortable

for their taste. The rest of us, I hope, will be permitted without hindrance to carry through to their conclusion our labors in the depths.

Vast scholarly energy has been invested in clarifying the relations among the workers in the "underworld of psycho-analysis," with the purpose of showing how the discoverers of the logic of the unconscious failed to use their knowledge in such a way as to overcome the natural human propensities toward competition, selfishness, fear, and jealousy. Most of these studies have been written in a psychoanalytic spirit, using Freud's own concepts to analyze the causes of the divisions within his movement. In doing so, they merely repeat, sometimes in a more even-handed way, the hostile gestures of interpretation that were employed at the time. They demonstrate, therefore, the endless capacity of psychoanalysis to generate and then to capitalize upon suspicion. Even the master is fair game so long as the suspicion is couched in psychoanalytic terms. What has not been sufficiently appreciated, however, is the degree to which the theoretical vocabulary of psychoanalysis creates the perils of dissension to which the movement has been so remarkably vulnerable. In giving credit solely to selfish motives in the event of intellectual dissent from orthodox teaching, it made every extension of the theory not initiated by Freud himself a potential occasion for suspicion. No wonder psychoanalysis, as Freud complained, brought out the worst in everyone.

One of the strangest and most absurd, indeed delusional, aspects of Freud's behavior was his willingness to brand those who would not submit to his authority as paranoids. Freud actually believed that the break-up of his friendship with Wilhelm Fliess had had the power to induce "a dreadful case of paranoia" in his former collaborator. The diagnosis of paranoia helped Freud rationalize the hostility that arose between the two men when Fliess discovered that Freud had carelessly disseminated some of Fliess's ideas about human bisexuality, leading to their publication. Fliess's paranoia was entirely in Freud's imagination! As Frank Sulloway reasonably speculates, Freud's cavalier way of disseminating Fliess's intellectual property shows his own desire for revenge against a man he felt had forsaken him.

In the midst of another break-up occurring some years after, Freud wrote to Jones of Alfred Adler observing, "He is not very far from paranoia, his distortions are gorgeous." A couple of months later he added,

"As to the internal dissension with Adler, it was likely to come and I have ripened the crisis. It is the revolt of an abnormal individual driven mad by ambition, his influence upon others depending on his strong terrorism and sadismus." To James Jackson Putnam, an American supporter with whom he was much less intimate, Freud was equally frank, denouncing Adler as "a gifted thinker but a malicious paranoiac." His innovations were "paranoivelties." The malice on Freud's part is apparent, but that does not mean he did not believe what he was saying. He seems no less sincere in making these charges than he was in making his claims that psychoanalysis had encountered extraordinary cultural resistance. . . .

Late in his career Freud even went so far as to disclaim that he had the temperament of a physician:

> After forty-one years of medical activity, my self-knowledge tells me that I have never really been a doctor in the proper sense. [. . .] I have no knowledge of having had any craving in my childhood to help suffering humanity. My innate sadistic disposition was not a very strong one, so that I had no need to develop this one of its derivatives. In my youth I felt an overpowering need to understand something of the riddles of the world in which we live and perhaps even to contribute something to their solution.

This is a chilling admission from the most famous of therapists. We might think to ascribe Freud's posture to modesty were it not supported by a long record of comments in which he expresses distaste for his patients and for human beings as a group: "In my experience most of them are trash."

It is further to be noted that the "overpowering need" to solve "the riddles of the world" discovered by Freud at the core of his nature is hardly a point of modesty. Freud positions himself bravely as a descendant of Oedipus. It is no part of his version of the myth that Oedipus investigated his origins in order to save his people; Freud's Oedipus is, like himself, entirely an intellectual hero. There is also something peculiar in the terms of Freud's disclaimer. It is because Freud has no strong "innate sadistic disposition" that he lacks the qualities of a physician. In other words, physicianly care can only be a disguise for a more fundamental sadism, which must be hypocritically masked from conscious awareness in the guise of affectionate concern. One must be cruel, unconsciously, in order to be kind. Now we can see that Freud's lack of solicitude for humanity is actually a virtue, part of his clear-sightedness, honesty, narcissistic independence, and freedom from animus. What it asserts, with a peculiarly sinister form of self-congratulation, is a primal father's notion of virtue.

To illustrate Freud's performance in the role of primal father, I am going to choose the most extreme example of the Freudian egotistical sublime. It is the example of Freud's treatment of an adherent who remained loyal to him even in the act of suicide, a fact that did not make up in Freud's view for his threatening endowment of talent. The story of Victor Tausk has been insightfully reconstructed by Paul Roazen. Tausk killed himself shortly after his return from service in the World War. One of the circumstances surrounding Tausk's dejection, apparently, was Freud's refusal to analyze him and his subsequent command that Tausk's assigned analyst, Helene Deutsch, humiliatingly his junior in the movement, be withdrawn so that Tausk could not interfere in her analysis with Freud. Freud disliked Tausk because Tausk had a way of developing Freud's own ideas very much in the way Freud himself intended to develop them. Freud came to view Tausk's analysis under the direction of his own analysand as an indirect way for Tausk to get at him. A primal father cannot share his women, so Freud forced Helene Deutsch to choose between himself and Tausk, with disastrous consequences. . . .

Freud reported the suicide to Tausk's former lover, his sycophantic devotée, Lou-Andreas Salomé: as a former friend of Nietzsche and lover of Rilke, her adherence to the psychoanalytic movement and attachment to its founder were sources of considerable pride to Freud. The note of triumph over a former rival for Salomé's regard is impossible to mistake:

> . . . In his letter to me he swore undying loyalty to psychoanalysis, thanked me etc. But what was behind it all we cannot guess. After all he spent his days wrestling with the father ghost. I confess that I do not really miss him: I had long realized that he could be of no further service, indeed that he constituted a threat to the future.

Roazen's account of this episode leaves little doubt that the "father ghost" with whom Tausk was struggling was Freud himself. Tausk's friends "in that tiny subculture" took it for granted that "if Freud dropped a man it could lead to his self-extinction." Tausk was not the only example. Freud's letter reveals a primal father's superiority, which is responsible to no one. . . . It is taken for granted that the future interests of the movement override any individual concern for Tausk's welfare; indeed, the meaning of his existence is altogether identified with his contribution to that future. Freud's sense of destiny justifies the dictates of his pride and fear with a flawless theoretical economy. . . .

During the battles of his later life Freud comported himself with an Olympian superiority to human feeling, refusing to admit satisfaction in the world's homage, which he had so relentlessly pursued, refusing to utter good wishes to his admirers—this being an unacceptable concession to the "omnipotence of thoughts"—and declaring any altruism that might have characterized his life to be something mysterious and not necessarily admirable: "Why I—and incidentally my six adult children as well—have to be thoroughly decent human beings is quite incomprehensible to me." Only Freud had the strength—and the entitlement—to live out this much of the wisdom of psychoanalysis. His paranoid suspicion toward the world grew up from a fundamental mistrust of his own nature, which he learned to convert into a supreme intellectual advantage.

In the light of the facts presented here, let us now review Freud's own account of his discovery of psychoanalysis: the naive modesty with which he set his findings forth, the hostile response—imaginary—with which they were received, and the slow recognition of the immense importance that this hostility betokened for his achievement. Now that we have become familiar with the suspicious manner in which Freud habitually treats his own motives, his claim to the unselfish idealism of the discoverer rings distinctly false. Yet there is a strange conviction here, too, the conviction of a man whose sense of worth is powerfully sustained by an opposition that is the product of his imagination:

> I did not at first perceive the peculiar nature of what I had dis-
> covered. I unhesitatingly sacrificed my growing popularity as a
> doctor, and the increase in attendance during my consulting
> hours, by making systematic enquiry into the sexual factors
> involved in the causation of my patients' neuroses; and this
> brought me a great many new facts which finally confirmed
> my conviction of the practical importance of the sexual factor.
> I innocently addressed a meeting of the Vienna Society for

Psychiatry and Neurology with Krafft-Ebing in the chair, expecting that the material losses I had willingly undergone would be made up for by the interest and recognition of my colleagues. I treated my discoveries as ordinary contributions to science and hoped they would be received in the same spirit. But the silence which my communications met with, the void which formed itself about me, the hints that were conveyed to me, gradually made me realize that assertions on the part played by sexuality in the aetiology of the neuroses cannot count upon meeting with the same kind of treatment as other communications. I understood that from now onwards I was one of those who had "disturbed the sleep of the world," as Hebbel says, and that I could not reckon upon objectivity and tolerance. Since, however, my conviction of the general accuracy of my observations and conclusions grew even stronger, and since neither my confidence in my own judgement nor my moral courage were precisely small, the outcome of the situation could not be in doubt. I made up my mind to believe that it had been my fortune to discover some particularly important facts and connections, and I was prepared to accept the fate that sometimes accompanies such discoveries.

I pictured the future as follows:—I should probably succeed in maintaining myself by means of the therapeutic success of the new procedure, but science would ignore me entirely during my lifetime; some decades later, someone else would infallibly come upon the same things—for which the time was not now ripe—would achieve recognition for them and bring me honour as a forerunner whose failure had been inevitable. Meanwhile, like Robinson Crusoe, I settled down as comfortably as possible on my desert island. When I look back to those lonely years, away from the pressures and confusions of to-day, it seems like a glorious heroic age. My "splendid isolation" was not without its advantages and charms.

The reader who has assented to the foregoing analysis of Freudian psychology will hardly need a commentary upon this passage. One can only admire the rhetoric by which Freud creates his grandiose, magical, almost cosmic drama of unself-conscious virtue that was met with, instead of applause, an unexpected and meaningful silence, a "void" gathering round it, full of disturbing "hints," and then the sudden recognition that the "world's sleep" had been inadvertently troubled, with ominous consequences that would forever set the innocent inquirer beyond the pale of human consideration. So what can he do but decide to believe in himself, gather his "moral courage," which was not "precisely small," and await in "splendid isolation" the verdict of the future? Hostility, suspicion, strange significance, heroic isolation, and embattled self-reliance—all the paranoid vices and virtues are here. . . .

Let there be no mistake about the kind of explanation that I am proposing in order to illuminate the form of psychoanalytic thought and the source of its allure. I am not turning Freud's idea of paranoia back upon him. That would be merely to repeat his own self-reduction. What I am drawing to attention is the fact that his self-conception, his conception of the human subject, is given in the image of the paranoid, and that this gesture is inherently self-fulfilling. The power of psychoanalysis lies in the ingenious manner in which it permits reductive thinking to extend its authority by means of an absolute psychological suspicion, leading to the construction of a most gratifyingly systematic paranoia. Freud the theorist displays every feature of paranoid thinking. Yet all of these features, so inseparable from Freud's personality, spring with unassailable logic from the premises of his science. In this paranoia we are not dealing merely with a psychologically aberrant condition but, rather, with a self-sustaining intellectual dynamic. It is the prevalence of this intellectual dynamic that causes modern people to see themselves so movingly reflected in personalities like those of Rousseau, Nietzsche, and Freud, allowing these agitated and frequently deluded intellectuals to assume a prominent place in history without embarrassment.

19

Sons and Killers*

François Roustang

Although Freud announced to the world that he had devised a sure technique for healing psychoneuroses and for obliging the repressed unconscious to yield up its stubbornly guarded treasures, he never spelled out that technique in a way that might render it available to other physicians. Nor was this a casual oversight: the founder of psychoanalysis wanted to control its future course through a personal laying on of hands, which would then be duplicated in the next generation by disciples whom he had analyzed and overseen. Thus Freudianism was to be propagated not through the free dissemination of its method but through apostolic succession, with the usual churchly emphasis on orthodoxy of doctrine and ritual (Falzeder, 1994). But sooner or later, of course, there would have to be a new pope, anointed by the abdicating Freud but somehow—how, exactly?—accepted as supreme leader by all the other candidates for that eminence.

Like John Farrell in Chapter 18, François Roustang sees that a movement focused on loyalty to Freud the man was foredoomed to tempestuousness. In the text that follows, however, Roustang leaves Freud's paranoid style largely out of account. Here it is not the master's need for enemies but simply his standing as the absolute dispenser of favor and blame that infantilizes his "sons," leaving them desperate to outdo one another in viciousness toward those branded as heretics and thus as suit-

* From *Dire Mastery: Discipleship from Freud to Lacan* (Baltimore, MD: The Johns Hopkins University Press, 1982), pp. 1–16.

able objects of contempt. At the same time, anxiety over succession only heightened the tendency toward ruthless intrigue. Freud was already middle-aged when he launched his "science," and nobody among his band but Carl Jung, who was already beginning to experience manic religious visions of his own (Noll, 1994, 1997), resembled a plausible heir.

Roustang does not question Freud's "discovery" of the unconscious dynamics that make every group an artificial and unstable achievement. Hence, for him, the squabbling that broke out within the psychoanalytic second generation was an ironic instantiation of the master's theory. On this reading, the only un-Freudian element in the comedy was Freud's having imagined in the first place that he could secure his immortality through the obedience of a restive horde.

But where else, one might ask, could Freud the pseudoscientist have turned? All authority had to be vested, as long as humanly possible, in the Viennese man-god (in Karl Abraham's words, "our work . . . is identical with your person") because there was nowhere else for it to alight; and the descent into sectarianism was made inevitable not by the inherent character of all groups but by the absence of any empirical ground of appeal from the free-for-all. As Max Graf, the father of "Little Hans," observed in retrospect, "Within the space of a few years, I lived through the whole development of a church history" (Graf, 1942, page 473). The development of other pseudosciences displays the same pattern, though without the unique Freudian signature—namely, the invoking of unconscious causation by all parties as a means to exculpate oneself, outmaneuver a rival, or ascribe mental illness to deviant theorists.

Both this chapter and the previous one make reference to Freud's "Committee," a secret inner circle formed in 1912 at the urging of Sándor Ferenczi and Ernest Jones when the looming defection of Jung threatened to plunge the psychoanalytic movement into chaos. The other initial members, besides Freud himself, were Karl Abraham, Hanns Sachs, and Otto Rank, soon to become a schismatic in his own right—as was Ferenczi at the end of his career. The Committee, however, managed to remain in operation until 1926, devoting itself, in conspiratorial stealth and with Freud's enthusiastic approval, to upholding his latest contortions of theory and to annihilating his adversaries through malicious gossip, exclusion from official journals, and the planting of demeaning critiques in those same journals. Eventually, not even Freud could keep his disciples' gang mentality focused on the designated targets; they had each other to fear and suspect as well. (The very existence of the Committee remained undisclosed until 1944. For a full discussion, see Grosskurth, 1991.)

Of particular folkloric interest, not just in the cohort studied by Roustang but for decades thereafter, is the continually entertained hope that the repsychoanalyzing of psychoanalysts will render them tractable to reason as understood by one faction or another. Unsurprisingly, nothing of the kind occurred. Indeed, the question of who should analyze whom became a sore point in its own right. One scholar, broadly sympathetic to Freudian ideas, surveyed the profession up to World War II and concluded that

> self-analysis was either not practised after analysis at all, or it did not help much; the dissolution of the so-called transference neurosis hardly ever took place after analysis; . . . the blurring of the borders of professional and intimate relationships was the rule and not the exception; and even allegedly normal, unneurotic people, famous analysts, needed two, three, four, or more long-term analyses without ever overcoming certain problems that would almost certainly, were they known, exclude them from analytic training today. . . . (Falzeder, 1994, page 188)

Even now, the eccentric, hate-filled, wildly unethical spirit of the early psychoanalytic movement remains largely unexplored. Enough is known, however, to dispel any idea that Freud's therapeutic innovation could render its own practitioners "normal."

François Roustang is an independent writer who lives in Paris. In addition to *Dire Mastery*, from which the following selection is drawn, his books include *Psychoanalysis Never Lets Go* (1983), *The Lacanian Delusion* (1990), and *Qu'est-ce que l'Hypnose?* (1994).

Only a few weeks before his death, Karl Abraham wrote, in his last letter to Freud:

> You know, dear Professor, that I am very unwilling to enter
> once again into a discussion of the film affair. But because of
> your reproach of harshness (in your circular letter), I find
> myself once more in the same position as on several previous
> occasions. In almost twenty years, we have had no difference of
> opinion except where personalities were concerned whom I,
> very much to my regret, had to criticize. The same sequence of
> events repeated itself each time; you indulgently overlooked
> everything that could be challenged in the behaviour of the per-
> sons concerned, whilst all the blame—which you subsequently
> recognized as unjustified—was directed against me. In Jung's
> case your criticism was that of "jealousy"; in the case of Rank
> "unfriendly behaviour" and, this time, "harshness." Could the
> sequence of events not be the same once again? I advanced an
> opinion which is basically yours as well but which you did not
> admit into consciousness.

Oddly enough, "this time" does not concern a quarrel between people.
In this instance, Abraham was not criticizing anyone whom Freud considered with indulgence; rather, he had accepted the idea of a film on psychoanalysis, about which Freud felt very reluctant. This error, which
Abraham does not notice, and the way in which he connects this incident
to the cases of Carl Gustav Jung and Otto Rank, clearly reveals that in his
eyes there could be no quarrel between Freud and himself unless Freud
became too attached to someone else. Neither he nor his master could be
blamed when something went wrong between them; it could only be
someone else's responsibility. As long as they were alone, as long as Freud
left the others alone, everything was just fine.

Might not this very exclusive passion be the basis for Abraham's
astonishing lucidity? In 1908 he was the first to criticize Jung's positions and to provoke a conflict. But Freud, in the end just as lucid, agreed
with Abraham on the theoretical level. Freud, however, had serious
motives for showing consideration for Jung; for he remained attached
to him, and, hoping that Jung would be the Aryan to bring psychoanalysis out of the Jewish ghetto, Freud made him his sole heir. This is why
Freud immediately perceived between Abraham and Jung a "rivalry," a
"sensitivity about priorities," a "competitiveness that has not been over-

come." Behind this important theoretical debate in the history of psycho-analysis is the underlying rivalry, and the honest Abraham admits to Freud:

> My manuscript for Salzburg contained a remark which would certainly have satisfied [Eugen] Bleuler and Jung; on a sudden impulse I omitted to read it out. I deceived myself momen-tarily by a cover-motive, that of saving time, while the true reason lay in my animosity against Bleuler and Jung. This was caused by their latest and far too conciliatory publications, by Bleuler's Berlin paper, which made no reference to you, and by other slight incidents. The fact that I omitted to name Bleuler and Jung obviously means: "They turn aside from the theory of sexuality, therefore I shall not cite them in con-nection with it." It naturally did not come into conscious thought at that moment that this omission might have serious consequences.

Abraham acknowledges that he was unconsciously, that is, very effec-tively, trying to provoke hostility. The fundamental reason for his ani-mosity lies in the attempt by Bleuler and Jung to achieve notoriety without mentioning Freud. . . .

When it came to helping Abraham to set up his practice, Freud began to impose conditions: "If my reputation in Germany increases, it will certainly be useful to you, and if I may refer to you as my pupil and follower—you do not seem to me to be a man to be ashamed of that description—I shall be able to back you vigorously." Abraham accepted. He was welcomed into the circle of Freud's family and said he would always feel "deeply indebted" to Freud. How could he bear to see others occupying a privileged position in the eyes of the master, when they were hardly interested in discharging their debt to their creditor? For Abraham, the wish was that "the followers of your science may increase in numbers" and that "theoretical contributions," always in reference to Freud, are the only ways in which to "eventually succeed in paying some of this debt." Anyone who does not pledge himself in similar terms must be excluded from the master's circle. For years Abraham was to devote himself to this end, in spite, and no doubt because, of Freud's hesitations. No matter how much Freud "for the sake of the cause" tried to reconcile the two men, who are "both too valuable," it was to no avail.

For Freud possesses the key to the rivalry between these two disciples. In 1908, he clearly prefers Jung and continues to consider him the hope of the psychoanalytic movement. After his stay in Zurich, he is full of illusions and unable to visit Abraham (an "appearance of unfriendliness," in his own words) on his way through Berlin before going on to see Jung. Freud was so embarrassed by this incident that he proposed to give up his role as creditor: "I owe you a debt that will one day be paid off. You know it was not easy for me between the two of you. I wish to dispense with neither of you, and I can tell neither how much liking I have for the other." In this sentence, Freud implies that he wants to have a unique and incomparable relationship with each man. This is a typically parental statement, which children cannot accept because it frustrates them and because they perceive it as the disguised preservation of a power that wants to dominate.

No matter how much Freud insists, "I ask both to make sacrifices, not to me personally but to the cause that matters," it does not seem very convincing, to say the least, since four years later, Freud writes of a breach in his relationship to Jung: "Then the vacillation took place behind my back; when I found out about it, it was over. This time I have felt obliged to react to the changed behaviour towards me and in so doing to lay down the armour of friendship and show him that he cannot at his pleasure assume privileges to which no-one is entitled." . . . When he takes a sorrowful tone to answer Abraham, "I see with dismay that you depreciate yourself in relation to me, building me up in the process into a kind of imago instead of describing me objectively," his humility is feigned, for it is precisely because Jung touched the imago of the uncontested master that he must perish, and perish at the hands of all the faithful. For there is nothing better than a crime perpetrated by one and all to ensure the cohesion of the horde.

Freud was to open the campaign with several works. *Totem and Taboo* "will serve to cut us off cleanly from all Aryan religiousness. Because that will certainly be the consequence." Or again: "Jung is crazy, but I have no desire for a separation and should like to let him wreck himself first. Perhaps my *Totem* paper will hasten the breach against my will." When we compare this "against my will" to "will serve to cut us off clearly," Freud's insincerity becomes obvious. Especially since he goes on to write *On the History of the Psycho-Analytic Movement* as part of the same strategy; the book was to be "vigorous and plain-speaking." It would even be a "bombshell" which should have a great effect. Freud's correspondent understood perfectly, since he wrote, "I have already written to you about the 'History,' I have read it over and over again and have increasingly come to see how important a weapon it is." And a little later, "Your 'History' will result in the resignation of Jung." In the meantime, Abraham himself is working on a criticism of Jung's works which Freud applauds and says deserves "a civic crown" (doubtless because it will greatly help to eliminate the traitor) and is "excellent, cold steel, clean, clear and sharp." The steel from which daggers are made. Weapons, a bombshell, cold steel, quite an arsenal and clearly revealing the intentions of Freud's faithful followers.

A vast plan is devised to remove Jung from his position as director of the *Jahrbuch*. All the psychoanalytic groups will become involved. Ernest Jones, Rank, Hanns Sachs, and Sándor Ferenczi, "who has been the hot head in the whole business," all agree. Freud hopes that Abraham is "in full command of [his] group," but he still impatiently awaits the reaction from London. When it arrives in March 1914, he sums up the whole affair with triumphant impudence: "I enclose Jones's letter. It is quite remarkable how each one of us in turn is seized with the impulse to kill, so that the others have to restrain him. I suspect that Jones himself will produce the next plan. The usefulness of cooperation in the committee is very well illustrated by this."

During this period, the activities of each member of the group, which were also scientific (leaving aside *Totem* and *On the History*, Abraham's contribution is the most precise, encompassing, and penetrating criticism of Jung written by any Freudian), were based on the *Impuls totzuschlagen*, so that the "usefulness of cooperation in the committee" (Abraham, Ferenczi, Jones, Rank, Sachs) is at its zenith in the assassination plot. At this point, the psychoanalytic association behaved like a gang of delinquents or killers. This was perfectly clear to Freud, who said, during a congress of psychoanalysis, "Did you ever see such a gang?" and who later wrote to Georg Groddeck, describing his disciples as "the other lions in the congress menagerie." . . .

Of course, the crime is not without its counterpart, love, not without the "pleasure and satisfaction" of having eliminated the rival. Abraham worked against Jung, but it was all for Freud; he was unable to free himself from the credit accorded to him, as we can see, for example, in the anxious sentence, "I always have the feeling that I cannot really do enough for our cause, since my obligation to you is too great in every respect." Which is why his criticism of Jung was seen as a present to Freud, but a present at once delightful and odious: "I am glad to be able to reciprocate with the enclosed gift which I have just completed. I have put a lot of work into this unpleasant review but I do not regret it, because only by doing it have I come to recognize the complete sterility of the Jungian 'School.'"

Instead of seriously considering the importance of this inextinguishable debt, instead of seeing that this gift, far from paying anything, is a demand for a privileged recognition that would incur an even greater debt, Freud responds by promising Abraham fame through the new *Jahrbuch*: "You will automatically find yourself in an extremely influential position." He fulfills the wishes of his disciple, who had sent him a new "gift," his photograph, by writing, "Your picture will return tomorrow from the framer's, and will then take the place of Jung"—not the place of that of Jung, but *den Platz von Jung*, "the imaginary place": the very place Abraham wanted, the unique place of the successor, which Freud had given to Jung. When Freud confessed to Abraham that he could "tell neither how much liking I have for the other," he could only stir up jealousy and create a situation in which Abraham and Jung would have to fight to the death. His knowledge of the transference should have warned him; but he himself was caught up in the relationship with his disciples, which he scarcely analyzed at all, and in a style that weighed heavily on the entire history of the psychoanalytic movement. . . .

When trouble with Rank and Ferenczi breaks out in 1924 because of their recent publications, Abraham is of course on the front line to lead the attack. He is delighted that Freud has been forced to make concessions to him, and to mistrust the theories of his closest collaborators. . . . Abraham is not trying to break up the committee but to diminish Rank and Ferenczi by making them out as small Jungs, although they are not deceitful or brutal; despite their "pleasant qualities," they are nonetheless sent off to join Jung in the darkness outside. . . .

At this point a very important question arises, which will reappear often in the history of the psychoanalytic movement. It seems that only two solutions are open: either to stay within the psychoanalytic mainstream, which implies accepting a permanent allegiance to Freud, or to act independently and find oneself rejected from psychoanalysis, to cease to count for it. . . .

Freud warned Groddeck about this in 1917:

I understand that you are requesting me urgently to supply you with an official confirmation that you are not a psychoanalyst, that you do not belong to the members of the group, and will be able to call yourself something special, and independent. Obviously I am doing you a service if I push you away from me to the place where [Alfred] Adler, Jung and others stand. Yet I cannot do this; I have to claim you. I have to assert to you that you are a splendid analyst who has understood for ever the essential aspects of the matter. The discovery that transference and resistance are the most important aspects of treatment turns a person irretrievably into a member of the savage horde.

And further on in the same letter: "Experience has shown that an untamed ambitious individual sooner or later jumps up and turns into an eccentric to the detriment of science and his own career."

For Freud's closest disciples, acknowledging his rights over them, belonging to the horde, and advancing the science of psychoanalysis all go together. Abraham wrote, for example, that he would do everything possible to prevent the committee from disintegrating, "I promise you, dear Professor, in advance, that it will be done on my part in a non-polemic and purely factual manner and only with the wish to serve you and our work, which is identical with your person." Jones agrees: "You know that it is essentially for you that we are all working, which is why your inspiration means so much to us all." As for Ferenczi, when Freud discreetly insinuates that he does not fully agree with the contents of his book on *The Development of Psychoanalysis*, Ferenczi answers in a ten-page letter that he is "shattered" by this remark and excitedly protests "that he could never dream of departing by a hair's breadth from Freud's teaching."

When the behavior of Freud's disciples reaches such a pitch, Freud begins to worry and tries to straighten things out. He replies to Ferenczi, "As for your endeavor to remain completely in agreement with me, I treasure it as an expression of your friendship, but find this aim neither necessary nor easily attainable." He does not draw the right conclusions from these incidents and does not pursue his analysis of what can only be called the infantilism of his disciples. This much is obvious from his utter bewilderment a few months later when he is confronted by Rank's hostility; he does not understand, even afterward, what was hidden behind the "affectionate solicitude of this pupil." He admits with disconcerting naïveté, "For fifteen years I have known him as someone who was affectionately concerned [. . .], who always took my side in a quarrel and, as I believed, without any compulsion to make him do so." It appears that Freud not only failed to question the partisan attitude of his disciples but even found it very satisfying. Why was he unable to perceive that those whom he willingly called his colleagues entertained an amorous passion for him, the consequence of which was quite predictable as well as inevitable? . . .

At once striking and astonishing, the same processes are repeated with every one of Freud's close collaborators, given their personal history and geographic situation. At work in each case were: attachment to Freud's person, demand for privileged recognition, jealousy of the others, and conflict about the inheritance. Wilhelm Stekel, who had left Freud as early as 1913, wrote to him in 1924 to ask that their differences be forgotten. According to Jones, "Things would have been different if only Freud had recognized in time that the pre-war dissensions had arisen from mutual jealousy in demands for his love rather than pretensions to his intellect." He may not have been altogether wrong, since the same facts, seen from another perspective, are found in Sachs's panegyric of Freud:

> It was Freud's enduring wish to be relieved from wearing the insignia of power. He went out of his way in his search for the right man to whom he could entrust the leadership of the psychoanalytic movement; when he thought he had found him, he tried to invest the man of his choice—Adler, Jung, Rank— with full authority. This was a tactical error, since it is a well-known historical fact that of all persons who are likely to get into sharp opposition to the reigning monarch, the likeliest is the crown prince. . . .

Personal obedience was not enough to guarantee faithfulness to the Freudian way of thinking nor to sustain what was necessary for the analysis. When one considers on the one hand the mysticoclinical ideas of Lou Andreas-Salomé, which Freud hardly criticizes and even encourages, and on the other hand the reductive interpretations of Anna Freud, which subvert psychoanalysis in the most decisive way, one is convinced that the confidence Freud had in these women is equal only to their admiration of him and their submission to him. They explicitly questioned neither Freud himself nor his work, thanks to which they could transform psychoanalysis into a Russian novel or a school textbook. . . .

Obedience to Freud and to the cause, this search for refuge in the founder, the paternal understanding, the demands for loyalty, the solicitude regarding money (once someone has entered the circle, he must be helped, be sent patients, be lent money, etc.), and the acceptance into Freud's family that change the disciples into clients in the Roman sense of the term (i.e., dependents of a patrician family)—the conglomeration of all these features presents to us the figure of a very intricately organized society.

Such features did not arise by chance in the relationships between the first psychoanalysts, but were codified when the International Psychoanalytic Association was founded in 1910. Freud proposed that the association be given a chief (*ein Oberhaupt*) who, on the death of the founder (*der Führer*), would be his successor, his *Ersatz,* prepared to instruct and admonish. The association would also choose a leadership whose business it would be to declare, as Freud puts it in *On the History of the Psycho-Analytic Movement,* "All this nonsense had nothing to do with analysis; this is not psychoanalysis." Freud continues, "Moreover, it seemed to me desirable, since official science had pronounced its solemn ban upon psychoanalysis and had declared a boycott against doctors and institutions practicing it, that the adherents of psychoanalysis should come together for friendly communication with one another and mutual support." It was declared that the aim of the association would be to "foster and further the science psycho-analysis founded by Freud, both as pure psychology and in its application to medicine and the mental sciences," and "to promote mutual support among its members in all endeavours to acquire and to spread psychoanalytic knowledge."

It is astonishing to see Freud, without wincing, gather together the psychoanalysts by uttering statutes of which not even the most traditional societies would disapprove. There is nothing to prevent us from admitting that all this amounts to laying the foundations of a new church. There is and there can be only one *Führer,* Freud, the founder of psychoanalysis. After his death, the *Führer* will be replaced by an *Ersatz,* who must obediently submit, for if Jung was a failure in this respect, it was because Freud "had lighted upon a person who was incapable of tolerating the authority of another, but who was still less capable of wielding it himself, and whose energies were relentlessly devoted to the furtherance of his own interests." Such clichés can also be heard in religious societies: the right to command is in proportion to the perfection of the obedience.

Not only would the association have a single representative of the *Führer,* but only the authority of the *Ersatz* would spread internationally to declare truth and error and to react against anathema and boycott. Lastly, the association would support charity, as it is called elsewhere, between members in view of what must also be called their mission: "to acquire and to spread psychoanalytic knowledge." Later on, in *The Question of Lay Analysis*, Freud will actually express the fantasies that already have a hold on him:

> Our civilization imposes an almost intolerable pressure on us and it calls for a corrective. Is it too fantastic to expect that psychoanalysis in spite of its difficulties may be destined to the task of preparing mankind for such a corrective? Perhaps once more an American may hit on the idea of spending a little money to get the "*social workers*" of his country trained analytically and to turn them into a band of helpers for combatting the neuroses of civilization.—"Aha! a new kind of Salvation Army!" Why not? Our imagination always follows patterns.

Freud indeed uses well-worn models. Without even noticing it, in laying the rules for his association, he does nothing other than take up the norms of even the most obvious societies, the "artificial crowds" (the Church, the army) whose unconscious structures he was to analyze in *Group Psychology and the Analysis of the Ego.* . . . There is a complete contradiction between the aim of psychoanalysis, which, along with its rules, must remain an artifact, and the constitution of a society around an irreplaceable leader whose thinking is adopted and who is acknowledged as the master. Here the contradiction is even more violent, since, in order to be constituted, the society uses processes such as the transference, which properly belong to the analytic cure. . . . The group around Freud was constituted through the transference onto him—which can be seen in the statutes of the association. This involved very real things like the use of power and the circulation of money. The surreptitious shift of the analytic transference into the realm of real social relations creates the ambiguity and even the untenability, by definition, of the psychoanalytic society. . . .

Freud would have founded a church if the association had had the mission of spreading a new gospel. Instead, as he himself said when he arrived in America, he was bringing the plague, that is, among other things, the discovery of the compromises that are the cement of all societies. Thus, the International Psychoanalytic Association, whose aim was to promote mutual aid and the doctrine of submission to the leader, could only be a misunderstanding. . . . Only when it sees itself as a gang of killers, as an assembly of madmen, or, according to Freud, as a savage horde, does a psychoanalytic society take on the only form suited to it, the only image that it can uphold without misrepresenting psychoanalysis. . . .

If Freud was unable to criticize radically the psychoanalytic association, if he did not draw the consequences of his theoretical and practical views, it is because he had a personal need to have disciples and to work for them. . . . This is why Jung's reproach to Freud that he "misuse[s] psychoanalysis to keep [his] students in a state of infantile dependency" and that he is "responsible for their infantile behaviour" is not completely unfounded. And when he replied to Jung that "I have become accustomed to the opposite reproach, to wit, that I concern myself too little with the analysis of my 'students,'" he fails to realize that he is confirming Jung's opinion, that is, what is diametrically opposed in fact amounts to the same thing. To help his disciples advance in their analysis would be the best method to avoid infantile dependence, but it would also lead them to give up being "partisans for the cause," to become only scholars or practitioners in a specific field. . . .

Alfred E. Hoche's definition of the group of psychoanalysts which Freud reports in On the History of the Psycho-Analytic Movement, "a fanatical sect blindly submissive to their leader," is not so absurd as Freud would have us believe. One can even add that if the facts make this definition absurd, it is because they confirm it. The sight of "the psychoanalysts tearing one another limb from limb" is, as we have seen, a consequence of their attachment to Freud and each one's wish to be the sole heir, and, therefore, to be forced to eliminate the other partisans, his rivals. That Freud describes his disciples as a savage horde can be related to what he says in *Totem and Taboo*: the sons kill each other in order to take the place of the father. We propose the following hypothesis: when creating his own myth, Freud simply looked around him.

But then the myth also supposed that, after the father's death, the sons would come to an understanding in order to avoid a massacre.

The Marriage Counselor*

Lavinia Edmunds

We close with another chapter about Freud and his followers, this time with a more intensive focus on a single case, that of the unfortunate Horace Frink, whom Freud had chosen to spearhead the psychoanalytic movement in America as head of the New York Psychoanalytic Association. Instead, Frink's life disintegrated under the combined strain of his depressive tendency and the effects of Freud's imprudent advice, which would end by devastating three other people in the bargain.

In a sidebar to this article of 1988 that set forth the dimensions of the Frink tragedy, Lavinia Edmunds explained that Horace Frink's daughter, Helen Frink Kraft, had found in her cellar, in the 1940s, a packet of melancholy letters from her mother at the time of her divorce from Horace. Only in the 1970s did Mrs. Kraft realize the potential significance of the letters and begin investigating the incidents surrounding them. Her work was complemented by the research of Nancy McCall, Nancy Heaton, and Ruth Leys in the files of the eminent psychiatrist Adolph Meyer, covering the period when Meyer was treating Frink and corresponding with Freud. Meyer was a key precursor of the biological orientation to psychiatry which, by today, has largely reduced the Freudian symbol-hunting approach to a historical curiosity. Thus Meyer's shock and anger at Freud's mishandling of Frink can be considered portentous.

Freud's catastrophic intervention in Frink's marriage vies with the

* From "His Master's Choice," *Johns Hopkins Magazine*, April 1988: 40–49.

Emma Eckstein and Viktor Tausk affairs (pages 44–45, 54–55, 242–243 above) as the most shocking evidence not just of his icy remorselessness but also of his penchant for self-interested rationalizations. More generally, the Frink story illustrates several themes featured in our earlier chapters. The Freud with whom we are now well acquainted knew that his therapeutic and scientific claims for psychoanalysis could not withstand scrutiny from outsiders and that his own, continually evolving, version of the theory had no claim to objective precedence over any other. As a result, he bent his major efforts to controlling access to the levers of power and to exacting loyalty from his lieutenants. He was also preoccupied with the need for money, not for himself but for the effective spread of his movement. The Frink case, we will see, stands at the dangerous crossroads of those two desires on Freud's part. His challenge to Frink—get divorced and remarried to a richer woman, or you will turn homosexual!—sounds more like a voodoo curse than the counsel of a modern sage. Yet many another of Freud's patients was saddled with a no less arbitrary diagnosis.

Readers may nevertheless be taken aback when they see that Freud still wanted Frink to serve as his American deputy after learning that Frink was a suicidally inclined depressive. They would be less surprised, however, if they understood how shorthanded Freud was for emotionally stable disciples. Between 1902 and 1938, at least 9 of the 149 members of the Viennese Psychoanalytic Society died at their own hands (Falzeder, 1994, page 182). As Freud wrote to Jung with his customary detachment, "Do you know, I think we wear out quite a few men" (Freud and Jung, 1974, page 413).

A year before he died, Horace Frink was asked by his daughter Helen what message he would convey to Freud if he could. "Tell him he was a great man," said Frink, "even if he did invent psychoanalysis."

Lavinia Edmunds was on the staff of *Johns Hopkins Magazine* when the following text was published there. She is now an independent writer working out of Baltimore.

His emotional state was like "an automobile skidding," Horace Frink told a young resident at Phipps Psychiatric Clinic. Frink, a psychoanalyst anointed by Sigmund Freud to lead his movement in the United States, was now a patient himself, placing himself under the care of psychiatrist Adolph Meyer in May 1924. His rugged good looks had faded, the hair thinned around the temples.

The Phipps Clinic, at Johns Hopkins Hospital, was not a bad place for anyone then deemed a lunatic. Meyer, Phipps's founder and director, saw the clinic as a bridge between the prison-like asylums of the day and normal living. No one was there against his will. From the ward, there was a view of a lovely courtyard with a Japanese garden. Nearby were an exercise room, a resident hydrotherapist who oversaw a variety of soothing baths, and a social worker. Even the bars over the windows were made to look decorative.

None of this was enough to lift Frink's depression. For almost three years now, as long as he'd been married to his second wife, he'd suffered long bouts of depression, occasionally interrupted by spurts of manic exuberance. Frink had appealed to Meyer, a professor from his medical school days at Cornell, for help. Meyer's technique called for the patient to recount his "life story" to better understand it. Wrote Frink: "I doubt if I could give you a history of my difficulty inside an hour and a half."

Freud, his mentor and analyst, had pronounced his analysis complete, refusing to see him further, even as Frink's depression was deepening. Freud had promised Frink happiness once he left his wife, Doris Best, and two children for New York heiress Angelika Bijur. But in no time, the supreme happiness had degenerated into a hopeless mismatch.

Only four years earlier, Frink had been considered one of the most brilliant and witty men in the burgeoning field of psychoanalysis. First attracted to Freud's work in hypnosis, Frink had used it successfully with neurotic patients as an assistant in the Cornell clinic. In 1918 he had written a popular book, *Morbid Fears and Compulsions*, which gave Americans a humorous, insightful interpretation of Freud's theories. A founding member of the New York Psychoanalytic Society—the core of Freud followers in the United States—Frink had been unanimously elected as its president just a year before, in 1923. But in a strange quirk of fate, Freud had since concurred in Frink's ouster from the leadership because of his mental health. He had been unable to practice psychoanalysis or attend a meeting.

Frink's case upset Meyer. He had supported Freud, too, as a founding member of the American Psychoanalytic Association. But now the Swiss-born psychiatrist was heading in new directions, seeking more scientific ways of examining the mind through biology and developing standardized questionnaires for patients. "Freud was never scientific," he told his students.

From his first examination of Frink, Meyer was struck by Freud's meddlesome role in Frink's relationship with Bijur. As it unfolded over the next few months, Meyer would label the case "nauseating": "The attitude of Freud was evidently one of encouragement and suggestion rather strongly in contrast to his usual pretension that these factors are left out of consideration."

In February 1921, Horace Frink had sailed for Europe to undergo analysis by Sigmund Freud. Frink, then 38, was one of many young intellectuals drawn to 19 Berggasse in Vienna to study under "the master," as they called him. Those who sought training in analysis paid $10 an hour on Freud's couch, delving into their dreams and fantasies. Very simply, Freud taught analysis, in part, by performing it on the student.

The process was riveting to Frink, who stayed in Vienna from March to June, a time he would recall to Meyer as manically happy and unreal. . . . It was heady stuff by day, and at night the world of Vienna was open to him. Frink, staying at a hotel, loved to put on his tuxedo and go dancing or to the opera.

Freud favored Frink over the other Americans, if only for his morbid sense of humor. In a letter to American follower A. A. Brill, Freud wrote that Frink "shows signs of deep understanding rarely to be met with and he has learned so much by his own neurosis that I have a high opinion of his chances as a healer." And Abram Kardiner, another of the early psychoanalysts, later commented to psychology historian Paul Roazen that Frink seemed more brilliant and charming than the others. In addition, Roazen points out, Frink was a Gentile among mostly Jews, a factor the Jewish Freud thought would be important if he wanted to reach beyond New York intellectual circles.

While Frink traveled in those circles, trying to start his psychoanalytic practice in New York, the bank heiress Angelika Bijur was in the city's top social echelon with her older husband, Abraham Bijur. Some years after Angelika had become Frink's patient in 1912, the two had fallen in love. In Frink, Bijur was discovering a life of self-fulfillment, she would tell

Meyer: "Dr. F.'s lovemaking freed me from the prison in which I had shut myself. [. . .] As I found myself, he seemed to find himself and want me."

In his analysis of Frink, Freud openly encouraged this sexual liberation. Later in 1921, in a letter to Abraham Bijur's analyst defending his conduct in the case, Freud explained:

> I simply had to read my patient's mind and so I found that he loved Mrs. B., wanted her ardently and lacked the courage to confess it to himself. [. . .] I had to explain to Frink what his internal difficulties were and did not deny that I thought it the good right of every human being to strive for sexual gratification and tender love if he saw a way to attain them, both of which he had not found with his wife. [. . .]

But Frink was in turmoil over whether to divorce his wife to marry his former patient. After agonizing about it for the first six weeks of analysis with Freud, Frink decided to ask Bijur to marry him. "Following the decision, or tentative decision, was a period of great conflict," he would later recall to Meyer. "I could not reconcile myself to give up my children."

In a letter to Meyer, Angelika Bijur would remember finding Frink in a state of depression after he had completed his first stint with Freud:

> In July after five months of analysis, I joined Dr. F[rink] in Vienna as a result of his pleading letters in which he said he needed me to bring his analysis to a successful issue. Upon my arrival I found Dr. F. emersed in what I now know as a depression. Freud had said he should let me come and that he would be cured long before I ever got there. When I saw Freud, he advised my getting a divorce because of my own incomplete existance [. . .] and because if I threw Dr. F. over now he would never again try to come back to normality and probably develop into a homosexual though in a highly disguised way.

Following Freud's advice, Bijur and Frink met Abraham Bijur in Paris in July. His wife told him they had fallen in love and planned to marry, with Freud's blessing. Throughout the meeting, Bijur later wrote, Frink just sat there, lapsing into a "dazed ineffectual personality." Abraham Bijur was shocked and furious at the revelation. Only a few days before, he and his wife had made love and she had given him a $5,000 pair of pearl studs. The three—Abraham, Angelika, and Horace—returned to New York on separate steamers.

By the time he arrived, Frink had mustered his resolve. He went directly from the ship to his wife to tell her he wanted a divorce. Doris later wrote that she would do whatever would make him happy.

But the resolve of both Frink and Bijur dissolved again, as quickly as it had formed. The couple had serious doubts about the wisdom of leaving their spouses, about their compatibility, and about Frink's looming mental illness. In a letter to Frink on September 12, 1921, Freud reassured them:

> I answered to a long & desperate cable from Mrs. B. by the words: No mistake, be kind and patients. I hope it was not oracular. She had inquired whether I was sure of your love for her or confessed myself mistaken about it. So you see I have not changed my mind about your affairs which I think is perfectly intelligible. [. . .]
>
> It is true you are taking all possible pains to put me in the wrong. Yet I know I am right.
>
> [. . .] As for your wife [Doris], I do not doubt her kind intentions but her letters are cool and reasonable. I am sure if the storm has passed she will become what she has been before.
>
> Mrs. B is a treasure of a heart. Tell her she is not to blame analysis for the complications of human feeling which is only exposed not created by analysis. [. . .] I don't think continued analysis can be of any use for you [. . .] your case is complete.

Frink was ecstatic. As Bijur would note to Meyer, Frink worshipped Freud; his attitude "was that of a child to an all-wise father as demonstrated by his acceptance and obedience to Freud's views. I at the time felt Freud to be the greatest authority we could trust and was happy. [. . .]" After receiving the Freud letter, Frink immediately wrote Angelika that he had the seal of approval from the man they'd put in charge of their souls:

Angie dearest,

I am enclosing a copy of the Freud letter which I hope may be as much of a comfort to you as it has been to me. I want to preserve the original. Our grandchildren may be interested to read it sometime.

I am very, very happy.

[. . .] We haven't yet perceived the strength of the rightness of our own position. [. . .] And we are right dear. [. . .] You'll be my inspiration but not from a distance. We may keep four people unhappy and deprive two of the chance of glorious happiness. [. . .] [We are] capable of greater love than they. We, I believe, have experienced greater unhappiness than they. [Our] ultimate triumph will be a great one. [. . .]

I can easily believe Freud is right in thinking that once this is passed she [Doris] will become as she was before. She has shown signs of it already.

Horace

Yet that fall, as he practiced psychoanalysis, Frink once again was overwhelmed by guilt. He wept frequently and complained that he'd lost his sexual attraction to Angelika. When Frink wrote to Freud for advice, Freud (who had just learned that he had mouth cancer) replied on November 17, "I am too far away to extend any influence. [. . .]"

The impending divorces and quick marriage of a leading psychoanalyst and a former patient threatened to become a scandal. To avoid it, Frink told his wife to take the children and settle somewhere out West incognito for a while. According to Ernest Jones in *The Life and Work of Sigmund Freud*, "In New York, the wildest rumors were current, one being that Freud himself was proposing to marry the lady."

Doris Best, an innocent from the New York countryside, didn't even tell neighbors where she was going. Her marriage had had its difficulties: Horace had fallen out of love and dabbled in affairs. She had refused to embark upon analysis with her husband. Faced with his departure, she was both compliant and depressed, roaming from hotel to rooming house with her baby, Helen, and son, Jack, looking for ways to save money.

March 6, 1922
Albuquerque, New Mexico

Dear Horace,

We arrived here last night and find things very nice. Helen was fine on the boat, but awful on the train. [. . .] I am so tired from her I could cry. They are charging us $18 a day so I should like to get a cottage or make some other arrangements. [. . .] I felt so ill today I could not do anything but I'll try to see a lawyer to-morrow and be sure the [divorce] laws here are O.K. [. . .] If you know definitely that I am to settle here I think I can get something much less and begin to save another month. I do hope you are feeling better. I seem to have lost my grip entirely since I arrived here. I never wanted to be looked after so much in my life. [. . .]

Doris

Bijur's furious husband wasn't so compliant. He prepared to tell the world of Frink's moral crime through an open letter to Freud, which he planned to run as an ad in New York newspapers:

Dr. Freud:

Recently I am informed by the participants, two patients presented themselves to you, a man and a woman, and made it clear that on your judgment depended whether they had a right to marry one another or not. The man is at present married to another woman, and the father of two children by her, and bound in honor by the ethics of his profession not to take advantage of his confidential position toward his patients and their immediate relatives. The woman he now wants to marry was his patient. He says you sanction his divorcing his wife and marrying his patient, but yet you have never seen the wife and learned to judge her feelings, interests and real wishes.

The woman, this man's patient, is my wife. [. . .] How can you know you are just to me: how can you give a judgment that ruins a man's home and happiness, without at least

knowing the victim so as to see if he is worthy of the punishment, or if through him a better solution cannot be found?

[. . .] Great Doctor, are you savant or charlatan?

Doktor, please write me the truth. The woman is my wife
whom I love. [. . .]

Perhaps fortunately for Frink, Bijur died of cancer in May 1922 before
he could publish the letter. His analyst sent a copy to Freud, who wrote
back that the letter was silly and appealing to hypocritical public opinion
in America.

In March Doris Best Frink had gone to Reno to file for divorce. So had
Angelika Bijur, sometime that same month, although their paths did not
cross. Later that year, as Frink's condition worsened, Freud agreed to take
him back as a patient. Frink was in Vienna again from April to July 1922.
He would recall "fogginess" and "queer feelings," especially toward Angelika, who looked "queer, like a man, like a pig." Two months later Bijur
and Frink attended the Seventh International Psychiatric Conference in
Berlin, as did Freud. There Freud gave Bijur a photograph of himself
with the inscription "To Angie Frink, in memory of your old friend, Sigmund Freud, September 1922," addressing Angelika as if she were already
married.

Frink and Angelika went to Paris during October, but Frink could
not shake his depression and guilt. Freud agreed to take him back
once more, and for three weeks in November and December, Frink was
more manic than ever. Unbeknownst to Bijur, Freud had sent a doctor to
stay overnight with him. Bijur was concerned about Frink's stupor, but
she had no idea that Frink was subject to manic episodes or that he had
experienced depression as early as 1908 (as he would later tell Meyer).
Under analysis for the third time, Frink hallucinated—in "a delirium," he
would recall. In Freud's room, crammed with antiquities, Frink paced fre-
netically around the Oriental carpet designs, took gargoyles from the walls.
At his hotel room, his mood shifted from minute to minute: "elation,
depression, anger, fear, every emotion." He mistook his bathtub for a grave.

Then Frink's depression lifted. "Suddenly on December 23, Freud said
he felt the analysis was complete, that Dr. F. was using it now to maintain
his neurosis, that he should get married, have children and would soon
be well living under the happy condition which he had won for himself,"
Angelika would write to Meyer.

December 27, 1922: Angelika and Horace married in Paris. Frink would recall feeling "queer and dreamlike." They honeymooned in Egypt. When they returned to New York in February, they avoided a public scandal, although most in the New York Psychoanalytic Society knew of Frink's shaky mental state and the unsavory marriage. Frink, fresh from analysis and Freud's choice for president of the group, did not win favor with the other Americans, as Sandor Lorand, Frink's friend and fellow analyst, later recalled:

> For getting along with the other analysts, Frink's personality was not the very best. [. . .] Those who had been analyzed by Freud [. . .] formed a small clique. There was much hostility between two or three men. Everybody wanted power, and all wanted to be president of the New York society. They all knew Frink was being guided by Freud in his marriage, and there was bad blood. Some of his enemies might have thought him schizophrenic, but he was not. He was depressed; depressed and aggressive, that was it.

Freud, who tirelessly looked for ways to promote himself in the United States, worried that the Frink case, if publicized, might harm his movement. As early as November 1921, in a letter to Frink, Freud said he had asked Angelika not to "repeat to foreign people I had advised her to marry you on the threat of a nervous breakdown. It gives them a false idea of the kind of advice that is compatible with analysis and is very likely to be used against analysis." Freud was acutely aware of the need for an appropriate leader in the United States and thought Frink was the one. Once the word of the master spread, Frink was unanimously elected president of the New York Society in January 1923, although he was still on his honeymoon.

When Bijur and Frink returned a month later, Frink was struggling to keep himself together and deliver lectures to the society on the latest of Freud's teachings. On April 26, Frink was scheduled to lecture on the technique of analysis when he heard that his former wife, Doris, was dying of pneumonia. He promptly took the train to Chatham, New York, where she and the children had settled, but the attending physician advised against admitting him to her room. Doris Best died May 4. "After her death we let him come," Doris's sister-in-law would recall. He sat by her bedside for 30 minutes. "We were sitting in the parlor. When he came downstairs, he stared ahead, looking neither left nor right. He left the house without speaking to us or looking at us and we never saw him or heard a word from him again." Frink and Bijur took custody of his two children.

Soon after, Frink plunged deeper into a state of confusion and hostility against his new wife. He left the house one night without a word: another time he gave her a black eye. He was soon out of favor with the psychoanalytic society, and by March of 1924 its acting president read a letter discussing Frink's absence due to ill health. That May Frink committed himself to Phipps.

Reliving the time in Vienna, Horace and especially Angelika were beginning to see themselves as victims of psychoanalysis rather than its beneficiaries. When Bijur wrote Freud that the marriage was collapsing, Freud telegraphed back: "Extremely sorry. The point where you failed was money." It had occurred to Bijur that Freud had promoted their marriage as a source of funds for his movement in the United States. In November 1921 Freud had written Frink:

> May I still suggest to you that your idea Mrs. B had lost part of her beauty may be turned into her having lost part of her money. [. . .] Your complaint that you cannot grasp your homosexuality implies that you are not yet aware of your phantasy of making me a rich man. If matters turn out all right let us change this imaginary gift into a real contribution to the Psychoanalytic Funds. [. . .]

Money was an issue in their marriage, Bijur would note in a letter to Meyer. Bijur was glad to support Frink so that he could do his important work—she'd paid for his analysis with Freud, her own analysis had given him the bulk of his earnings for two years, and now she was paying his hospital bills. Frink cringed at his dependence on her.

Feeling mistreated by Freud (more and more as the years went on), Bijur tried to be a wiser consumer with Meyer. Always strong and opinionated, she wrote Meyer long letters expressing skepticism about analysis ("I have so far not met any analist who does not appear to me an obvious neurotic, lost in their theory and unable to deal with life. [. . .]")

She demanded to know how and when Frink could be cured. If not, she needed to make plans to get on with her life.

Meyer was irritated by her efforts to interfere. With some sense of impending doom, Meyer sought to create for Frink some neutral ground, away from his wife, until he could rebuild his emotions.

May 12, 1924

Dear Mrs. Frink,

I am afraid the situation concerning Dr. Frink is very difficult for you to grasp impersonally and objectively and the task correspondingly bewildering to you. [. . .] It is a definite sickness and not merely a psychoanalytical tangle to be dispelled by more and more analysis. [. . .] It is tremendously important to suspend all counting on fixed dates. [. . .] The main thing is to get the best possible ease and poise and patience into your own life. For the time being, Dr. Frink simply has to be looked upon as in neutral hands. [. . .]

Two days later he wrote that there is "a definite depression which I consider curable." Frink agreed to "a definite plan of activities" and "determined to give part of his time to work on a book, which I think like his previous book, shows very keen capacity for devotion to work. And I think he will take up some work in our Psychological Laboratory." It was "a promising start."

Bijur decided she needed to get away to Scandinavia with her step-daughter, Helen, and her adopted daughter. Her psychologist George Kirby worried about her and wrote Meyer on May 22 that she was "quite depressed" and "spends much of her time alone in her house, except of course, for the presence of servants and the children." Bijur had told Kirby she would not go to Scandinavia, of course, if Meyer could promise a "rapid recovery or tell her she was needed."

When Meyer allowed her one visit with her husband, in a Baltimore hotel, it was a disaster. She wrote to Meyer afterward, on June 24:

I found him less well—He showed no tenderness to me. At previous visits—while there did occur violent emotional storms if we remained together more than twenty-four hours he did show definite humanness of feeling of me as an individual. [. . .]

What he told me was that he had discovered a fundamental falacy in Freud's exposition of a certain problem and that he was going to stir this up (as he put it) by first printing (a book) and showing how erroneous were the conclusion he (Freud) drew. [. . .]

Dr. Frink's expression, his excited tone & manner a general trembling of his mouth and face showed the emotions (that lay back of this tack of "showing Freud up" and that the point at issue was merely a means to an end. [. . .])

In the early morning when I awoke I couldn't help crying quietly and believed he could not hear, but he did hear me. He asked me why I cried [. . .] in a far away tone that implied he saw no reason for crying. I made light of the matter and said it was because he was going away to which he answered, "I don't understand. I don't understand."

Frink could not shake his vague despondency. Freud had been so positive about his down side, as if he could use it somehow in analyzing others. Freud had written him February 20, 1922:

For fun it is, all of it: your repressed sadism is coming up in the shape of excellent grim humor, but harmless too. I never was afraid of it. And while you are half playing with half torturing yourself and those around you, you are steadily & consequently pursueing the way which will lead to the "right solution."

In an effort to keep Frink in "neutral" territory, Meyer arranged for him to spend the summer away, first at a sanitorium and then at a ranch in New Mexico. Frink loved the exercise, experimented with sleep patterns, and sought out companions, but he felt himself growing suicidal.

August 1, 1924
Cimarron, New Mexico

[. . .] Even when I was well I was not one of those persons who thought suicide always inexcusable. It would seem to me that

for me to commit suicide would be the best thing for everybody concerned. But if I have a chance of getting well, I'd hate
to see it destroyed by one of these impulses. . . .

[. . .] I should hate to practice psychoanalysis again after
what it has done to me. But there is no other way in which I
could make a living. I'm too sick and depressed to go without
trained help. My old punch and energy is all gone. I can hardly
recognize myself anymore.

Meanwhile, Bijur had instructed her lawyer to write Meyer on July 31:
"Mrs. Frink has definitely decided to obtain her freedom from Dr. Frink."
Meyer wrote to psychologist Kirby August 12 in exasperation, upset that
Mrs. Frink

puts down the entire matter on a vague and probably exaggerated notion of homosexuality on the part of Dr. Frink. It makes
me hot to deal with that kind of over-condensation of a much
broader philosophy of domination which evidently she
enjoyed when it was a question of mere husband-wife dominance but which I feel is more sweeping—I say "hot" at
Freudism rather than at Mrs. F. . . .

He told Bijur's lawyer, "Mrs. F. realizes now what others, not blinded
by love, might have realized before the disastrous development that mere
Freudian love-philosophy cannot guarantee safety and success in life as a
whole. Man is too complex a subject for that."

Watching the self/marriage destruction, Meyer was more than ever
turned off by the notion of the Freudian unconscious and the need to discover its repressed sexual urges. In the essay "Hedonistic Views of History," written later that year, Meyer worried that Freud's philosophy was
opening up the Victorian Pandora's box of sexuality, which would be far
more difficult for the next generation to cope with.

Back at the clinic in the fall, Meyer told Frink about his wife's intention
to get a divorce. Frink "suppressed tears with great difficulty," wrote resident F. I. Wertheimer. "Patient was very upset during the last few days
and cried on several occasions." At one point, Wertheimer quoted Frink
as saying, "I wish I had stayed with my first wife. If she were alive, I'd
return to her now."

Frink grew more manic as plans were made for the divorce. The Frinks decided to iron out details of a financial settlement in New York and go to Paris November 12 to end the marriage officially. "His last words to me were that if things would go through and there would not be a reunion afterward, he would bet they both would be dead in a year," Meyer wrote to Kirby. . . .

Frink went to New York to meet with attorneys, staying with his old friend and physician Swepson Brooks. There, on October 27, he took an overdose of Veronal and Luminal. A hardened Angelika, believing that Frink was inventing schemes to win her back, told her lawyer that she would regard death by suicide the same as death by pneumonia. It was all the same to her. She wanted out.

Frink tried suicide again, and this time was more convincing. In a curiously dispassionate letter to Wertheimer on December 2, he detailed his "adventures":

> I was supposed to sail for France Nov. 12. About three days before that date, I woke up from sleep greatly depressed, and in a very hasy state of mind, proceeded to cut the ulnar artery in my arm at the bend of the elbow. The blood spurting out made an astonishingly loud noise and woke up the nurse asleep in the room with me. He grabbed the artery and yelled for Brooks. Had he not done so, I would have been dead in a couple of minutes more. Whether I am to be congratulated or not remains to be seen.

In spite of his wife's "hellish" behavior, he added, "there is much to be said on her behalf—she is not well herself and marriage to a lunatic certainly has its dark side."

Bijur again footed the bill for him to be institutionalized, this time at McLean Hospital in Waverly, Massachusetts. On December 9, 1924, his psychologist, F. H. Packard, wrote Meyer that Frink had shown some improvement and began to crystallize some of his feelings about Freud, too:

> He is very bitter against Freud. He says that Freud does not at all understand psychoses, that the field of psychoanalysis is limited to psychoneuroses, that Freud himself knew this

and never should have attempted to treat him when he was in a psychotic condition and that his treatment and advice was all harmful and detrimental to his best interests. [. . .] His wife is very bitter against Freud and in a way against Frink. [. . .]

Meyer kept in touch with his former patient and accompanied him in 1925 at the divorce proceedings. He wrote that Frink "wanted to shake hands but she refused steadfastly." Gentlemanly to the end of the affair, Meyer took Angelika back to the train and escorted Horace back to his room.

Reunited with his children, Frink briefly practiced psychoanalysis in New York, until he felt another manic episode coming in 1927. The next year he and the children moved to an inn in Hillsdale, New York, near where his ancestors had settled. There he lived a relatively tranquil life, without experiencing a major psychotic incident, except in the final year of his life, according to his daughter, Helen Frink Kraft. . . .

Although he never wrote another book, and practiced little psychoanalysis, Frink did seem happy and never mentioned Freud's role in his life to his children. The family moved to Chapel Hill, where Jack was attending the University of North Carolina. Frink lectured at the university occasionally, had a few patients, and in 1935 married Ruth Frye, a teacher he met in Southern Pines.

Kraft recalls one incident a week before her father died that haunted her long afterward. "He called me to the living room. I went in and took a chair beside him and waited for him to speak. Almost 20 minutes went by. He looked up and started out of his reverie and he began to cry. Then he apologized and said something was the matter and went upstairs to his room." Later, he reminisced over a watercolor of the Paris Opera House, where he and Bijur had attended an opera in happier days: "Angie was radiant in a velvet cloak. We stood looking over Paris. She turned to me and said, 'Horace, with your brains and my money, we can have the world.' "

The next day he committed himself to Pine Bluff Sanitarium in Southern Pines, and a week later, on April 19, 1936, Horace Frink died of heart disease at age 53. A packet of love letters was found by his bedside. Included was a letter from his first wife, Doris, addressed to him in

Vienna, offering love and wisdom that he never quite grasped during his immersion in psychoanalysis.

> After you left tonight, I wanted to pack my bag and follow. I am anxious that you should come to some decision which will bring you peace and happiness as soon as possible. If you decided to try things as they are, I will gladly make any sacrifice but I am not sure that with every effort I can make I shall be able to give you what you want. [. . .] Although I cannot say it to you I feel that you have had great unhappiness and I am anxious that you should have just as great happiness. I cannot feel that it lies where Freud thinks it does. [. . .] To be to you what you desire would give me absolutely the greatest joy in the world. [. . .]

WORKS EDITORIALLY CITED

Anzieu, Didier. (1986). *Freud's Self-Analysis*. London: The Hogarth Press.

Appignanesi, Lisa, & Forrester, John. (1992). *Freud's Women*. New York: Basic Books.

Balmary, Marie. (1982). *Psychoanalyzing Psychoanalysis: Freud and the Hidden Fault of the Father*, trans. Ned Lukacher. (First published 1979). Baltimore: Johns Hopkins University Press.

Basseches, Harriet I., with Nancy R. Goodman. (1996). Grassroots group boosts Freud exhibit momentum. *The American Psychoanalyst*, 30 (3): 33.

Benson, Ronald M. (1996a, February 11). Update Freud exhibit. (E-mail message to members of the American Psychoanalytic Association.)

———. (1996b). Task force keeps Freud exhibit alive. *The American Psychoanalyst*, 30 (3): 32–33.

Bernheimer, Charles, & Kahane, Claire, eds. (1985). *In Dora's Case: Freud-Hysteria-Feminism*. New York: Columbia University Press.

Blum, Harold. (1995, July 31). [Opening Remarks]. Annual Conference, International Psychoanalytical Association, San Francisco, CA. Private audiotape.

Bonomi, Carlo. (1997). Freud and the discovery of infantile sexuality: A reassessment. In *Freud under Analysis: History, Theory, Practice: Essays in Honor of Paul Roazen*, ed. Todd Dufresne. Northvale, NJ: Jason Aronson, pp. 35–57.

Borch-Jacobsen, Mikkel. (1996a). Neurotica: Freud and the seduction theory. *October*, 16: 15–43.

———. (1996b). *Remembering Anna O.: A Century of Mystification*, trans. Kirby Olson in collaboration with Xavier Callahan and the author. New York: Routledge.

Brenneis, C. Brooks. (1997). *Recovered Memories of Trauma: Transferring the Present to the Past*. Madison, CT: International Universities Press.

Busse, Gerhard. (1991). *Schreber, Freud und die Suche nach dem Vater: Über die Real-itätsschaffende Kraft einer Wissenschaftlichen Hypothese*. Frankfurt-am-Main: Peter Lang.

Cavell, Marcia. (1993). *The Psychoanalytic Mind: From Freud to Philosophy*. Cambridge, MA: Harvard University Press.

Ceci, Stephen J., & Bruck, Maggie. (1995). *Jeopardy in the Courtroom: A Scientific Analysis of Children's Testimony*. Washington, DC: American Psychological Association.

Cioffi, Frank. (1970). Freud and the idea of a pseudo-science. In *Explanation in the Behavioural Sciences*, ed. Robert Borger. Cambridge: Cambridge University Press, pp. 471–499.

———. (1972). Wollheim on Freud. *Inquiry*, 15: 171–186.

———. (1974, February 7). Was Freud a liar? *The Listener*, 91: 172–174.

———. (1998). *Freud and the Question of Pseudoscience*. Chicago: Open Court.

Cixous, Hélène. (1975). *The Newly Born Woman*, trans. Betsy Wing. Minneapolis: University of Minnesota Press.

Collins, Bradley. (1997). *Leonardo, Psychoanalysis and Art History*. Evanston, IL: Northwestern University Press.

Crews, Frederick. (1986). *Skeptical Engagements*. New York: Oxford University Press.

———. (1996). Forward to 1896? Commentary on papers by Harris and Davies. *Psychoanalytic Dialogues*, 6: 231–250.

———, et al. (1995). *The Memory Wars: Freud's Legacy in Dispute*. New York: New York Review.

Daly, Martin, & Wilson, Margo. (1990). Is parent-offspring conflict sex-linked? Freudian and Darwinian models. *Journal of Personality*, 58: 163–189.

Davidson, Donald. (1982). The paradoxes of irrationality. In *Philosophical Essays on Freud*, ed. Richard Wollheim and James Hopkins. Cambridge: Cambridge University Press, pp. 289–305.

Dawes, Robyn. (1994). *House of Cards: Psychology and Psychotherapy Built on Myth*. New York: The Free Press.

Degler, Carl N. (1991). Has sociobiology cracked the riddle of the incest taboo? *Contention*, 1: 109–130.

Domhoff, G. William. (1996). *Finding Meaning in Dreams: A Quantitative Approach*. New York and London: Plenum Press.

Dunlap, Knight. (1913–1914). The pragmatic advantage of Freudo-analysis. *Psychoanalytic Review*, 1: 149–152.

Edmunds, Lavinia. (1988, April). His master's choice. *The Johns Hopkins Magazine*, pp. 40–49.

Edmundson, Mark. (1997, July 13). Save Sigmund Freud: What we can still learn from a discredited, scientifically challenged misogynist. *New York Times Magazine*, pp. 34–35.

Ellenberger, Henri F. (1970). *The Discovery of the Unconscious: The History and Evolution of Dynamic Psychiatry*. New York: Basic Books.

——. (1972). The story of "Anna O": A critical review with new data. *Journal of the History of the Behavorial Sciences*, 8: 267–279.

Erdelyi, Matthew Hugh. (1985). *Psychoanalysis: Freud's Cognitive Psychology*. New York: W. H. Freeman.

——. (1996). *The Recovery of Unconscious Memories: Hypermnesia and Reminiscence*. Chicago: University of Chicago Press.

Erickson, Mark T. (1993). Rethinking Oedipus: An evolutionary perspective of incest avoidance. *American Journal of Psychiatry*, 150: 411–416.

Erikson, Erik H. (1962). Reality and actuality. *Journal of the American Psychoanalytic Association*, 10: 451–474.

Erwin, Edward. (1993). Philosophers on Freudianism: An examination of replies to Grünbaum's *Foundations*. In *Philosophical Problems of the Internal and External Worlds: Essays on the Philosophy of Adolf Grünbaum*, ed. John Earman et al. Pittsburgh: University of Pittsburgh Press, pp. 409–460.

——. (1996). *A Final Accounting: Philosophical and Empirical Issues in Freudian Psychology*. Cambridge, MA: The MIT Press.

Esterson, Allen. (1993). *Seductive Mirage: An Exploration of the Work of Sigmund Freud*. Chicago: Open Court.

——. (1998). Jeffrey Masson and Freud's seduction theory: A new fable based on old myths. *History of the Human Sciences*, 11 (1): 1–21.

Etchegoyen, Horacio. (1996). President's column. *Newsletter of the International Psychoanalytical Association*, 3 (1): 2.

Eysenck, Hans J. (1985). *Decline and Fall of the Freudian Empire*. New York: Viking Penguin.

——, & Wilson, Glenn D. (1973). *The Experimental Study of Freudian Theories*. London: Methuen.

Falzeder, Ernst. (1994). The threads of psychoanalytic filiations: Or psychoanalysis taking effect. In *100 Years of Psychoanalysis: Contributions to the History of Psychoanalysis*, ed. André Haynal and Ernst Falzeder. Geneva: Cahiers Psychiatriques Genevois, 1994, pp. 169–193.

Farrell, John. (1996). *Freud's Paranoid Quest: Psychoanalysis and Modern Suspicion*. New York: New York University Press.

Ferenczi, Sándor. (1988). *The Clinical Diary of Sándor Ferenczi*, ed. Judith Dupont, trans. Michael Balint and Nicola Zarday Jackson. Cambridge, MA: Harvard University Press.

Fine, Sidney & Esther. (1990). Four psychoanalytic perspectives: A study of differences in interpretive interventions. *Journal of the American Psychoanalytic Association*, 38: 1017–1048.

Fish, Stanley. (1986, August 29). Withholding the missing portion: Power, meaning and persuasion in Freud's "The Wolf-Man." [*London*] *Times Literary Supplement*, pp. 935–938.

———. (1989). *Doing What Comes Naturally: Change, Rhetoric, and the Practice of Theory in Literary and Legal Studies*. Durham, NC: Duke University Press.

Fisher, Seymour, & Greenberg, Roger P. (1985). *The Scientific Credibility of Freud's Theories and Therapy*. (First published 1977). New York: Columbia University Press.

Forrester, John. (1990). *The Seductions of Psychoanalysis: Freud, Derrida, and Lacan*. Cambridge University Press.

———. (1997). *Dispatches from the Freud Wars: Psychoanalysis and Its Passions*. Cambridge, MA: Harvard University Press.

Frank, Joseph. (1976). *Dostoevsky: The Seeds of Revolt 1821–1849*. Princeton: Princeton University Press.

Freud, Sigmund. (1950). *Aus den Anfängen der Psychoanalyse: Briefe an Wilhelm Fliess, Abhandlungen und Notizen aus den Jahren 1887–1902*. Introduction by Ernst Kris. Edited by Marie Bonaparte, Anna Freud, and Ernst Kris. London: Imago.

———. (1953–1974). *The Standard Edition of the Complete Psychological Works of Sigmund Freud*, 24 volumes, translated by James Strachey. London: Hogarth Press.

———. (1974). *Cocaine Papers*. Notes by Anna Freud. Edited by Robert Byck. New York: Stonehill.

———. (1985). *The Complete Letters of Sigmund Freud to Wilhelm Fliess, 1887–1904*, trans. and ed. Jeffrey Moussaieff Masson. Cambridge, MA: Harvard University Press.

———. (1993). *The Case of the Wolf-Man: From the History of an Infantile Neurosis*, introd. Richard Wollheim, etchings and woodcuts by Jim Dine. San Francisco: Arion Press.

———, & Jung, C. G. (1974). *The Freud/Jung Letters: The Correspondence between Sigmund Freud and C. G. Jung*, ed. William McGuire. Trans. Ralph Mannheim and R. F. C. Hull. Princeton: Princeton University Press.

Gabbard, Glen O., Goodman, Sheldon M., & Richards, Arnold D. (1995). Psychoanalysis after Freud: A response to Frederick Crews and other critics. *Psychoanalytic Books*, 6: 155–173.

Galatzer-Levy, Robert M. (1997). Psychoanalysis, memory, and trauma. In *Trauma and Memory: Clinical and Legal Controversies*, ed. Paul S. Applebaum, Lisa A. Uyehara, & Mark R. Elin. New York: Oxford University Press, pp. 138–157.

Gartner, Richard B. (1997). (Ed.). *Memories of Sexual Betrayal: Truth, Fantasy, Repression, and Dissociation.* Northvale, NJ: Jason Aronson.

Gay, Peter. (1989). *Freud: A Life for Our Time.* First published 1988. New York: Anchor Doubleday.

Gellner, Ernest. (1996). *The Psychoanalytic Movement: The Cunning of Unreason.* (First published 1985). Evanston: Northwestern University Press.

Gifford, Sanford. (1996). The Library of Congress and the fear of controversy. *The American Psychoanalyst.* Vol. 30 (2): 2, 16.

Gitlin, Todd. (1996, January 22). The big mouse. *The New Republic,* p. 14.

Glymour, Clark. (1983). The theory of your dreams. In *Physics, Philosophy and Psychoanalysis: Essays in Honor of Adolf Grünbaum,* ed. R. S. Cohen and L. Laudan. Dordrecht: D. Reidel, pp. 57–71.

Goodheart, Eugene. (1977). *The Reign of Ideology.* New York: Columbia University Press.

Graf, Max. (1942). Reminiscences of Professor Sigmund Freud. *Psychoanalytic Quarterly,* 11: 465–476.

Grosskurth, Phyllis. (1991). *The Secret Ring: Freud's Inner Circle and the Politics of Psychoanalysis.* Reading, MA: Addison-Wesley.

Grünbaum, Adolf. (1984). *The Foundations of Psychoanalysis: A Philosophical Critique.* Berkeley and Los Angeles: University of California Press.

———. (1986). Précis of *The Foundations of Psychoanalysis,* and author's response to 39 reviewers: Is Freud's theory well-founded? *Behavioral and Brain Sciences,* 9: 217–284.

———. (1993). *Validation in the Clinical Theory of Psychoanalysis: A Study in the Philosophy of Psychoanalysis.* Madison, CT: International Universities Press.

———. (1996, February 6). Critique of Freud's neurobiological and psychoanalytic dream theories. [Lecture, Center for Philosophy of Science, University of Pittsburgh.].

———. (1997). One hundred years of psychoanalytic theory and therapy: Retrospect and prospect. In *Mindscapes,* ed. Martin Carrier & Peter Machamer. Pittsburgh: University of Pittsburgh Press, pp. 323–359.

Habermas, Jürgen. (1971). *Knowledge and Human Interests,* trans. J. J. Shapiro. Boston: Beacon Press.

Hale, Nathan G., Jr. (1971). *Freud and the Americans: The Beginnings of Psychoanalysis in the United States,* 1876–1917. New York: Oxford University Press.

———. (1995). *The Rise and Crisis of Psychoanalysis in the United States: Freud and the Americans, 1917–1985.* New York: Oxford University Press.

Hedges, Lawrence E. (1994). *Remembering, Repeating, and Working through Childhood Trauma: The Psychodynamics of Recovered Memories, Multiple Personality, Ritual Abuse, Incest, Molest, and Abduction.* Northvale, NJ: Jason Aronson.

Herman, Judith Lewis. (1992). *Trauma and Recovery.* New York: Basic Books.

Hirschmüller, Albrecht. (1989). *The Life and Work of Josef Breuer: Physiology and Psychoanalysis.* New York: New York University Press.

Hobson, J. Allan. (1988). *The Dreaming Brain.* New York: Basic Books.

Israëls, Han. (1989). *Schreber: Father and Son.* Madison, CT: International Universities Press.

————, & Schatzman, Morton. (1993). The seduction theory. *History of Psychiatry,* 4: 23–59.

Janet, Pierre. (1925). *Psychological Healing: A Historical and Clinical Study,* trans. Eden and Cedar Paul. 2 volumes. London: Allen & Unwin.

Jensen, Ellen M. (1984). *Streifzüge durch das Leben von Anna O./Bertha Pappenheim: Ein Fall für die Psychiatrie; Ein Leben für die Philanthropie.* Frankfort-am-Main: ZTV.

Jones, Ernest. (1953–1957). *The Life and Work of Sigmund Freud,* 3 volumes. New York: Basic Books.

Jung, Carl Gustav. (1953–1980). *The Collected Works of C. G. Jung,* 17 volumes. Ed. Gerhard Adler, Michael Fordham, and Herbert Read. Trans. R. F. C. Hull. Bollingen Series XX. Princeton: Princeton University Press.

Jurjevich, R. M. (1974). *The Hoax of Freudism: A Study of Brainwashing the American Professionals and Laymen.* Philadelphia: Dorrance.

Kaley, Harriette. (1997). Where credit is due. *The American Psychoanalyst,* 31 (1): 15.

Kerr, John. (1993). *A Most Dangerous Method: The Story of Jung, Freud, and Sabina Spielrein.* New York: Alfred A. Knopf.

Kihlstrom, John F. (1987). The cognitive unconscious. *Science,* 237: 1445–1452.

Krüll, Marianne. (1986). *Freud and His Father,* trans. Arnold J. Pomerans. (First published 1979). New York: Norton.

Kurzweil, Edith. (1989). *The Freudians: A Comparative Perspective.* New Haven: Yale University Press.

————. (1996). A politically correct Freud? *Partisan Review,* 63: 236–241.

Lakoff, Robin Tolmach, & Coyne, James C. (1993). *Father Knows Best: The Use and Abuse of Power in Freud's Case of Dora.* New York: Teachers College Press.

Lear, Jonathan. (1995, December 25). The shrink is in: A counterblast in the war on Freud. *The New Republic,* pp. 18–25.

————. (1996). [Review of *Memory Wars*]. *Journal of the American Psychoanalytic Association,* 44: 580–587.

Lehrer, Ronald. (1995). *Nietzsche's Presence in Freud's Life and Thought: On the Ori-*

gins of a Psychology of Unconscious Mental Functioning. Albany: State University of New York Press.

Levy, Donald. (1996). *Freud Among the Philosophers: The Psychoanalytic Unconscious and Its Philosophical Critics*. New Haven: Yale University Press.

Library of Congress. (1995). Sigmund Freud: Conflict and culture: Exhibition summary and background. [Official announcement of the forthcoming exhibition.]

———. (1996, February 27). Library schedules Freud exhibition for 1998. [Press release.]

Loftus, Elizabeth, and Ketcham, Katherine. (1994). *The Myth of Repressed Memory: False Memories and Allegations of Sexual Abuse*. New York: St. Martin's Press.

Lothane, Zvi. (1992). *In Defense of Schreber*. Hillsdale, NJ: The Analytic Press.

Macmillan, Malcolm. (1977). Freud's expectations and the childhood seduction theory. *Australian Journal of Psychology*, 29: 223–236.

———. (1997). *Freud Evaluated: The Completed Arc*. 2nd edition. (First published 1991). Cambridge, MA: The MIT Press.

Mahony, Patrick. (1984). *Cries of the Wolf Man*. New York: International Universities Press.

———. (1986). *Freud and the Rat Man*. New Haven: Yale University Press.

———. (1995). *Les hurelements de l'homme aux loups*, trans. Bertrand Vichyn. Paris: Presses Universitaires de France.

———. (1996). *Freud's Dora: A Psychoanalytic, Historical, and Textual Study*. New Haven: Yale University Press.

Masson, Jeffrey Moussaieff. (1992). *The Assault on Truth: Freud's Suppression of the Seduction Theory*. 2nd edition. (First published 1984). New York: HarperPerennial.

Medawar, Peter. (1982). *Pluto's Republic*. New York: Oxford University Press.

Merck, Mandy. (1993). *Perversions*. London: Virago.

Merskey, Harold. (1992). Anna O. had a severe depressive illness. *British Journal of Psychiatry*, 161: 185–194.

Micale, Marc. (1995). *Approaching Hysteria: Disease and Its Interpretations*. Princeton: Princeton University Press.

Michels, Robert. (1996). [Review of *Memory Wars*]. *Journal of the American Psychoanalytic Association*, 44: 573–579.

———. (1997). Psychoanalysis and its critics. *Partisan Review*, 64: 515–537.

Nagel, Ernest. (1959). Methodological issues in psychoanalytic theory. In *Psychoanalysis, Scientific Method, and Philosophy*, ed. Sidney Hook. New York: New York University Press, pp. 38–56.

Nagel, Thomas. (1995). *Other Minds: Critical Essays 1969–1994*. New York: Oxford University Press.

Niederland, William G. (1959). Schreber: Father and son. *Psychoanalytic Quarterly*, 28: 151–169.

Noll, Richard. (1994). *The Jung Cult: Origins of a Charismatic Movement*. Princeton: Princeton University Press.

———. (1997). *The Aryan Christ: The Secret Life of Carl Jung*. New York: Random House.

Obholzer, Karin. (1982). *The Wolf-Man Sixty Years Later: Conversations with Freud's Controversial Patient*, trans. Michael Shaw. London: Routledge & Kegan Paul.

Ofshe, Richard, & Watters, Ethan. (1996). *Making Monsters: False Memories, Psychotherapy, and Sexual Hysteria*. 2nd edition. (First published 1994). Berkeley: University of California Press.

Orr-Andrawes, Alison. (1987). The case of Anna O.: A neuropsychiatric perspective. *Journal of the American Psychoanalytic Association*, 35: 387–419.

Pendergrast, Mark. (1996). *Victims of Memory: Incest Accusations and Shattered Lives*. Revised edition. (First published 1995). Hinesburg, VT: Upper Access.

Phillips, James. (1996). From the editor. *Newsletter for the Advancement of Philosophy and Psychiatry*, Vol. 4, No. 1: 1, 10–11.

Polanyi, Michael. (1958). *Personal Knowledge: Towards a Post-Critical Philosophy*. Chicago: University of Chicago Press.

Popper, Karl R. (1962). *Conjectures and Refutations*. New York: Basic Books.

Powell, Russell A., & Boer, Douglas P. (1994). Did Freud mislead patients to confabulate memories of abuse? *Psychological Reports*, 74: 1283–1298.

———. (1995). Did Freud misinterpret reported memories of sexual abuse as fantasies? *Psychological Reports*, 77: 563–570.

Prager, Jeffrey. (1996). On the abuses of Freud: A reply to Masson and Crews. In *Debating Gender, Debating Sexuality*, ed. Nikki Keddie. New York: New York University Press, pp. 315–323.

Prozan, Charlotte Krause. (1993). *The Technique of Feminist Psychoanalytic Psychotherapy*. Northvale, NJ: Jason Aronson.

———. (1997). (Ed.). *Construction and Reconstruction of Memory: Dilemmas of Childhood Sexual Abuse*. Northvale, NJ: Jason Aronson.

Rice, James L. (1993). *Freud's Russia: National Identity in the Evolution of Psychoanalysis*. New Brunswick, NJ: Transaction.

Ricoeur, Paul. (1970). *Freud and Philosophy*, trans. Dennis Savage. New Haven: Yale University Press.

Roazen, Paul. (1969). *Brother Animal: The Story of Freud and Tausk*. New York: Knopf.

———. (1975). *Freud and His Followers*. New York: Alfred A. Knopf.

Robinson, Paul. (1993). *Freud and His Critics*. Berkeley and Los Angeles: University of California Press.

Rorty, Richard. (1996, September 22). Sigmund on the couch. *New York Times Book Review*, p. 42.

Roth, Michael S. (1995, October 5). [Letter to signers of petition (Swales et al., 1995).]

———. (1996a, March/April). The Freud flap. *Tikkun*, pp. 40–41.

———. (1996b, May 24). The fracas over Freud. *Chronicle of Higher Education*, p. A60.

Roudinesco, Elisabeth. (1996, January 26). Le révisionisme antifreudien gagne aux Etats-Unis. *Libération*, p. 7.

——— et al. (1996, March 25). [Petition to Library of Congress.]

Roustang, François. (1982). *Dire Mastery: Discipleship from Freud to Lacan*, trans. Ned Lukacher. Baltimore: The Johns Hopkins Press.

Safouan, Moustapha. (1988). *Le transfert et le désir de l'analyste*. Paris: Le Seuil.

Sand, Rosemarie. (1993). On a contribution to a future scientific study of dream interpretation. In *Philosophical Problems of the Internal and External Worlds: Essays on the Philosophy of Adolf Grünbaum*, ed. John Earman et al. Pittsburgh: University of Pittsburgh Press, pp. 527–546.

Schapiro, Meyer. (1955–56). Two slips of Leonardo and a slip of Freud. *Psychoanalysis*, 4: 3–8.

———. (1956). Leonardo and Freud: An art-historical study. *Journal of the History of Ideas*, 17: 147–178.

Scharnberg, Max. (1993). *The Non-Authentic Nature of Freud's Observations*. 2 volumes. Stockholm: Almqvist & Wiskell International.

Schatzman, Morton. (1973). *Soul Murder: Persecution in the Family*. New York: Random House.

———. (1992, March 21). Freud: Who seduced whom? *New Scientist*, pp. 34–37.

Schimek, Jean G. (1987). Fact and fantasy in the seduction theory: A historical review. *Journal of the American Psychoanalytic Association*, 35: 937–965.

Schur, Max. (1972). *Freud: Living and Dying*. New York: International Universities Press.

Schweighofer, Fritz. (1987). *Das Privattheater der Anna O: Ein Psychoanalytisches Lehrstück; Ein Emanzipationsdrama*. Munich/Basel: Ernst Reinhardt Verlag.

Scruton, Roger. (1986). *Sexual Desire: A Philosophical Investigation*. London: Weidenfeld and Nicolson.

Shorter, Edward. (1997). What was the matter with "Anna O.": A definitive diagnosis. In *Freud under Analysis: History, Theory, Practice: Essays in Honor of Paul Roazen*, ed. Todd Dufresne. Northvale, NJ: Jason Aronson, pp. 23–34.

———. (1996). *A History of Psychiatry: From the Era of the Asylum to the Age of Prozac*. New York: John Wiley.

Showalter, Elaine. (1997). *Hystories: Hysterical Epidemics and Modern Media*. New York: Columbia University Press.

Smith, Dinitia. (1995, December 10). Freud may be dead, but his critics still kick. *New York Times*. Western Edition, p. E14.

Sprengnether, Madeleine. (1990). *The Spectral Mother: Freud, Feminism, and Psycho-analysis*. Ithaca: Cornell University Press.

Stannard, David E. (1980). *Shrinking History: On Freud and the Failure of Psycho-history*. New York: Oxford University Press.

Sulloway, Frank J. (1991). Reassessing Freud's case histories: The social construction of psychoanalysis. *Isis*, 82: 245–275.

———. (1992). *Freud, Biologist of the Mind: Beyond the Psychoanalytic Legend*. With a new preface. 2nd edition. (First published 1979). Cambridge, MA: Harvard University Press.

Swales, Peter J. (1982a, Spring/Summer). Freud, Minna Bernays, and the conquest of Rome: New light on the origins of psychoanalysis. *New American Review*, 1(2/3): 1–23.

———. (1982b). Freud, Minna Bernays, and the imitation of Christ. Privately printed.

———. (1982c). A fascination with witches. *The Sciences*, 27 (8): 21–25.

———. (1983). Freud, Martha Bernays, and the language of flowers: Masturbation, cocaine, and the inflation of fantasy. Privately printed.

———. (1986). Freud, his teacher, and the birth of psychoanalysis. In *Freud: Appraisals and Reappraisals: Contributions to Freud Studies*, Vol. 1, ed. Paul E. Stepansky. Hillsdale, NJ: The Analytic Press, pp. 3–82.

———. (1988a). Anna O. in Ischl. *Werkblatt*, No. 5: 57–64.

———. (1988b). Freud, Katharina, and the first "wild analysis." In *Freud: Appraisals and Reappraisals: Contributions to Freud Studies*, Vol. 3, ed. Paul E. Stepansky. Hillsdale, NJ: The Analytic Press, pp. 81–164.

———. (1989a). Freud, cocaine, and sexual chemistry: The role of cocaine in Freud's conception of the libido. In *Sigmund Freud: Critical Assessments*, 4 volumes, ed. Laurence Spurling. London: Routledge. 1: 273–301.

———. (1989b). Freud, Fliess, and fratricide: The role of Fliess in Freud's conception of paranoia. In *Sigmund Freud: Critical Assessments*, 4 volumes, ed. Laurence Spurling. London: Routledge. 1: 302–330.

———. (1989c). Freud, Johann Weier, and the status of seduction: The role of the witch in the conception of fantasy. In *Sigmund Freud: Critical Assessments*, 4 volumes, ed. Laurence Spurling. London: Routledge, 1: 331–358.

——— et al. (1995, July 31). [Petition to head of the Manuscript Division, Library of Congress.]

———. (1997). Freud, filthy lucre, and undue influence. *Review of Existential Psychology and Psychiatry*, 23: 115–141.

Swanson, David, Bohnert, Philip J., & Smith, Jackson H. (1970). *The Paranoid*. Boston: Little, Brown.

Szasz, Thomas. (1978). *The Myth of Psychotherapy: Mental Healing as Religion, Rhetoric, and Repression*. Garden City, NY: Anchor Press/Doubleday.

Thalberg, Irving. (1982). Freud's anatomies of the self. In *Philosophical Essays on Freud*, ed. Richard Wollheim and James Hopkins. Cambridge: Cambridge University Press, pp. 241–263.

Thornton, Elizabeth. (1986). *The Freudian Fallacy: Freud and Cocaine*. London: Paladin.

Timpanaro, Sebastiano. (1976). *The Freudian Slip: Psychoanalysis and Textual Criticism*, trans. Kate Soper. London: NLB.

———. (1992). *La "fobia romana" e altri scritti su Freud e Meringer*. Pisa: ETS.

Torrey, E. Fuller. (1992). *Freudian Fraud: The Malignant Effect of Freud's Theory on American Thought and Culture*. New York: HarperCollins.

Van Til, Reinder. (1977). *Lost Daughters: Recovered Memory Therapy and the People It Hurts*. Grand Rapids, MI: Erdmans.

Von Eckardt, Barbara. (1982). The scientific status of psychoanalysis. In *Introducing Psychoanalytic Theory*, ed. Sander L. Gilman. New York: Brunner/Mazel, pp. 139–180.

Wallace, Edwin R., IV. (1983). *Freud and Anthropology: A History and Reappraisal*. New York: International Universities Press.

Webster, Richard. (1995). *Why Freud Was Wrong: Sin, Science, and Psychoanalysis*. New York: Basic Books.

Weiss, Edoardo. (1970). *Sigmund Freud as a Consultant: Recollections of a Pioneer in Psychoanalysis*. New York: Intercontinental Medical Book Corporation.

Welsh, Alexander. (1994). *Freud's Wishful Dream Book*. Princeton: Princeton University Press.

Whyte, Lancelot Law. (1960). *The Unconscious before Freud*. New York: Basic Books.

Wilcocks, Robert. (1994). *Maelzel's Chess Player: Sigmund Freud and the Rhetoric of Deceit*. Lanham, MD: Rowman & Littlefield.

Wittgenstein, Ludwig. (1958). *The Blue and Brown Books*. Oxford: Basil Blackwell.

Wollheim, Richard. (1981). *Sigmund Freud*. (First published 1971). Cambridge: Cambridge University Press.

———. (1993). *The Mind and Its Depths*. Cambridge, MA: Harvard University Press.

Wolpe, Joseph, & Rachman, Stanley. (1963). Psychoanalytic evidence: A critique based on Freud's case of Little Hans. (First published 1960). In *Critical Essays on Psychoanalysis*, ed. Stanley Rachman. New York: Macmillan, pp. 198–220.

Wortis, Joseph. (1975). *Fragments of an Analysis with Freud.* (First published 1954). New York: McGraw-Hill.

Zalewski, Daniel. (1995, November/December). Fissures at an exhibition. *Lingua Franca.* pp. 74–77.

Zaretsky, Eli. (1996, January/February). [Letter.] *Lingua Franca,* p. 76.

INDEX